NETWORKING THE DESKTOP:

CABLING, CONFIGURATION, AND COMMUNICATIONS

NETWORKING THE DESKTOP:

CABLING, CONFIGURATION, AND COMMUNICATIONS

DENI CONNOR
MARK ANDERSON

AP PROFESSIONAL

Boston   San Diego   New York
London   Sydney   Tokyo   Toronto

This book is printed on acid-free paper. ∞

Copyright © 1995 by Academic Press, Inc.

AP PROFESSIONAL
1300 Boylston St., Chestnut Hill, MA 02167

An Imprint of ACADEMIC PRESS, INC.
A Division of HARCOURT BRACE & COMPANY

United Kingdom Edition published by
ACADEMIC PRESS LIMITED
24–28 Oval Road, London NW1 7DX

Connor, Deni
  Networking the Desktop: Cabling, Configuration, and Communications / Deni Connor,
Mark Anderson.
     p.   cm.
  Includes bibliographical references and index.
  ISBN 0-12-185865-0
  1. Local area Networks (Computer Networks)   2. Computer Network
Protocols.
3. Distributed Operating Systems (Computers)
I. Anderson, Mark, 1956-   II. Title.
TK5105.7.C676   1995
004.6'8--dc20   95-10184
                                                     CIP

Printed in the United States of America
95 96 97 98   IP 9 8 7 6 5 4 3 2 1

CONTENTS

I Network Operating Systems

II Specifications, Standards, Protocols, and Interfaces

III Protocol Suites

IV Network Implementation Features

Appendices

ACKNOWLEDGMENTS

DENI CONNOR

Every LAN has a legacy that every network manager inherits and should remember when he or she is brought in to manage it. People also have legacies they inherit that give them their personalities and give reason to the things they do. I have my own legacy—it gives me the ability to string words together and explain concepts in coherent sentences. I don't know whom I inherited these features from, but would like to thank those from my earliest memories—my grandparents, Paul E. and Winifred Lorentz and Orson and Lillian Nielsen.

MARK ANDERSON

This work is dedicated to my son Kevin, to "Beege" for her support, and to the loving memory of my parents Helen and Robert. I would also like to thank Thomas-Conrad Corp. for providing me the time and opportunity to explore LANs. Special thanks to Annette, Bob, and Peter Sierant for their guidance, help, and editing.

ABOUT THE AUTHORS

DENI CONNOR

Deni Connor is the editor of *NetWare Solutions*, a monthly magazine for NetWare system managers. She is the former media relations manager for Thomas-Conrad Corp. and a former technical editor at *LAN Times* magazine. Connor is the co-author of AP PROFESSIONAL's *LAN Survival: A Guerrilla Guide to NetWare* and IDG's *NetWare for Dummies*. She has written for *Computerworld, Datamation, PC Today, PC Novice, Reseller Management, Windows User*, and *Computer Shopper*. Deni lives in Austin, Texas, with her husband Terry, a LAN software contractor.

MARK ANDERSON

Mark Anderson is a systems test engineer for Thomas-Conrad Corp. in Austin, Texas. He has written for *NetWare Solutions* and *LAN Times*. Anderson is the coauthor of AP PROFESSIONAL's *LAN Survival: A Guerrilla Guide to NetWare* and has written several chapters in Sam's Publishing's *Unleashing Novell DOS*. Mark lives in Austin, Texas, with his son Kevin.

INTRODUCTION

Take a look at how you spend your day as a network manager. If you're the average network administrator, you have 14–20 users per file server, and an average of 16 total users. You may have more users or fewer, but the job you do and the tasks you perform don't change much. You install workstation after workstation, configure LAN drivers to fit the system configuration, set up applications for users, and assist them when they have problems. It seems that you never have enough time to do every task management expects of you, or that you never get a chance to attend training classes or teach users how to work with the LAN. Yet you're accountable for everything having to do with the LAN, including some tasks that should not be your responsibility. Here's how you may spend a typical day:

8 a.m.   You receive a call from Linda in accounting. She can't log into the network. You find that someone moved her desk and her workstation during the night to make room for the new accounting clerk's desk. Your network consists of thin Ethernet, and someone forgot to lock the barrel on the T-connector after he or she moved the workstation. You find that it is loose. Problem solved.

8:30 p.m. Sally calls next. She is trying to run the month-end reconciliation of the company's accounts again this month. She complains that once again, the reconciliation is going "ever so slowly." You've heard this complaint time and time again. Sally's in luck. You'll be changing her workstation from

2.5 megabit per second (Mbps) ARCNET to 16Mbps token-ring next month. You'll be upgrading her accounting co-workers as well.

9 a.m.   Next, the president of the company calls you. She asks why you've installed the latest, greatest, fastest, and most quickly emerging technology on her workstation. She can't get anything done: Her workstation keeps losing its connection with the file server, and she keeps losing the work she's doing, including your next personnel evaluation. You tell her that the technology you chose is the latest and greatest, that the press thinks it's great, and that so-and-so across town installed it a month ago. You also tell her the technology is so new it's not out of the standards committee yet. As you put it, she should be glad. She always gets the best, and the company she runs is on the "bleeding edge." Bad choice of words. You know immediately that you'll learn from this one.

9:05 a.m. You join the ranks of job hunters. The LAN adapter you installed in the president's machine was too new, too great, too fast—and too unpredictable. Sometimes it is a case of the best, the fastest, and the newest not being good enough. You should have known better. Perhaps you should have tried it on your workstation first.

This book centers around events like the preceding occurrences. It tells you how to manage your day and make the best decisions you can about network standards, access methods, protocols, cabling, network topologies, and network specifications. These choices influence how well you do your job and how well your users do theirs.
        We'll look at:

1.   current network operating systems,
2.   available cabling for networks,
3.   access methods you can use,
4.   established, emerging, and de facto standards,
5.   interface specifications that govern your network operating system,
6.   rules for installing all these factors, and
7.   how to make them all work so you can spend more planning for future responsibilities.

Networking the Desktop: Cabling, Configuration, and Communication is part of an open-ended series on desktop networking. At present, several other books in this series are planned. They are *Networking the Desktop: NetWare* and *Networking the Desktop: Windows*. Both these books are companions to this book, however, none of the books require

others. Two other books are presently planned on OS/2 LAN Server
and networked applications. As we said, the *Networking the Desktop*
series is open-ended. If you have ideas for other books, let us know.

Is This Book Right for You?

Networking the Desktop: Cabling, Configuration, and Communication is for
the everyday network manager who is responsible for installing,
upgrading, and maintaining the local-area network. It includes information on wide-area network standards and expansion from single-
server to multiserver networks.

The book is one in a series that concentrates on desktop management
and encompasses information you need running a NetWare, Windows
NT Advanced Server, LAN Manager, Banyan VINEs, or LAN Server
network, or any of several peer-to-peer networks.

What will You Learn?

This book is a tutorial on planning, installing, configuring, and managing workstations on your network. You'll learn how to connect those
workstation to other environments such as IBM's Systems Network
Architecture or UNIX workstations. You'll receive in-depth instructions
on installing and configuring each piece of available client software for
the network operating system you choose.

How Is This Book Organized?

This book is grouped into four sections, which progress from general
topics to more specific and rely on concepts you have learned in the
previous sections. The sections are:

Part I.   Network Operating Systems
Part II.   Specifications, Standards, Protocols, and Interfaces
Part III.   Protocol Suites
Part IV.   Network Implementation Features

Each section is divided into numerous chapters.

Part I: Network Operating Systems tells you what network operating systems are available and discusses how each pertains to the desktop environment. For instance, in NetWare, Novell's client/server-based network operating system, you will learn about the different NetWare versions, and also about the clients that can operate with NetWare. The chapters on Microsoft include information on Microsoft's LAN Manager as well as Windows NT Advanced Server, and Microsoft's peer-to-peer operating system, Windows for Workgroups.

Part II: Specifications, Standards, Protocols, and Interfaces talks about the underpinnings of network communication. These chapters discuss the network and data communication standards and the organizations that govern them, the specifications that dictate how networking takes place, the protocol suites that network operating systems attempt to conform to, and the interfaces that make networking easier both for users and for software and hardware developers.

Part III: Protocol Suites discusses two of the more popular suites of networking protocols, TCP/IP and AppleTalk.

Part IV. Network Implementation Features details the nuts and bolts of networking: topologies and media. It is intended to be a hands-on discussion for implementing these technologies and using them every day. It also discusses the meat of network operating systems: access methods stipulate how data communication takes place between nodes on the network. You'll learn how to choose the best network access method for your installation and how to configure it properly. This section also relates the idiosyncrasies of each network access method, and describes the characteristics of data-link protocols.

Each chapter in *Networking the Desktop: Cabling, Configuration, and Communication* is meant to serve as a reference for managing and maintaining the workstation on your network, whether the network operating system is NetWare, Windows NT Advanced Server, or IBM's LAN Server. Throughout chapters you will find Tips and Traps you will want to use or avoid.

We want you to use this book as a reference whenever you are working at the desktop level. If this book helps you improve your networking capabilities, let your peers know. Also, if we've omitted anything you think is necessary, please let us know.

Deni Connor
Mark Anderson
May 1995

NETWORK OPERATING SYSTEMS

I

The network operating system is a control mechanism that allows single-user PCs to share resources and information. It stores, locates, and allows access to files. The network operating system also manages resources on the network, such as printers or users, and prioritizes the resources' access to services. It is responsible for security of the LAN and for tracking the use of resources. A variety of network operating systems are available, each with varying services. Among the most popular are NetWare, LAN Manager, Windows NT 3.5, LAN Server, and LANtastic.

The pros and cons of different network operating systems incite a hot debate among users, critics, and analysts. Many people prefer NetWare, the network operating system that 70 percent of networked workers use. Versions of Netware are available for small, medium, and large LANs, as well as multiple server enterprise networks. Others prefer Microsoft's networking implementation, NT 3.5, or its earlier precursors, Windows NT Advanced Server and LAN Manager. Microsoft is developing a networking strategy that will allow it to capture a significant number of users, from those with small networks to those with large networks. From IBM, LAN Server has commanded a market share in organizations that prefer IBM-only systems. And, for those users with large-scale wide-area IBM connectivity concerns and an affinity for UNIX, Banyan VINES has been a logical choice. Small offices and workgroups that need file- and printer-sharing, but not high performance, have adopted peer-to-peer network operating systems such as Artisoft's LANtastic, Novell's Personal NetWare, or Microsoft's Windows for Workgroups.

Whatever alliances a user forms, most midsize-to-large networks are heterogeneous, and even more attach and communicate with diverse devices such as mainframes, minicomputers, and UNIX. Large NetWare LANs may use LAN Server servers as application servers or Windows NT 3.5 servers for databases.

This section describes the predominant client–server and peer-to-peer network operating systems in use today. Since this book is directed to workstation management, we focus on the workstation environment these systems offer. With the diverse variety of client operating systems, network operating systems should accommodate as many clients as possible. Some do better at this than others.

NETWORK TYPES

WHAT IS A NETWORK?

Simply put, a network consists of one entity that communicates with another or many entities. Networks may consist of groups of computers, people, telephone systems, or other devices. As the term applies to computers, a network is a collection of intelligent or non-intelligent devices that exchange information and are connected to each other with some type of medium. IBM mainframe computers transfer data to minicomputers; non-intelligent terminals present mainframe-based data to users for processing; PC-based file servers share information and processing power with the PCs on user desktops. PC workstations connect to other workstations and share their resources and processing power. The term network has become commonly applied to collections of PCs that share resources and information with each other and with mainframe- or minicomputer-based systems.

NETWORK COMMUNICATIONS

Networks allow communication between physically separate computers connected via media. Communications between two partners exists under the control of a series of networking protocols or rules responsible for ensuring the safe delivery of data to its destination.

In any communication, four entities are required: sender, receiver, message, and medium. Computers that have messages to send must identify the receiver of the message—its destination. The message consists of the data to be communicated, and a collection of header, identifying, and error checking information. Messages travel across the medium to their destination.

Communications takes place via a series of rules called *protocols*, which govern the format of the data, how it is sent, and how it is received. Protocols allow each node on the network to receive data it will understand.

Several network implementations exist, each distinguished by series of common characteristics. They are host/terminal, in which a central host distributes and receives information from non-intelligent terminals; peer-to-peer communications, in which individual PCs share their resources with other PCs on the network; and client/server networks, in which a central PC called a *server* shares information and resources with individual PC stations connected to the network. Client/server and peer-to-peer communication are the subjects of this book. Host/terminal relationships will be discussed when they are pertinent to tying the LAN, WAN, internetwork, or enterprise-wide nodes to a host computer to allow communication.

Host/Terminal Implementations

In host/terminal networks, a central machine with a processor and access to a large amount of disk storage controls the services it provides to non-intelligent terminals or intelligent workstations that emulate terminals on user desktops. (See Figure 1-1 on page 5.) Most host/terminal systems use expensive mainframes or minicomputers as the host, and inexpensive devices for user input. Applications operate on the mainframe and are conveyed to the terminals, which only act as input devices for entering instructions and requests. Host/terminal networks were created when computer processors were expensive, and their use has diminished as PC prices have dropped. At present, the price of intelligent PCs equals that of non-intelligent terminals, also called *dumb terminals*.

With the trend toward downsizing, many companies are moving data and applications off traditional host/terminal networks as the processing power and capabilities of client/server networks increase.

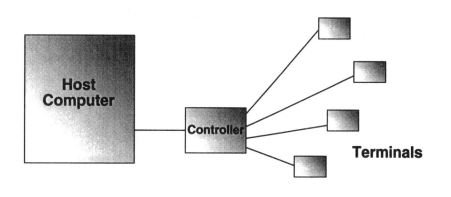

Figure 1-1. *A host/terminal network.*

Peer-to-Peer Implementations

In a peer-to-peer network, nodes with the same or similar characteristics share data and resources with peer machines on the network. (See Figure 1-2 on page 6.) The ability to share resources and data presumes that each device on the peer-to-peer network is intelligent and capable of processing information without relying on its peers. In most peer-to-peer networks, no single machine controls the resources available to the network and no central management is available. Each machine, under the control of the user, is capable of sharing information on its disk drives and requesting information stored on other workstations' disk drives. Each workstation may act as a server or workstation.

While peer-to-peer networking is inexpensive and has the advantage of sharing information among peer-type machines, it has several disadvantages. Because no device serves as the dedicated file- and print-server, performance is diminished. Also, when individual workstations power down, access to applications may be denied, and because the peer-to-peer networking relies on each workstation playing its own part in the backing up of shared data, data may be lost. While slower than client/server implementations, peer-to-peer networks have gained popularity in small and large offices and the workgroups and departments at many companies where simple file-and printer-sharing are the only requirements. The most popular peer-to-peer network

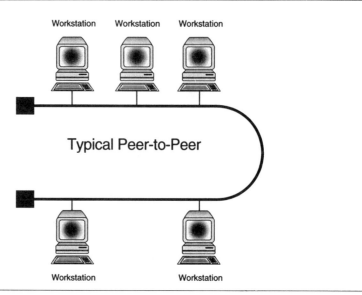

Figure 1-2. *A peer-to-peer networking implementation.*

implementations for PCs are Microsoft's Windows for Workgroups, Artisoft's LANtastic, Performance Technology's POWERLan, and Novell's Personal NetWare. Saber Software's GraceLAN is popular for networking Macintosh computers.

CLIENT/SERVER IMPLEMENTATIONS

Client/server networks are characterized by dedicated machines that provide resources such as printer- and file-sharing to intelligent, client workstations. In a client/server network, each device has its own role, and clients are able to perform many processing functions on their own. When clients need resources that are not available locally, they request them from the server. (See Figure 1-3 on page 7.)

Servers may be dedicated to a variety of services, including file sharing (file servers), printing (print servers), database management (database servers), and communications (communication servers). The client/server methodology allows services and resources to be distrib-

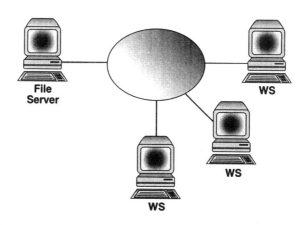

Figure 1-3. *A client/server network.*

uted to the source that can provide the best functionality, processing power, and performance.

Client/server networks allow applications to be distributed among multiple machines. Tasks and processes within the same application may be shared among a number of processors and report to a single processor. Because the client/server architecture is built in scalable form, easy expansion and incremental growth is possible without large up-front equipment replacement costs.

The server operating system, called the *network operating system,* provides central data storage and management, security properties, administrative management functions, and multiple protocol and client support. It distributes these services to its clients and centralizes the management of these resources. Servers normally congregate the CPU-intensive operations of an application and rely on individual workstations to make requests for its services.

Communication between the server and its clients occurs via protocols and interprocess communications such as NetBIOS, the Internetwork Packet Exchange/Sequenced Packet Exchange (IPX/SPX) protocols, or the Transmission Control Protocol/Internet Protocol. The server uses protocols such as the Network File System (NFS), the NetWare Core Protocol (NCP), or the AppleTalk Filing Protocol (AFP) that rule the way clients request resources and the server responds to requests. In NetWare, for example, the workstation makes an NCP request to open a file resident on the file server. The server acknowledges the request and sends the file to the workstation. Transport of the NCP request between the server and workstation is encapsulated in an NetWare IPX packet, which is further enclosed in a packet designated by the network access method. At the destination, successive layers strip off information to reveal the original request.

Client/server systems allow many client operating systems, and because of their centralized node management and control, increase performance. Tasks are offloaded to machines with faster processors and among a variety of clients. The client/server request/response mechanism in which each request elicits a response reduces network traffic and enhances the use of resources. Because servers can prioritize their response to requests, data transmission is more effective.

Common client/server implementations are Microsoft's Windows NT Advanced Server, Novell's NetWare v2.x, v3.x, and 4.x, IBM's OS/2 LAN Server, and Banyan VINEs. Each of these client/server implementations has strengths and weaknesses. NetWare, for example, is known for its file and printer-sharing capabilities, while Microsoft's Windows NT Advanced Server and IBM's OS/2 LAN Server are known for their strong database and application server capabilities. While homogenous networks consisting of servers and workstations ruled by a single network operating system are prevalent, heterogeneous networks are becoming more common and making use of the strong characteristics of a particular network operating system.

Each network operating system is also increasing the client operating systems it supports; Novell's NetWare at present supports the largest number of clients. As network operating system vendors pursue interoperability among server operating systems and attempt to provide their services on as many user desktops as possible, universal client support will grow.

LANs, WANs, AND MANs

Client/server implementations take many forms depending on the geography they cover, the communication methods and protocols they use, and the applications they make use of. In an attempt to achieve optimal performance, the response times various protocols and technologies offer define many networking implementations.

It is difficult to separate and categorize the types of networks. The boundaries among them tend to blur, depending on current English usage and technology. At present, the implementations are divided into local area networks (LANs) and internetworks. Internetworks may consist of collections of local area networks, campus-wide networks, metropolitan area networks (MANs), wide-area networks (WANs), and enterprise-wide networks. These definitions constantly change depending on convenience and user.

Consider this scenario: You have a business, which is part of a national chain. At your location, you have a network with two file servers. The first file server in the accounting department is small—it contains only one network adapter that connects it to four workstations. The other network contains three LAN adapters, connecting to 120 workstations. Each network communicates with the other—they share word processing applications and electronic mail. They also communicate via leased lines with a mainframe in the same city that belongs to a service bureau that processes the company's orders. Each day, users also upload daily sales orders to a network at an industry distributor located in another city. (See Figure 1-4.)

If you were asked to describe this network with a single term, you might be stymied. The network meets the characteristics of a LAN—part of it exists within a confined area. It also can be called an *internetwork*—it has two interconnected file servers in the same area, each with

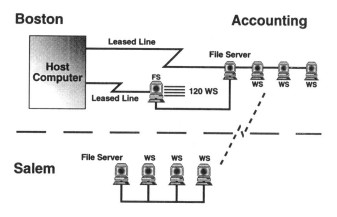

Figure 1-4. *The network at ABC Company.*

multiple networks connected to them, as well as connections to a geographically separate network. The network can be called a *metropolitan-area network* because it stretches across a metropolitan area. Or, it can be an enterprise network—it performs the networking operations of a single corporate entity. The network also may be a wide area network because it makes use of third-party telecommunication services. To insist that this network falls in any one category is limiting, and definitions really don't matter as long as the individual components can be defined in a relatively concise manner. Based on users' insistence, however, categorizing everything they are presented with, here are the definitions commonly ascribed to these different networks.

LANs

A local area network, called a *LAN*, is limited to the interconnected clients of a single server in a local area—most often a single building, a group of buildings at a site, or a single department or workgroup. (See Figure 1-5.) LANs are normally owned by a single corporate entity, individual, or organization. Nodes and servers connect to each other via physical media such as coaxial or twisted-pair. They do not rely on third-party services provided by common carriers or other service providers.

In a LAN, requests and responses flow across the physical media to their destinations. Within the corporate entity, each LAN has a unique network address. The size of a LAN is limited by the access method

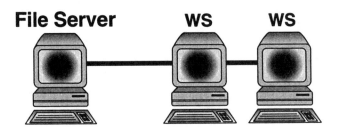

Figure 1-5. *A local area network.*

and the network operating system in use. Practically, you will not see networks reaching these limitations without segmentation into separate networks.

A single file server may contain several network adapters to divide and segment network traffic into manageable components. The nodes extending from each network adapter share a unique network address, and hence their own network. Collections of networks attached in this manner are called *internetworks*.

Internetworks

An internetwork is a group of interconnected LANs. (See Figure 1-6.) These LANs may be at a single site, in a single building, or spread across metropolitan areas, cities, or countries. Internetworks consist of multiple servers, and a large number of devices, each responsible for their own workgroups or departments. Management of the internetwork may be centralized in one location or dispersed to each individual LAN. Many LANs become internetworks when the amount of traffic expands beyond the capabilities of a single file server or when the application needs of the network require division. Internetworks may be the property of multiple corporate entities and incorporate third-party communication services.

Several types of internetworks exist: campus-wide networks, wide-area networks (WANs), metropolitan area networks (MANs), and enterprise networks.

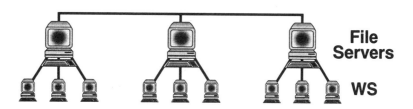

Figure 1-6. *An internetwork.*

Campus-Wide Networks

A campus-wide network consists of a collection of networks joined together by physical media over a geographically local distance of several buildings. It is normally owned by a single corporate entity, and each individual LAN may be managed separately or hierarchically by a single, centralized computer. (See Figure 1-7 on page 13.)

Metropolitan Area Networks

Within a large metropolitan area of approximately 50 miles, internetworks exist that use third-party public or private network services to communicate with each other. Because of the relatively local distance covered, the response time is faster than WANs, but slower than LANs. Metropolitan-area networks are typically under the control of a single corporate entity. (See Figure 1-8 on page 13.)

Wide-Area Networks

A wide-area network, consisting of multiple LANs, spans a large geographic area. It uses publicly owned communication lines and third-party service providers to make the link between LANs. (See Figure 1-9 on page 13.) WANs may be owned by several corporate entities. Because they rely on third-party telecommunication services, their response time is generally slower than LANs.

The LANs within a WAN may be connected by dial-up or leased lines, Dataphone Digital Service (DDS), a Public Data Network (PDN) that uses X.25, or T1 or T3 lines. The protocols used for LAN-to-LAN communication differ from the typical one request elicits one response mechanism. In wide-area links, it is desirable to receive many responses to a single request, thus saving internetwork traffic and decreasing the propagation delay between networks.

Two common forms of wide-area protocols exist: packet-switched and circuit-switched. In packet switching, a high-speed channel contains multiplexed packets that are routed as full packets, not frames. In circuit-switching, which is not as efficient as packet-switching, frames are routed over leased or private lines to their destinations, leaving an open connection between frame transmission. Frames from the same packet may take different paths to their destination. Circuit-switched

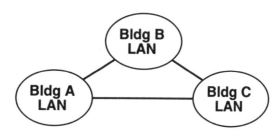

Figure 1-7. *A campus-wide network.*

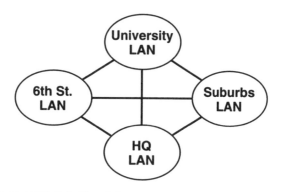

Figure 1-8. *A metropolitan area network.*

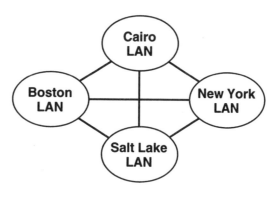

Figure 1-9. *A wide-area network.*

networks are composed of phone line, microwave, and satellite transmission.

Several packet-switching networks exist. They are the Integrated Services Digital Network, frame relay, Switched Multimegabit Data Service (SMDS), and the Asynchronous Transfer Mode (ATM).

Although ISDN was introduced in 1979, it was only in 1992 that the Bell Operating Companies defined their ISDN strategy. ISDN is a connectionless service that carries voice, data, and video. It has two services: basic rate ISDN (BRI) and primary rate ISDN (PRI). BRI allows voice and data to be transmitted on telephone lines as two 64 kilobits per second (Kbps) channels. In PRI, 23 64Kbps second channels are supported. Users of ISDN are billed a monthly fee plus connection charges.

Frame relay, a packet-switching technology for data, is designed to replace point-to-point lines. It operates at T1 speeds and makes use of permanent virtual circuits. A proposal is in place for switched virtual circuits, which would allow less expensive temporary connections.

SMDS is a packet-switching technology that is an alternative to leased lines. It operates at T1 to T2 speeds and is flexible in configuration. With SMDS, you do not need to predesignate all sites that will make use of SMDS. SMDS is provided by common carriers.

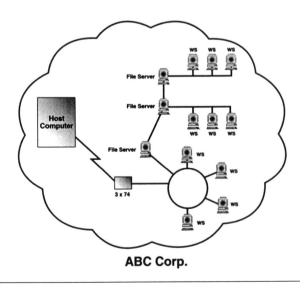

ABC Corp.

Figure 1-10. *An enterprise network.*

ATM, which allows the transmission of voice, data, and video, is offered by service providers such as Wiltel and PacBell. It is a fiber-optic based cell-switching network that allows up to 53-octet packet transmission.

Enterprise Networks

A term presently in vogue is *enterprise network*. This term describes little more than a network owned by a single corporate entity. It may consist of a local area network, a campus-wide network, a MAN, or a WAN. Some people define an enterprise-wide network as the network that operates the company's mission-critical applications, those applications that would harm the revenues of a company it they were not available. However, the description of a mission-critical application is arguable. Many users describe mission-critical applications as the large databases and legacy applications carried over from mainframe systems. Word processing or a desktop publishing system for a magazine publisher or the accounts receivable system in a dentist's office qualify as mission-critical applications—their performance is critically tied to the assets and future of the corporation. (See Figure 1-10 on page 14.)

NETWARE

2

Novell Inc.'s NetWare network operating system, which has approximately 72 percent market share, evolved over the last 11 years to its currently sold versions: NetWare v3.12 and NetWare 4.10. For its network operating system based on the client–server model, Novell estimates that there are presently 2,700,000 NetWare file servers and 40 to 60 million NetWare users. Each NetWare network has an average of 15 users per file server.

NetWare, a multitasking network operating system, provides networking for diverse clients, among them DOS, Macintosh, OS/2, Windows, and UNIX workstations. It is optimized as a file server and uses a proprietary directory and file structure to provide quick file access.

NetWare's strengths are its wide client support, portability to other operating system platforms such as Digital's VMS or the Macintosh, extensive security, and the ability to incorporate different LAN access methods and route them from one to another.

EVOLUTION OF NETWARE

Novell Inc. evolved from an Orem, Utah–based company called Novell Data Systems, which marketed printers and peripherals and a Zilog Z-80–based computer of its own manufacture that used the CP/M operating system. Its first product, a star-topology network operating system, used the Motorola 68000 processor in the file server and connected to CP/M-based workstations via a 232 kilobit per second (Kbps) modified RS-422 connection.

In the early 1980s, Novell Data Systems filed for bankruptcy reorganization. Safeguard Scientific oversaw the organization, and the company was renamed Novell Inc. Its first product, created by a group of former Brigham Young University programmers who called themselves SuperSet, allowed IBM PCs to access the 68000-based Novell Data Systems file server. In 1983, Ray Noorda joined the company as president and chief executive officer, and the company started marketing its network operating system, ShareNet. This implementation was subsequently S-Net with the release of the IBM PC/XT.

S-Net gave way to G-Net when Novell transferred its network operating system to an all-PC base. G-Net was named according to the type of network adapters it used; they were based on Gateway Communications' two megabit per second (Mbps) broadband adapters.

Novell's next operating system version was introduced when it became clear that DOS-based computers would dominate the desktop. Called NetWare/86, this version formally integrated the concept of request and response, which is still the core of NetWare today. In a request/response-based system, the network operating system oversees requests from individual network devices. Because control is exerted by the network operating system, a variety of client systems can be supported.

NetWare/86 was replaced by Advanced NetWare v2.0 in 1986, which linked different access methods, such as ARCNET or Ethernet, within the file server or externally by a dedicated workstation bridge. Advanced NetWare v2.0 was based on the Intel 80286 processor and offered multitasking, multiuser support. This version of NetWare also gave the option of operating in dedicated or nondedicated mode. In nondedicated mode, the machine designated as the file server also could operate as a workstation. Nondedicated mode significantly affected network performance, especially when the workstation portion of the file server was requesting service.

From 1986 to 1987, Novell also introduced System Fault Tolerant (SFT) NetWare and SFT NetWare Level II. These versions allowed disk mirroring and duplexing and incorporated a feature called *Hot Fix* that allowed data from defective areas of the disk to be redirected to good areas and for the defective area to be marked unusable. SFT NetWare also added the Transaction Tracking System, a feature still used to preserve the integrity of database transactions in the event of failure during a database operation.

In 1987, Novell introduced Entry Level Support (ELS) NetWare, which allowed groups of up to four users to access the file server. It was followed by ELS Level II, which allowed more users. That year, Novell also introduced SFT NetWare v2.1, which incorporated HotFix, disk mirroring, and Transaction Tracking.

Just short of the new decade, Novell introduced NetWare/386 version 3.0 in September of 1989. Using 386- and 486-based machines as file servers, this was the first implementation of NetWare for large-sized LANs. In 1992, Novell introduced SFT Level III, which allows mirroring and duplexing of file servers. The next year the company released NetWare 4.0.

Figure 2-1 on page 20 lists some NetWare milestones.

The currently marketed versions of NetWare are NetWare v3.12, NetWare SFT Level III, and NetWare 4.10. In this book when we discuss NetWare, we will refer to v2.2, v3.11, v3.12, SFT Level III, or NetWare 4.10.

According to statistics of its readership gathered by *NetWare Solutions* magazine, 11.9 percent have purchased NetWare v4.x; 85.3 percent use NetWare v3.x; and 33.5 percent use NetWare v2.x. These statistics roughly parallel those of the industry. Although v2.x, represented mainly by NetWare v2.15c and NetWare v2.2 users, is no longer marketed by Novell, it still accounts for a large share of Novell's networking market. The remainder of this book will treat versions of NetWare v2.x as a viable network implementation.

NetWare Operational Principles

NetWare is a file-server based network operating system in which user software resides on the file server. Each workstation loads a shell program (NETx.COM, NETx.EXE, VLM.EXE, or an OS/2 daemon) that directs network requests to the file server and DOS or OS/2 requests to the workstation's local drive.

NOTE: The Macintosh client's shell is built into the Macintosh operating system as is the UNIX shell.

Communication between the shell and the file server occurs at the Open Systems Interconnection (OSI) Model's Network Layer via the Internetwork Packet Exchange (IPX) protocol.

Year	Version
Early 80s	ShareNet, S-Net, NetWare/G
1983	NetWare/86 for the 8086 processor NetWare/68 for the 68000 processor
1985	Advanced NetWare version 1.0
1986	Advanced NetWare version 2.0 System Fault Tolerance Level I
1987	NetWare ELS I SFT 2.1 Advanced NetWare v2.10
1988	ELS II 2.12 NetWare for VMS OS/2 clients ODI specification
1989	ELS II 2.15 NetWare for Macintosh Portable NetWare NetWare/386 version v3.0
1990	ELS I 2.12 NetWare/386 version 3.1
1991	NetWare 2.2 NetWare v3.11
1992	NetWare SFT III
1994	NetWare 4.0
1995	NetWare 4.10

Figure 2-1. *Versions of Novell's NetWare make up a 72 percent market share.*

In NetWare, multiple file servers as well as multiple network access methods exist. NetWare's architecture allows operation independent of access method—Novell networks operate on token-ring, Ethernet, ARCNET, and the Fiber Distributed Data Interface (FDDI), to name a few. NetWare also supports a multitude of workstation clients. Client software is available for DOS, OS/2, UNIX, and Macintosh users.

NetWare owes its "openness" to the Open Data-Link Interface (ODI) specification, which allows diverse client operating systems to access the network and a variety of protocols to traverse different access methods.

In most implementations, NetWare communication consists of a request-response mechanism. For every request made, the receiver of the message responds. On the client workstation, the shell, now called the *requester* or *redirector*, processes requests for the file server, whether those requests are to open a file or send a message to another workstation.

Two databases control access to NetWare. They are the bindery in versions of NetWare previous to 4.x and the NetWare Directory Services database in NetWare 4.x and up. These databases contain network object information (properties) including the object's rights to the network and to other objects. When a user logs in to the network, his or her username is checked with the bindery to determine the services he or she can receive.

While NetWare's primary communication protocol is IPX, it also operates with a variety of other network protocols including TCP/IP and NetBIOS, and thus can connect to a diverse collection of devices such as UNIX workstations, minicomputers, and mainframe computers. NetWare supports routing and bridging from one network to another, from one access method to another, and from one network protocol to another.

NetWare v2.2

NetWare v2.2, based on the Intel 80286 processor, is designed for small businesses and for departmental servers. Although an older version of NetWare than is presently available, it outperforms Artisoft's LANtastic, a peer-to-peer network operating system, and most other peer-to-peer network operating systems on the market.

According to a 1994 study by International Data Corp. of Framingham, Massachusetts, in 1991, 792,000 licenses to NetWare v2.x were in use. These figures contrast slightly to 801,000 licenses in 1992 and 700,000 licenses in 1993.

Features

NetWare v2.2 allows a file server to access 12 megabytes of RAM and supports maximum volume sizes of 255MB. It supports DOS-, Macintosh-, and OS/2-based workstation clients. NetWare v2.2 allows up to four LAN adapters in the file server. These adapters support internal routing between networks. It also supports System Fault Tolerance (SFT) Level I and II, which allow disk mirroring and duplexing. NetWare v2.2 is the last version of NetWare that allows the server to operate in nondedicated mode. (See Figure 2-2 for a description of some other features of NetWare v2.2.)

Limitations

NetWare v2.x is based on a 16-bit operating system, which limits its use in larger networks. Further, it does not support UNIX clients, cannot span data over multiple hard disks, and has a limited amount of RAM and disk capacity per volume. NetWare 286 does not dynamically allocate memory to network operating system resources and is thus not as flexible as NetWare v3.x and 4.x. In addition, NetWare v2.x supports Value-Added Processes (VAPs) which load into server memory. VAPs, which are difficult to use and thus, have little third-party support, can not be dynamically loaded and unloaded from server memory.

Although NetWare v2.2 is still supported by Novell Services and Support, it is no longer sold.

Clients

NetWare v2.x supports DOS-, Macintosh-, and OS/2-based client workstations. It does not support UNIX or the Open Systems Interconnection's (OSI) File Transfer, Access Method (FTAM) clients. (In 1994, Novell sold its interests in FTAM after OSI standards did not materialize in the quantities previously expected.)

Feature	Quantity/Size
RAM supported	16MB
# of users	5, 10, 50, 100
Maximum disk space	2GB
Maximum file size	255MB
# of open files maximum	1,000

Figure 2-2. *NetWare v2.2 features.*

NETWARE V3.X

NetWare v3.x has more NetWare users than the other version of NetWare and is still being installed in large numbers for mid-sized and larger LANs. According to IDC, 128,000 units of NetWare were sold in 1991 followed by 416,000 in 1992, and 733,000 in 1993.

Features

The key new feature of NetWare v3.x is the dynamic allocation of resources. Formerly, when resources were loaded into the file server memory, they remained resident in memory until the file server was "downed." NetWare's dynamic memory allocation allows programs to be loaded as they are needed and unloaded when they are no longer in use.

Another new feature of NetWare v3.x is the introduction of NetWare Loadable Modules (NLMs), which replace the Value-Added-Processes (VAPs) used in NetWare v2.2. NLMs, programs which become an integral part of the network operating system when loaded from the file server console, include LAN drivers, server management utilities, and application NLMs.

NetWare v3.11 includes these features:

- Allows up to 32 terabytes (TB) of disk storage
- Supports up to 100,000 open files
- Allows files of up to four gigabytes (GB)
- Supports up to 250 users (a 1,000-version was delivered
- Uses NetWare Loadable Modules (NLMs)
- Allows up to 32 physical drives to be linked to form a virtual volume
- Supports 18 LAN adapters per server
- Allows dynamic allocation of resources

NetWare v3.12, the current version of NetWare, uses the Packet Burst NetWare Core Protocol (NCP), which is particularly useful in internetworked or high-traffic environments and allows bursts of data to be transmitted without waiting for acknowledgment of packet receipt. Its other distinctive features include the use of the Virtual Loadable Module (VLM) DOS requester as a substitute for the DOS redirector used in previous versions. The DOS requester runs on the DOS client workstation and allows the workstation to request and receive network services as well as make use of DOS when necessary.

NetWare v3.12 also contains Novell's Message Handling Service and First Mail, an entry-level electronic mail system. NetWare 3.12 was the first version of NetWare to ship with a DOS media manager, which allows CD-ROM drives to be incorporated into the network.

Limitations

The limitations of NetWare v3.x are its lack of a directory services structure that allows multiple networks to be managed as a single entity, its inability to suballocate disk space and save space, and its lack of file compression. In addition, in NetWare v3.x, NetWare Loadable Modules (NLMs) can not run in protected mode.

Clients

NetWare v3.x supports DOS, Windows, UNIX, OS/2, FTAM, and Macintosh files.

SYSTEM FAULT TOLERANCE LEVEL III

While fault tolerance in some form has been available in NetWare for several years, implementations of NetWare have not been able to offer full redundancy for file servers. System Fault Tolerance Level I permitted mirrored directory entry tables (DETs), file allocation tables (FAT), and Hot Fix, which allowed for data protection in the event of failure. System Fault Tolerance Level II incorporated the Transaction Tracking System, disk mirroring and duplexing. It was with the advent of System Fault Tolerance Level III that full server mirroring and duplexing became available.

In SFT Level III, two file servers are connected with a special connection called a *Mirrored Server Link (MSL)*. When operational, the second server mirrors the memory and disk contents of the first server, effectively hiding failures or unavailability of the server's RAM and hard disk space. SFT Level III, while protecting data on the server, does not protect the network from NLM or system software failures.

SFT Level III is configured with two file servers of the same memory, disk, LAN adapter, and video display configuration. It allows the servers to be separated from each other by 100 feet if coaxial Mirrored Server Link adapters are used, or four kilometers (Km) with more expensive fiber-optic adapters. The Mirrored Server Link (MSL) consists of a LAN adapter in each file server, joined by the cable, and directed by the SFT Level III network operating system. While allowing full redundancy and 100 percent uptime, SFT Level III is expensive— like NetWare, its cost is based on the number of concurrent connections required. Several vendors offer MSL implementations. Among them are Eagle, Thomas-Conrad, and Plaintree Systems. (See Appendix B for the addresses and telephone numbers of these vendors.)

The SFT Level III operating system consists of two parts: a mirrored server engine and non-mirrored I/O engines. The mirrored server engine services the requests; the I/O engines perform identical I/O requests on each mirrored server. These requests are processed on each server concurrently by the separate hardware. SFT Level III is a subset of NetWare v3.11 and as such does not provide Macintosh or NFS support.

Several alternatives to SFT Level III exist. These alternatives do not offer the full capabilities of NetWare SFT Level III, but provide serviceable and less expensive implementations. Vendors who offer such options are Vinca, Ornetix, MiraLink, and Horizons Technology.

NetWare 4.x

NetWare 4.10 is Novell's latest network operating system implementation and is intended to be a client-server operating system for enterprise networks. It implements NetWare Directory Services, in which users have rights to devices or entities. Rather than viewing the network as the file server logged into by the user, in NetWare 4.0, a user logs into the network and is granted access to specified servers and devices. According to International Data Corp., 51,000 copies of NetWare 4.0 were purchased in 1993.

Features

NetWare 4.1 introduces three other important features: file compression, disk suballocation, and data migration. File compression allows data to be compressed for storage based on frequency of use and decompressed when needed. In disk suballocation, files can be saved in less than their traditional four-kilobyte block if the number of bytes of data are not sufficient to fill the entire block. Data migration provides services and methods for the management of frequently used data, the migration of infrequently used data to alternative storage mechanisms such as CD-ROM, and the archiving of unused historical data. Migration also includes demigration mechanisms that allow classes of data to be moved from one form of storage to another.

In NetWare 4.x, the bindery, a database of the objects on the network, is replaced by NetWare Directory Services. These objects may be users, groups, servers, and printers or their associated queues. Objects consist of container and key objects. Key or leaf objects apply to alias object names, bindery objects, computers, and directory maps. In addition, groups, servers, printers, users, and volumes are objects.

NetWare 4.0 offers improved network backup support by providing tape spanning ability in which data may be spanned over numerous tapes or tape sets.

Important to internetworking is 4.0's use of the NetWare Core Protocol (NCP) burst mode protocol, which speeds internetwork communications by allowing bursts of data to be sent without the one-for-one packet acknowledgment Novell's NetWare Core Protocol normally requires. A number of new utilities also are available in NetWare 4.0, including Windows-based administration utilities that replace common NetWare utilities such as SYSCON and FILER.

NetWare 4.x is available in 5, 10, 25, 50, 100, 200, 500, and 1,000-user versions. It provides the ability to operate NetWare Loadable Modules in Ring 3, thus enabling the testing of NLMs in a secure, protected environment. It also supports SFT Level III and redundant Mirrored Server Link (MSL) adapters.

Limitations

The present migration utilities that permit the migration of NetWare v2.2 or v3.11 data are improved in NetWare 4.10 and directory services administration is simplified.

Clients

NetWare 4.x supports DOS, Windows, OS/2, Macintosh, and UNIX clients.

NOVELL'S FUTURE DIRECTION

With the acquisition of WordPerfect and its office productivity packages in 1994, Novell is moving to make networking pervasive. 1994 saw the introduction of a new CEO chairman and president at Novell, Robert J. Frankenburg, formerly of Hewlett-Packard. To Frankenburg, pervasive computing extends to all areas: group activities, mobile users, and into the home. Novell has also announced plans to introduce a symmetric multiprocessing interface for NetWare v4.10 by the end of 1995, and NetWare and Novell's Intel-based UnixWare will have common management, security, and directory services. In 1996, Novell will introduce a new network operating system called SuperNOS, which is modular, distributed, and fault tolerant.

IBM's OS/2 LAN Server

3

BM's contribution to the client–server networking market is OS/2 LAN Server, which has been installed in 8 percent of the network market. The current version of IBM's network operating system is OS/2 LAN Server 4.0. The previous and the most commonly used version is OS/2 LAN Server 3.0, which was introduced in 1992.

The OS/2 LAN Server network operating system relies on IBM's 32-bit, preemptive multitasking personal computer operating system, OS/2, for many of its network characteristics. OS/2 LAN Server's networking strengths include its ability as an application server, its integration with IBM mainframe and minicomputer products, and its base operating system, OS/2. The large base of IBM-only organizations accounts for OS/2 LAN Server's broad acceptance into the client–server arena.

EVOLUTION OF LAN SERVER

IBM's first venture into the LAN operating system market was to connect IBM's PCs to its mainframe and minicomputer systems. This connection allowed the PCs to communicate with each other and to act as terminals in mainframe or minicomputer-connected environments. For IBM, PC-based networking was first implemented in 1984 as the IBM Personal Computer Network (PCN) and its associated IBM PC LAN

Program (PCLP). PCN was a limited peer-to-peer network for DOS-based IBM PCs. As a network operating system, PCN ran on top of IBM PC-DOS and used the NetBIOS protocol to communicate via the token-ring access method among individual PCs.

Tip:
Many people consider NetBIOS to be an application program interface (API). This book refers to NetBIOS as a protocol. NetBEUI, Microsoft's implementation of NetBIOS, is also a protocol. Both use APIs to function.

This implementation of token-ring became the basis of the Institute of Electrical and Electronic Engineers' (IEEE) 802.2 Logical Link Control sublayer in the Open Systems Interconnection Model (OSI). PCN provided file server capability and the remote booting of individually attached workstations. Although limited in features, PCN provided an excellent method for establishing token-ring network communications among PCs, and between PCs and IBM mainframe and minicomputer products. The network is still in limited use today.

When IBM introduced OS/2 in 1987, the company needed a network operating system that would take advantage of the features of the new PC operating system. In 1988, Microsoft and IBM developed LAN Manager and LAN Server, respectively. It was Microsoft's and IBM's intent, although not yet actualized, to make each networking product more fully compatible with the other. As IBM developed OS/2, it added to the functionality of LAN Server. Windows NT Advanced Server and Windows NT 3.5 have replaced LAN Manager.

The current version of LAN Server, 4.0, was introduced in the second half of 1994. However, most users still run 3.0, and the majority of this chapter is devoted to this version.

LAN Server Operational Principles

At its heart, LAN Server retains many of the features originally found in the IBM PC Network (PCN). Although the Transmission Control Protocol/Internet Protocol (TCP/IP) suite has become an important network component in LAN Server 4.0 for its widespread use and internetwork routing capabilities, NetBIOS is still the default protocol.

LAN Server is considered by many to be a peer-to-peer network, in which each workstation on the network may share its resources with other workstations. A dedicated file server is not necessary in LAN Server, as it is in current versions of NetWare.

Each machine on the LAN Server network is categorized as a server or a requester. The server consists of an OS/2 workstation running the OS/2 Requester as well as server programs, which allow the machine to share its resources and computing power with other workstations on the network.

The Domain Concept

IBM LAN Server is based on the *domain* concept, in which the network is divided into domains consisting of servers and workstations. Each domain contains a user account database that is stored on a *domain controller*. From version to version, IBM has retained the domain concept as a way to divide the resources on the network.

In LAN Server, a client logs onto the domain server, which gives it access to network resources within that domain. It then requests services from other network devices. In operation, one or two machines on the network may act as servers, while the rest of the devices act as requesters. Several types of servers and requesters exist:

- The Server
- The Domain Controller
- An Additional Server
- The Requester
- The OS/2 Requester
- The OS/2 Remote IPL Requester
- The DOS Requester
- The DOS Remote IPL Requester

The *server* provides file, print, remote boot, and serial services to other workstations on the LAN. Access to network resources is based on a security profile assigned to each device.

Tip:
Applications can run on LAN Server servers as well as workstations, thus allowing the workstation to use its processing power. In LAN Server, a common application of this principle is to run the server as an SQL server and run the SQL application on the

same machine. Under LAN Server 4.0, several servers can be used
in this manner.

A *domain controller* is a server within a group that controls and manages the group (domain). Each domain has a domain controller. This
machine maintains a database, called the *Domain Control Database
(DCDB)*, that maintains the list of users and group definitions. Security
for the network is maintained in individual Access Control Profiles
stored on the domain controller.

Tip:
There can only be one domain controller per domain. You can designate a backup domain controller to take over in the event the
domain controller fails. The information the domain controller
maintains is replicated on the backup domain controller.

Tip:
The file name for the master user and group definitions (profile) is
NET.ACC. The domain controller maintains this file and copies it
to all servers on the network.

Tip:
The domain controller must be installed and users defined before
users can login to the domain.

Tip:
A workstation can be a member of more than one domain. This
allows the workstation to log in to more than one domain simultaneously and use the differing resources of each domain. To do so,
your user name and machine must be defined in each domain
from which you are requesting services.

An *additional server* is a workstation on the network that shares its
resources with other workstations on the network. Many additional
servers can exist in each domain. The additional server receives its user
and group information from the domain controller. An additional server can act also as backup domain controller.

A *requester* is a workstation that allows a user to access shared resources and use the server's processing abilities. This is the "true" workstation, from which you can log on to the network, log off, and map drives to workstations whose resources you want to share. Currently LAN Server supports OS/2 and DOS requesters. From one of these workstations you can access domains for which you have the proper access control profile.

Requesters that also may use the file server as a boot device are called DOS remote IPL and OS/2 remote IPL requesters. In these machines, the workstation contains a ROM chip on the network adapter that allows the machine to boot without the assistance of a local drive and connect to the Remote Program Load (RPL) server. The ROM then causes the files required for booting to be transported over the network and stored in the DOS or OS/2 remote IPL requester's memory. The Remote Program Load runs the programs from a RAM disk created during the boot process.

OS/2 LAN Server Features

OS/2 LAN Server is licensed per server and by individual workstations. It provides fault tolerance in the form of disk mirroring and duplexing. LAN Server, as it was initially distributed, was designed as a direct replacement for Personal Computer LAN Program (PCLP). As a result it was designed around an IBM-centric view of the world. The finished product was a workable but very limited network operating system.

LAN Server 2.0

LAN Server 2.0 was a vast improvement over the original LAN Server. Version 2.0 was designed to work in conjunction with the latest version of OS/2, version 2.0. Its Installation and Configuration program, although primarily text-based, ran in the Presentation Manager environment.

IBM bifurcated the installation process and began installing LAN and Protocol drivers as separate entities using the LAN Adapter and

Protocol Support Program (LAPS). This design had two features. First, driver and protocol support are now independent of LAN Server installation, allowing IBM to use the program for other IBM products such as Communications Manager 2. Second, the separation of LAPS from LAN Server allowed easier development of original equipment manufacturer (OEM) drivers and information files called *Network Information Files (NIFs)*. The switch to Network Driver Interface Specification (NDIS)-based drivers allowed additional topologies to be supported, provided they used NDIS LAN drivers.

Network management was enhanced by features such as First Failure Support Technology/2, Alerter Services, and Timesource services. First Failure Support Technology/2 allows domain database replication; the Alerter Services allows the network manager to send messages to users across the network; and Timesource Services allows the synchronization of server and workstation time.

OS/2 LAN Server 2.0 also introduced remote booting of OS/2 LAN Requesters and DOS LAN Requesters. Security was increased by the use of User Profile Management (the means for creating LAN Server users), and enhanced file security when using the High Performance File System (HPFS).

IBM also introduced improved support for DOS LAN Requesters and Microsoft Windows support in OS/2 LAN Server. In addition, version 2.0 greatly enhanced performance.

LAN Server 3.0

LAN Server 3.0 provided additional functionality over LAN Server 2.0 in a number of ways. Fault tolerance was improved with real-time replication of the domain control database and the ability to mirror the boot drive. Also, data drives now could be mirrored, and fault tolerance could not be administered from a remote server.

Performance was improved by the use of sideband technology, which was designed to improve the performance of small random read and write operations. These performance enhancements were installed in the DOS and OS/2 requesters. Enhancements to the HPFS file system improved file I/O. Support for the DOS Windows environments was also improved.

Additionally, LAN Server 3.0 allowed remote operating system and requester installation from a central server. Virtual DOS support was added in the OS/2 multiple virtual DOS machine (MVDM) environment, which allowed multiple DOS applications to run concurrently. Peer services were added to the OS/2 requester to allow users to share resources without installing complete Server services.

LAN Server 4.0

With the introduction of LAN Server 4.0, the network operating system is now a mature networking product. The installation and configuration is fully graphical and replaces the text-based installation and configuration routines of LAN Server 2.0. LAN adapter and protocol support installation has become an integral part of workstation installation. TCP/IP support has been added as a primary network protocol.

The REXX script language was improved and added to LAN Server 4.0 to allow the network administrator to perform network administrative functions, including workstation and application installation, over the network without user intervention.

Finally, performance has been dramatically improved, as has user functionality, and integration with other network operating systems, including NetWare, has been tightened substantially.

SUPPORTED ACCESS METHODS

OS/2 LAN Server operates with several network access methods. They are token-ring, Fiber Distributed Data Interface (FDDI), Ethernet, 100BASE-T, 100BASE-VG and ARCNET. It uses the Network Driver Interface Specification v2.0 (NDIS) as a framework for the creation of network drivers. NDIS allows multiple network protocols including NetBIOS and TCP/IP to be bound to an individual workstation's LAN driver. In OS/2 workstations, the driver binds directly to the Protocol Manager for OS/2. DOS workstations must use the IBM LAN Support Program. The Protocol Manager uses the PCLP and the LAN Support version of NetBIOS to bind the LAN driver to the network protocol.

Up to four LAN adapters, each supporting 1,000 users, can be installed in each LAN Server server. However, because LAN Server's default network protocol, NetBIOS, is not a routable protocol, the server does not provide internal routing among individual adapters. Each LAN adapter operates independently of its companions in the server.

In addition, the server may operate by itself on the network or as part of a domain.

OS/2 LAN Server Limitations

Although the enhancements of LAN Server versions 2.0 to 4.0 have increased the functionality of the server product, several limitations still exist. The server product must be installed on an OS/2-based machine. This relieves the server product from having to deal with problems associated with support, but limits the currently supported file systems to OS/2- or DOS-based machines. Remote IPL also is limited to either OS/2 or DOS workstations.

While LAN Server 4.0 boasts tremendous speed increases, it is still slower than other network operating systems, including Novell's NetWare.

chapter

MICROSOFT SERVER-BASED NETWORKS

4

icrosoft networks consist of server-based and peer-to-peer implementations that support Microsoft Windows, DOS, OS/2,
NetWare, and Macintosh clients. In 1984, Microsoft developed its
first server-based operating system, MS-Net, based on MS-DOS version
3.1 with support for DOS workstation clients. The company followed
MS-Net in 1988 with LAN Manager, which supported DOS, OS/2, and
Windows clients. Microsoft implementations since that time have consisted of both peer-to-peer and server-based operating systems based
on the company's DOS-based Windows graphical shell environment.
The product was Microsoft Windows NT, introduced in the summer of
1993, which has both peer-to-peer and server-based implementations.
The current version of the server-based network operating system is
called *Windows NT Advanced Server*. It accounts for a 7% market share,
according to the International Data Group based in Framingham,
Massachusetts.

NT Advanced Server preserves many of the features of Microsoft's
LAN Manager such as the use of domains and multiple protocol support. In addition, Advanced Server supports DOS, OS/2, Windows,
and NetWare clients.

The next version, Windows NT 3.5, adds Macintosh client support
and allows up to 1,000 concurrent connections per domain controller.
(A domain controller is responsible for managing a group of workstations.) NT 3.5 has been updated to use Windows NT, a powerful 32-bit
operating system, which will carry Microsoft into the next century. NT

3.5, the replacement for NT Advanced Server, shipped in September 1994. The evolution of Microsoft server-based network operating systems is shown in Figure 4-1.

A large amount of confusion exists in the names Microsoft gives its network operating systems. Since 1993, each release of Windows NT has had separate client components based on Microsoft's Windows. Some of these clients are Windows 3.0 released in 1990, Windows 3.1, Windows 95 (also called *Chicago*), and the as yet unreleased and undocumented Cairo, an object-oriented operating system.

To further muddy the waters, Microsoft presently has two peer-to-peer network operating systems. The first is called *Windows for Workgroups*. The second is incorporated into Windows NT Workstation. Windows 95 will include peer-to-peer networking.

LAN MANAGER

Microsoft and IBM developed OS/2 as a preemptive multitasking operating system. The original OS/2 (v1.0) was a text interface; v1.1 introduced a graphical user interface that looked and operated like Windows. OS/2's graphical user interface was the Presentation Manager. Concurrent to the development of OS/2, Microsoft introduced LAN Manager, a networking product that was tied directly to the OS/2 v1.3 operating environment. (See Figure 4-2 on page 39.)

Network Operating System	Clients	Number of users
MS-Net	DOS	not specified
LAN Manager	OS/2, DOS, Windows, Windows for Workgroups, NT Workstation, and NetWare	not specified
Windows NT Advanced Server	DOS, Windows 3.0 and 3.1, NT 3.5 Workstation, Windows for Workgroups, NetWare	1,000
Windows NT 3.5	Macintosh (forthcoming), Windows 3.0 and 3.1, OS/2, DOS, NT 3.5 Workstation, Windows for Workgroups, NetWare	1,000

Figure 4-1. *The evolution of Microsoft's server-based operating systems.*

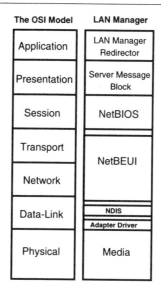

Figure 4-2. *LAN Manager and its relationship to the OSI Model.*

LAN Manager handles file- and print-sharing services for groups of workstations on a LAN. An updated version of OS/2's file system, the High Performance File System (HPFS), shipped with LAN Manager and provided services, including security, for multiple users. LAN Manager was implemented in two versions: LAN Manager v2.1 and LAN Manager 2.2. Although Microsoft has announced that it will continue to support and fix problems with LAN Manager, NT is designed as its replacement. This book discusses LAN Manager v2.1 and v2.2 interchangeably.

In LAN Manager, network devices are arranged into administrative groups called *domains*. A server called the *domain controller* exists in each domain. The domain controller manages the domain's security and resources.

In LAN Manager, two levels of security are provided, called the *logon process* and the *security protected subsystems*. The first provides logon security that requires users to enter their USERNAMEs and passwords to gain access to network resources. The second form of security is "share" security that requires users to enter passwords to access network resources. The domain controller is the repository of this information and is replicated in servers called *backup domain controllers*.

In LAN Manager environments, each network device provides services. Some devices provide network services such as file sharing, while others provide workstation services and request network services of network service devices. The devices that provide network services are called *servers*, while those that request network services from the server are called *workstations*. A server may be dedicated to providing services (a dedicated server) or non-dedicated and operable as both a workstation and a server.

LAN Manager Servers

To administer a LAN Manager server, you must use the NET ADMIN command. This command is a text-based utility that lets you add users and share files, printers, and communications devices. It also lets you monitor network performance.

The LAN Manager server module is installed after first installing OS/2 v1.3 on the computer that will act as the server. You must decide whether the server will provide server services or if it will act as a primary or backup domain controller. You must also determine the transport protocol the network will use. If you expect to use Remote Initial Program Load (RIPL) services for diskless workstations, you must also install a copy of MS-DOS and the necessary files for OS/2 RIPL support. While LAN Manager ships with third-party adapter drivers, additional drivers may be used by supplying the necessary Network Driver Interface Specification (NDIS) LAN driver and the NetWare Information File (NIF).

LAN Manager Clients

LAN Manager uses NDIS v2.0 adapter drivers to provide access to multiple protocols from a single network adapter in a client workstation. The network operating system supports the Institute of Electronic and Electrical Engineers (IEEE) 802.2 Data-Link protocols for Remote Initial Program Load (RIPL) of diskless OS/2 or DOS clients. It also supports token-ring, Ethernet, Fiber Distributed Data Interface (FDDI), and ARCNET access methods, as well as newer 100 megabit per second (Mbps) access methods that work with NDIS 2.0 drivers such as 100BASE-T and 100BASE-VG.

The LAN Manager network is accessed via a DOS-based text interface, Windows, or from the OS/2 command line. You bring up the user interface with the NET utility, which allows you to access shared files, printers, and communications devices or change the domain you want to use.

DOS workstation services install over any version of DOS by running the LAN Manager SETUP program. When installing workstations, you may use basic or advanced services options. You should choose advanced services for most installations, as it gives the workstation complete file and print service capability. You may also have the installation routine install services for extended memory managers and Windows. If you are using extended memory support, LAN Manager tries to load the drivers high. For Windows, it installs additional files to run the network administration programs under Windows.

To use shared resources, you use the NET utility. In DOS environments, this utility brings up text-based windows and dialog boxes that let you access shared network resources. You may then browse the network to find the shared devices and attach to them. One of the key features of DOS-based workstations is persistent connections. The existing connections from the last time you attached to the network are maintained in the LAN Manager workstation initialization file and restored when you next log in to the network.

Network Services

With LAN Manager v2.1, Microsoft introduced several features:

Auto-tuning for Network Performance
In auto-tuning, LAN Manager observes and records the network demands and adjusts network parameters for the next time the server is started. Microsoft has retained this feature in other Microsoft networking products such as Windows for Workgroups and NT Advanced Server.

Remote Administration
LAN Manager can be administered locally from the OS/2 server or remotely from any DOS, Windows, OS/2, or Windows for Workgroups workstation.

Disk Mirroring, Hot Fix, Duplexing, and File Replication

LAN Manager supports disk mirroring in which the information on one server disk can be mirrored to another drive on the same drive controller to ensure data integrity. It also supports Hot Fix, in which data is redirected to good sectors of the disk from bad sectors. Bad sectors are marked as bad and thereafter not used. In disk duplexing, data from one drive on one controller is also maintained on another disk on a separate disk controller, preventing data loss in the event of disk controller failure.

File replication synchronizes the files on one server to another server. The server originating the replication is called the *export server*; the destination server is called the *import server*.

Backup

LAN Manager includes Sytos backup software with each version. It also supports uninterruptible power supplies (UPSes) and data archiving for data protection and management.

TCP/IP Transport Support

To route data between non-routable NetBEUI networks, LAN Manager uses the Transmission Control Protocol/Internet Protocol (TCP/IP) as its default network transport protocol.

Management

LAN Manager is Simple Network Management Protocol-compliant (SNMP) and can be monitored with IBM's NetView network management software. In LAN Manager, MIB I data can be viewed but not changed because of Microsoft's perception of SNMP's poor security.

Remote Access Service

LAN Manager provides network access to remote workstations.

LAN Manager Direction

Once Microsoft embarked on the road to NT, the company made several decisions that would affect LAN Manager as a viable product. LAN

Manager servers only run Microsoft OS/2 v1.3, which limits the network operating system to a 16-bit operating system that dramatically affects performance. Because LAN Manager's primary transport protocol is NetBIOS, it is not routable. To route between LAN Manager networks, Microsoft added TCP/IP support.

Given its limitations, LAN Manager has distinct features that make it a product that many users keep installed until they consider that NT development is complete and stable.

WINDOWS NT

Windows NT is Microsoft's network operating system for the next generation of computers and applications. It is a platform-independent, modular operating system designed to work with most existing and future processors, file systems, and devices. NT design is based on the kernel architecture of the Digital VMS operating system model, which enforces a client/server model of operation on the operating system. (In a monolithic DOS environment, the operating system is organized to a set of procedures that allows any operating system to call any other procedure.)

NT Design Goals

NT was designed with several goals in mind:

Extensibility—The operating system must be able to grow and change as market requirements change.

Portability—The operating system must move easily between RISC and CISC processor platforms.

Reliability—The system must be robust and able to protect itself from malfunction and tampering.

Compatibility—The system must be able to interoperate with existing technology.

Performance—The system must be equally fast and responsive on all platforms.

To achieve these design goals, Microsoft designed the operating system to include preemptive multitasking, memory protection, virtual memory, symmetric multiprocessing, and built-in networking. The modular design provides the memory protection NT requires.

NT Architecture

NT's modular architecture consists of the Hardware Abstraction Layer (HAL), the kernel, the NT Executive, and the client environment subsystems. The kernel and the NT Executive, which make up the basic system, operate with the HAL, which increases portability between hardware platforms and operates below the kernel in privileged mode to access system data and hardware to make their access transparent to the operating system. The kernel and NT Executive handle thread scheduling, message passing, device drivers, and virtual memory allocation. Collectively these modules are referred to as *kernel mode*. The NT Executive serves as the interface between the kernel and the client subsystems. The client operating modules, called *environment subsystems*, handle file, memory, process, display, network, and other subsystems and operate in user mode. These processes, called *servers* and *redirectors*, send messages to the kernel to request access. Each subsystem operates in its own memory, which is protected from the rest of the system. Additionally, subsystems cannot directly access the kernel and HAL because they operate in a separate mode. The NT model provides an increase in overall throughput and reliability.

The NT Executive, kernel, and HAL operate in privileged mode (Ring 0). The other NT subsystems operate in user mode to separate individual processes from the operating system components. Individual subsystem processes run in their own memory areas and are protected from other system processes. Further, each application runs in its own protected memory. If an application crashes, the rest of the system is protected. No application or subsystem can directly address any operating system or hardware component.

NT Networking

The networking features of NT are an extension of LAN Manager. The system provides true 32-bit network performance. It has scalable performance ranging from simple peer-to-peer networking of the workstation product to the client/server model in the NT Server product (formerly called NT Workstation and NT Advanced Server of Windows NT v3.11). To take advantage of the NT operating system's 32-bit architecture, Microsoft developed NDIS 3.0.

NT Advanced Server operates with these network transport protocols:

1. Data-Link Control (DLC)
2. NetBEUI
3. Transmission Control Protocol/ Internet Protocol (TCP/IP)
4. NWLink (protocol that allows NetWare workstations to access an
   NT server)

NT Advanced Server also operates with a variety of network access
methods:

1. Token ring (both 4 and 16Mbps)
2. The Fiber Distributed Data Interface (FDDI)
3. Ethernet (10BASE-T, 10BASE-2, and 10BASE-5)
4. 100BASE-T
5. 100BASE-VG
6. ARCNET

 Tip:
ARCNET is only supported by Windows NT 3.5 and above.

NT is backward-compatible to LAN Manager and MS-Net.

Network Model

The NT networking module consists of the following components:

Providers—Each network contains providers. In Windows NT, the
provider allows NT-based machines to use network services. The
provider manages the commands between the user mode and the
kernel. Providers reside at the Application Layer of the OSI
Model.

User mode—User mode reflects the activities of the client and
resides at the Application Level of the OSI Model.

Executive services—Executive Services run in kernel mode to provide the interface between user environment subsystems and the
kernel. It operates at the Presentation Layer of the OSI Model.

Kernel mode—The kernel mode, which lies in the Presentation
Layer of the OSI Model, is the intelligence of Windows NT. It

schedules, monitors, and controls network activity. It operates at the Presentation Layer of the OSI Model.

I/O manager—The I/O manager encloses the LAN drivers, NDIS, the network transport protocols, the TDI, and the server and redirector programs. It corresponds to the Data Link through Session layers. It manages all I/O for the operating system.

redirector—Each workstation on a Windows NT network contains a software component called the redirector that allows it to handle requests for local or remote traffic. The redirector is the interface between the TDI and the Executive Services.

server component—Each server on a Windows NT network contains a software component called the server that allows it to handle requests for local or remote traffic. The server component provides the interface between the TDI and the Executive Services.

Transport Driver Interface—The Transport Driver Interface (TDI) provides a logical break point between Session Layer applications such as the redirector and servers and the network transport protocols. It straddles the Transport and Session Layers of the OSI Model.

Transport protocols—Windows NT supports a number of network transport protocols, including NetBIOS (NBF); TCP/IP; Data-Link Control, used to attach to mainframes and printers; and NWLink, which allows NetWare workstation to access Windows NT servers. NWLink is the NDIS-compatible version of Novell's Internetwork Packet Exchange (IPX). The network transport protocols are the interface between NDIS and the Transport Driver Interface (TDI). They reside at the Data-Link, Network, and Transport Layers of the OSI Model.

Network Driver Interface Specification (NDIS)—Microsoft and 3Com developed NDIS in 1989 to allow a single network adapter with one driver to communicate with several network transport protocols. NDIS is the interface between the LAN driver and the Media Access Control Layer of the OSI Model. NDIS has two versions, NDIS 2.0 and NDIS 3.0. Windows NT requires NDIS 3.0 drivers.

LAN drivers—The LAN drivers in Windows NT are NDIS v3.0 compliant, enabling them to communicate with several network transport protocols from the same LAN adapter. The driver provides the interface between the media and Windows NT. It resides at the OSI Data-Link Layer.

Medium—The medium provides the capability for devices on the network to communicate with each other. It resides at the Physical Layer of the OSI Model. (See Figure 4-3.)

System Requirements

The system requirements for NT are extensive—a minimum 386 processor with eight to 12 megabytes (MB) of RAM. A useable system, however, is a 486 with at least 16MB and a 200MB hard disk. The upper limits of NT are beyond the range of current hardware.

The NT Network Server

The NT server is 100 percent compatible with existing LAN Manager networks. The only change to the network structure is in the area of security. NT provides the full C2 security POSIX model requires. The security model for the NT server is designed around a security token.

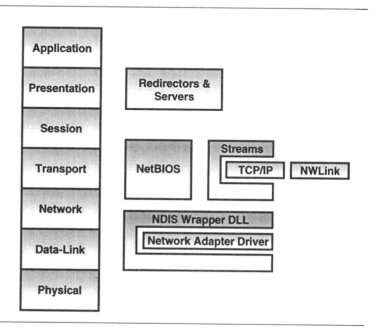

Figure 4-3. *NT's relation to the OSI Model.*

Logon security is maintained as a means of access to the operating system or the network. The logon procedure requires users to enter their USERNAMEs and passwords to start NT. If the network option is installed, users are automatically logged on to the network. When a user logs into the operating system or network, a security token is created for that user. The user account information is stored in the security account manager (SAM) database. The token includes the users' share and file-level security attributes as well as their passwords and USERNAMEs. Any network operating system or operating system access is compared to the security levels granted by the token. If the user's security level matches the security attributes in the token, access to the shared device is allowed.

The NT server is installed as part of the operating system. NT attempts to detect network adapters and install appropriate drivers. If it fails to detect an adapter configuration, or as happens occasionally, detects the incorrect adapter, you can make manual changes. Once the network is installed, changes are made to the network structure through the Windows' Control Panel Network option. These changes include adding or deleting adapters, transport protocols, or network software components. Binding information for network transport protocols can also be altered from the Control Panel's Network option.

Network administration is accomplished through the network administration icon located in the NETWORK group. This application lets you add or delete users and groups. You can change the security attributes for groups and individual users and determine and maintain user home directories and login scripts from this application. Only network administrators or equivalents may use this application.

File sharing is maintained through the NT File Manager. This application is similar to the Windows File Manager, with the exception that additional icons and menu items are added for file-sharing and connection to network drives.

Printer sharing is accomplished through the Print Manager application. Available printers are listed in the Print Manager window. An available printer may be shared by selecting the Share Printer As menu item or icon. A network printer may be attached by selecting the Connect Network Printer menu item or icon.

Network and system hard drives are maintained in the disk manager application located in the NETWORK folder. You may partition and format drives according to the FAT, NTFS, or HPFS file system you need. You may also duplex drives and add fault-tolerant, uninterruptible power supplies (UPSes) through the Control Panel located in the MAIN group.

NT Advanced Server Clients

Windows NT Advanced Server supports NDIS 3.0. Like NDIS 2.0, NDIS 3.0 allows a network driver to be bound to multiple protocols at the same time. NT Advanced Server supports DOS, Windows, Windows NT Workstation, OS/2, NetWare, or Windows for Workgroups workstations.

Direction

NT Advanced Server combines cross-platform networking and operating system software that is scalable to the resources available on the hardware components. The structure of this integrated operating system and network operating system provides ease-of-use and interoperability with other network operating systems such as NetWare, LAN Server, Banyan VINEs, or mainframes and minicomputers that is required for next level of client/server computing.

WINDOWS NT 3.5

The latest version of Microsoft's server-based network operating system is Windows NT 3.5. It is similar to NT Advanced Server, but includes a number of new characteristics.

Features

Like Windows NT Advanced Server, Windows NT 3.5 consists of server and client components. Unlike NT Advanced Server, which uses NetBIOS (NBF), Windows NT 3.5 uses Microsoft's version of the Internetwork Packet Exchange/Sequenced Packet Exchange (IPX/SPX) as its transport protocol. (IPX/SPX is Novell's implementation of the Xerox Network Services [XNS] protocol. Microsoft has rewritten it to their uses.) Windows NT 3.5 also supports Data-Link Control protocols required for mainframe and printer connections, TCP/IP transport, and NetBIOS (NBF), making it backward-compatible to Microsoft LAN Manager.

RAM and Dynamic Allocation

Windows NT 3.5 takes 4 to 8MB less RAM for cache buffer space, making it faster than NT Advanced Server. It also supports the Dynamic Host Configuration Program (DHCP), which lets the server dynamically allocate Internet Protocol (IP) addresses from a single address pool.

IP and Internet Support

NT 3.5 has a Windows Internet Name Service that maps IP addresses to USERNAMEs and support the Point-to-Point protocol and Serial Line Internet Protocol (SLIP). These components are part of the NT Remote Access Server (RAS).

Gateway Options and Migration

From an internetworking standpoint, NT 3.5 builds from NT Advanced Server, increasing the number of gateway sessions from 64 to 256. It is shipped with a migration tool that lets NetWare users migrate their networks to NT.

Security

The security in NT 3.5 has been enhanced, allowing for intruder detection and locking of inactive accounts.

Backward Compatibility

NT 3.5 also includes support for 16-bit workstations and has 32-bit administration tools.

Other Features

NT 3.5 also supports Microsoft's Windows Open Services Architecture (WOSA), which permits applications to operate across different network operating and operating system environments. It also incorporates the Plug and Play Specification, making adapter configuration easier.

Direction

Windows NT 3.5 is Microsoft's next-generation network operating system. While Windows NT market share is presently small (approximately 7 percent), many industry onlookers expect Microsoft server-based networks to significantly erode networks based on Novell's NetWare.

BANYAN VINES

5

Banyan Systems was founded in 1983 to make an enterprise network operating system. The result, Banyan VINES (Virtual Network System), is a nonpreemptive multitasking network operating system based on the client/server model. In non-preemptive multitasking operating systems, several tasks, called *processes*, perform at once, and none of the tasks is required to give up processor control to other tasks.

VINES takes its name from the root of the banyan tree, which as they spread take root to form another tree.

The VINES network operating system is based on AT&T UNIX version 5.3. While Banyan VINES consists of numerous releases, this book will only discuss the most recent versions, V4.x, V5.x, and V5.5.

FEATURES

Banyan VINES is a server-based networking implementation that operates with multiple UNIX servers and numerous DOS, Windows, OS/2, or Macintosh workstations. In VINES, each workstation, printer, directory volume, server, or other network device is an entity or *resource*. When users log in from workstations, they log into the network as a whole, rather than to an individual server. Users have access to entities existing in their user profiles, which contain the names of resources users have been assigned access rights to. The physical makeup of the network is transparent to users, as are the network's hardware complexities. To access printers or other network resources, the user doesn't need to know server names or directory paths. He or she simply needs to have rights to the resource, which are granted in his or her *user profile*. The rights specify the location of a resource and its properties. For this reason, Banyan VINES is called a *network-centric* instead of *server-centric* client/server implementation.

Devices and other network resources are maintained in access rights lists (ARL), which designate the users and other resources that are allowed access to them. The management of resources and access rights lists is maintained by the StreetTalk Global Directory Services (STDS) database, which is distributed among servers so each server knows at any time what entities have access to resources and how to locate them.

Banyan VINES uses proprietary protocols for network transport that are similar to the Transmission Control Protocol/Internet Protocol (TCP/IP) Suite's Internet Protocol (IP). VINES' primary transport protocol is called the *VINES Internet Protocol (VINES IP)*. VINES networks support token-ring, Ethernet, and ARCNET access methods.

Workstation Support

Banyan VINES supports DOS, OS/2, Windows, and Macintosh client workstations. DOS workstations must use MS-DOS v3.x or above and may contain Ethernet, token-ring, or ARCNET adapters. Adapter drivers may be monolithic drivers in which the driver is bound to the network transport protocol, NDIS-compatible drivers, or TOKREUI drivers (a NetBIOS variant). Each DOS workstation uses traditional file names with up to eight characters followed by an optional three-character extension. NDIS drivers are predominately used.

OS/2 workstations are also supported by Banyan VINES. OS/2 versions allowed are Microsoft OS/2 v1.2, IBM Standard and Extended Editions 1.2 and 1.3, Compaq's Standard Edition 1.21, and IBM OS/2 Extended Edition 2.0. Like DOS, OS/2 workstations use monolithic, NDIS, or TOKREUI drivers for the Ethernet, token-ring, or ARCNET adapters they contain. Because the VINES server is UNIX-based, Banyan VINES does not support OS/2's High Performance File System (HPFS).

Macintosh clients must use Macintosh System 6.07 or greater. They support Ethernet, token-ring, or LocalTalk access methods.

Diskless client workstations are supported in Banyan VINES V4.x only.

File System

The Banyan VINES File System (VFS) supports DOS, OS/2, Windows, and Macintosh clients. DOS, Windows, and OS/2 clients make use of Server Message Blocks (SMB), while Macintosh clients use AppleTalk Filing Protocol (AFP) naming and transport. Individual system administrators, responsible for groups of workstations, assign access rights and user profiles to client workstations that define the other network resources users have access to.

Banyan VINES' utilities support limited network backup and restore operations.

File Storage

The VINES File Service (VFS) manages file storage on a VINES server and consists of a file volume, client redirector software, and file management programs. The client redirector software provides client access to the server. Several file services can exist, each having its own StreetTalk name. In VFS, a disk can contain several physical file volumes, which use the DOS directory structure and provide mapping to offline data storage. Banyan VINES V4.11 limits file names to the 8.3 DOS format; V5.x allows heterogeneous formats with the exception of OS/2's HPFS.

Security

VINES security is integrated with StreetTalk and is based on IBM's Access Control Facility (ACF), which allows access rights to be assigned to network resources. In Banyan VINES, administration is decentralized to individuals within each group or at each server. No single super-supervisor exists. Banyan VINES is C2-compliant.

With VINES security, called *Vanguard*, an administrator can restrict access to the server console, files, directories, other utilities, and network utilities. Banyan VINES provides password security, and simultaneous login, login time, and location restrictions.

Each VINES server requires a hardware-based "server key," which attaches to the server's serial port, for operations.

Weak on fault-tolerant features, Banyan VINES supports disk mirroring and duplexing only if the hardware supports these features.

Management

Banyan VINES supplies a server-based network performance management tool called *MNET* that collects statistics on network operating system functions such as disk and processor usage, disk and file I/O, and other file system statistics.

In addition, VINES supports Simple Network Management Protocol (SNMP) client agents that can be controlled by HP Open View, AT&T, or Cabletron Spectrum enterprise network management software. VINES does not support the Common Management Information Protocol (CMIP) or IBM's NetVIEW. Both Banyan VINES V5.0 and V5.5 support remote console management from client workstations.

Administrative operations such as creation of users, user profiles, and access rights lists is controlled via the MUSER utility.

Messaging

VINES has integrated messaging called *Intelligent Messaging,* introduced in June 1993, that provides basic electronic mail functions and a messaging backbone that supports a variety of third-party front-end electronic mail packages. VINES Intelligent Messaging is multithreaded—local mail does not need to wait for delivery until remote mail is queued for sending. Intelligent Messaging is integrated with StreetTalk to offer full interoperability within the VINES directory structure.

VINES also has a more comprehensive Network Mail option available and supports the Simple Mail Transfer Protocol (SMTP) through an SMTP Mail Gateway option. It also supports the X.400 specification. An optional driver is available for interoperability between Microsoft Mail and Banyan messaging.

Internetworking

Banyan VINES is known for its enterprise, internetworking options. It provides automatic routing between adapters in a server, as well as Systems Network Architecture (SNA), Synchronous Server-to-Server, X.25, and serial communications capability options. The Banyan Intelligent Communications Adapter (ICA) consists of two adapters that let you connect a Banyan VINES network to different host computers or to public or private data networks. ICAs can support dial-in users and connections to other VINES servers.

Two ICAs exist. They are the ICA, which handles asynchronous, HDLC, Synchronous Data Link Control (SDLC), bisynchronous, X.25 and X.29 traffic. Up to four ICA adapters can exist in a server, negating the need for external routers. The ICAplus has two ports that support 384 kilobyte per second (KBps) transmission for fractional T1.

VINES SCS, which is based on DCA's Select Communications Server, supports DOS, Windows, and OS/2 clients and offers 3270 terminal and Advanced Program-to-Program Communications (APPC) to IBM mainframes. Integrated with the StreetTalk Directory Services, VINES SCS allows access to SNA servers. SCS allows up to 254 concurrent 3270 or APPC sessions and token-ring, SDLC, or X.25 connections.

Versions of VINES

Over the years, several versions of Banyan VINES have been released. Of these, most users presently operate V5.x networks.

VINES V4.x

Banyan VINES V4.x supports symmetrical multiprocessing (SMP), which divides tasks on a server-by-server basis, according to the device that best suits the processes' needs. VINES SMP supports up to eight 386- or 486-based processors and only DOS and OS/2 clients.

In V4.x, the VANGuard security system was first introduced, which allowed password protection and encryption and access rights designation.

VINES V4.x supports the Network Driver Interface Specification (NDIS) and allows OS/2, Microsoft Windows, Macintosh, and DOS client operation.

VINES V5.x

VINES V5.5, the latest version of Banyan VINES that was introduced in January 1993, incorporates many new features, including the ability to add multiple printers to a print queue, updated StreetTalk Directory Services, and various wide-area networking options. VINES V5.5 also supports management via a remote system console. It supports Macintosh clients without the purchase of a separate version of VINES, and sports a new file system and remote management. VINES V5.0 drops support for diskless PCs. It is the first version of VINES to use CD-ROM with online documentation that can be annotated for individual user needs.

The wide-area network additions to VINES include Integrated Services Digital Network (ISDN) and T1 Server-to-Server options and Source-Level Routing support to bridge remote token-ring LANs. In Source-Level Routing, VINES Internet Protocol (VINES IP) packets are routed over third-party bridges. VINES V5.0 also supports automatic routing between network adapters in the server without needing external routers. The internetworking options are these:

- A synchronous HDLC server-to-server option called SS/WAN
- An asynchronous server-to-server option called SS/WAN
- An X.25 server-to-server option
- A Systems Network Architecture (SNA) server-to-server option called SS/SNA

VINES V5.5 supports Windows clients and the Network Driver Interface Specification (NDIS) v2.01 for token-ring, Ethernet, and ARCNET access methods. It does not support NetBIOS for OS/2 clients. It has redesigned print services that allow administration, redirection of jobs from one queue to another, and LaserWriter support.

V5.5 also is the first version of VINES to support Redundant Arrays of Independent Disks (RAID) technology.

VINES for UNIX

Banyan has worked to extend its network operating system to other UNIX platforms. Among the platforms VINES supports are Hewlett-Packard's HP/UX, IBM's AIX, and SunSoft's Solaris.

ENS for NetWare

In 1992, Banyan made an entree in the NetWare community with the introduction of ENS for NetWare. It operates with NetWare v2.x and v3.x and provides directory services support for NetWare networks that are similar to those of Banyan VINES. In 1993, Banyan shipped ENS v1.1 that supported NetWare 4.01, Macintosh, and OS/2 clients, and SNA gateways. A version of ENS will also support Microsoft's Windows NT.

ENS allows users a single login to NetWare and Banyan VINES networks and allows them to print to any queue, whether it resides on a NetWare or VINES LAN. ENS supports CD-ROM storage and provides Internet connectivity from any server.

STREETTALK III

The strength of Banyan VINES is its directory services structure, called *StreetTalk III.* StreetTalk III is integrated with VINES Intelligent Messaging, VINES network management, and its security and system management features. It contains management features that allow an administrator to adjust and tune networks under his or her control.

In StreetTalk, each user or resource is assigned a three-part StreetTalk name. The first name is the individual's name; the second part is the group the individual belongs to; the last part of the name is the individual's organization. For example, Joe Standish works in the marketing department at Banyan Systems. His StreetTalk name may be jstandish@marketing@banyan.

Each server in a Banyan network maintains a StreetTalk database that it exchanges with other servers on the network on a regular basis.

NETWORK LAYER PROTOCOLS

Banyan VINES uses a variety of proprietary protocols for data communication between resources. Its default network transport protocol is the VINES Internet protocol, which also makes routing decisions based on routing tables it maintains. Banyan VINES also operates with SMB, NetBIOS, Named Pipes, NDIS, and the LAN Manager APIs. It supports NetBIOS through an emulator. The data transported on a VINES network is conveyed in a VINES Internet packet. VINES does not support Microsoft's NetBEUI or any Open Systems Interconnect (OSI) Model protocols.

VINES servers automatically route data between networks using different access methods and media. Because the frame size of these networks may differ, the VINES Fragmentation Protocol (FRP) breaks up packets into frames at the OSI Network Layer. These frames are reconverted to packets at the destination.

RELATION TO OSI MODEL

Although Banyan VINES has not adopted any OSI protocols, its networking model is similar to the OSI Model. The Application Layer of the OSI Model, Application encompasses VINES services such as file and print services, electronic mail, and NetBIOS emulation. At the session level, VINES uses remote procedure calls.

The transport layer contains VINES IPC, the VINES Sequenced Packet Protocol (SPP), and alternately TCP/IP's User Datagram Protocol (UDP). The network layer comprises the VINES Internet Protocol (VINES IP), the VINES Internet Control Protocol, the VINES Address Resolution Protocol, the VINES Routing Update Protocol, and the Internet Protocol (IP) used by the TCP/IP protocol suite. The VINES Internet Control Protocol provides cost of routing information. The VINES Routing Update Protocol (RTP) is responsible for resolving both Internet and LAN addresses. NetBIOS also exists at this layer.

VINES supports Ethernet, token-ring, ARCNET, X.25, and asynchronous HDLC Data Link Layer protocols. At the Physical Layer, VINES operates as a broadband or baseband technology, or uses the Point-to-Point or Transaction Processing (TP) protocols.

BANYAN VINES DIRECTION

Banyan has announced that it will introduce VINES V6.0 in the first half of 1995. VINES V6.0 has improved dial-in services, closer integration with NetWare, and support for X.500-based systems. In addition, Banyan VINES V6.0 can use TCP/IP as its network transport protocol, rather than only the proprietary VINES Internet Protocol (IP). VINES V6.0 will also include Banyans distributed network management architecture, DeMarc.

PEER-TO-PEER NETWORKS

6

If you are employed by a large corporation, you probably manage part of the company's WAN. If you work for a moderate-sized company, your users probably attach to a Novell NetWare, Banyan VINES, Microsoft LAN Manager, Microsoft Windows NT, or IBM LAN Server network. However, if you work for a small company with only a few users or you are a serious computer geek who has several computers at home, you probably use a peer-to-peer network to link computers together.

Peer-to-peer network's popularity grew with packages such as Artisoft's LANtastic and Performance Technologies' POWERLan. They are designed for small numbers of user with minimal network traffic generation and limited need for network services. The profits of Artisoft and Performance Technology, and the popularity of their peer networking software packages, did not go unnoticed. Two major network operating system vendors, Novell and Microsoft, each with their own server-based network operating systems, introduced peer-to-peer network operating systems to complement their existing products.

The attractiveness of peer-to-peer networks lies in their simplicity. Within a peer-to-peer network, computers are equal—all computers can act as servers, as servers and clients, or as clients. A file server with massive memory stores or a dedicated machine isn't required to provide file- and print-sharing services within a peer-to-peer network. No single computer is superior in the network hierarchy, and no machine is dedicated to providing file and printing services. Each computer acts as a server to share resources, as a server and workstation, or simply as a workstation to request resources from other network machines. Each user in a peer-to-peer network manages the resources on his or her workstation. Typically, no central network management exists. A workstation that has a printer attached and stores the shared copy of the word-processing application on its disk drive shares its resources with the rest of the network when users require printing or word-processing services. Other workstations attach to resources to run applications and send print jobs to the printer. As the user of a workstation, you are responsible for sharing your workstation, setting the rights of network users that can access your workstation's services, and making sure that your workstation is in working order.

The peer-to-peer network model is closely related, but still significantly different, from the client/server model, which requires one or more expensive networked computers with massive amounts of disk and RAM storage as file servers for the remainder of the network. In client/server networks, servers run the network operating system and are responsible for file, print, and other network services. Security, managed at the server, grants access to users. Network management is centralized at the server or at the network level as in NetWare 4.10 or Banyan VINES. Individual workstations can't share their resources, but simply run software that redirects requests for network services to the server and directs requests for DOS or OS/2 services to the workstation's local resources. Client/server implementations offer management capabilities and overall performance advantages over peer-to-peer network models, but are more expensive and difficult to implement.

Most peer-to-peer networks run as applications on DOS and are limited by DOS file structure requirements. The File Allocation Table (FAT) is maintained at the outermost track on the hard drive. When a hard drive receives a request for data, the head first moves to the outer edge of the hard drive and sequentially moves back and forth across the hard drive until it finds the entire file. As a result, hard drive access is the limiting factor on performance. As the number of users increase, network bottlenecks increase. This problem can be reduced by spreading applications across workstations.

Tip:
By contrast, a NetWare client/server network prioritizes and simplifies hard disk access so drive heads have only limited redun-

dant movement. In NetWare, the heads are in constant motion in the same direction across the physical disk, prioritizing file reads and writes by the closeness to the drive head to the desired memory location. This mechanism is called *elevator-seeking* and greatly increases network performance.

Peer-to-peer networks that run under OS/2 and Windows NT do not suffer hard drive access problems. The multitasking capabilities of OS/2 and Windows NT allow better hard drive access and greater caching capabilities than DOS. Peer networks have resurged with the advent of multiuser, multitasking operating systems. IBM has developed a peer component in LAN Server versions 3.0 and 4.0, and Artisoft has introduced LANtastic for OS/2.

Peer Workgroups

The best of both worlds would allow peer services for groups of users who work closely together and access to client/server networks when needed. Microsoft's network workgroup employs this concept. In a Microsoft workgroup, users are collected in logical groups to share resources among themselves, but can attach to client/server networks. The workgroup concept was first developed for Windows for Workgroups and extended to Microsoft Windows NT Workstation. It is a subset of the domain idea developed with LAN Manager and IBM LAN Server. The workgroup concept is also an integral part of Novell's Personal NetWare.

In a Microsoft Windows network, a workgroup is not a hard-and-fast physical separation of users or network devices. Any user can use the resources in another workgroup if he or she knows the resource's password. The password lets users easily locate devices; in the same way directories separate data and files into logical groups with similar characteristics. Resources on peer workgroup networks are defined by workgroup, user, and share names.

The best way to organize workgroups is by the company's organizational structure. This structure groups network users by department and job responsibilities and facilitates document-sharing by placing persons who work in the same department in the same workgroup.

BALANCING NETWORK OPERATIONS

Peer-to-peer networks access network files differently than client/server networks. Each user shares the resources of his or her PC with other users. Shared applications and files should be placed in a series of common subdirectories. (See Figure 6-1.)

In this figure, the directory COMMAPPS is for users that need access to all the applications on your hard disk. You should also set up a separate shared directory for each application. A user can then attach a drive for each application he or she wants to use. By restricting shared resource with passwords, you can limit users to only the devices they need. Resource restriction is called *share security* and is the most common form of security on peer-to-peer networks.

A problem can occur on shared networks when one user's workstation contains all the shared applications. Constant user access can cause applications to slow dramatically. The best method to combat application slowing is to distribute shared applications throughout the network. To determine which applications are used most, monitor the network and distribute applications so that no single user provides too many often-used applications on his or her workstation. This method of distributing shared resources is called *load balancing* and is essential for peer-to-peer networks with large numbers of users. Because no single machine is designed as a file server in a peer-to-peer network, some load balancing is necessary for healthy network operation.

```
C:\
    \COMAPPS
        \WORD
        \EXCEL
        \PAINTSHOP
        \PARADOX
        \DATA
```

Figure 6-1. *A peer-to-peer shared directory structure.*

NOVELL PEER-TO-PEER NETWORKS

Prior to 1992, Novell only made client/server networking products. When the market for high-quality peer-to-peer networks increased, Novell introduced NetWare Lite, a DOS-based peer-to-peer network. Later, Novell purchased Digital Research and its product DR-DOS operating system. Novell combined a new version of DR-DOS called *Novell DOS*, which has multitasking features, and introduced Personal NetWare and the Personal NetWare Desktop Server. Personal NetWare clients can access NetWare networks.

NetWare Lite

The first version of Novell's peer-to-peer networking architecture, NetWare Lite, used a variant of the NetWare Core Protocol (NCP) called the *NetWare Lite Protocol*. It used IPX as its network transport protocol and adopted the Open Data-Link Interface (ODI) Link Support Layer (LSL) and LAN drivers. NetWare Lite version 1.1 adopted NCP, which allowed NetWare Lite clients or servers to access NetWare Lite and NetWare client/server networks. NetWare Lite clients ran on Intel 8088- or 80286-based computers; NetWare Lite servers required 80286-based or above machines. Instead of using the NetWare redirector, NETX.EXE, workstations ran SERVER.EXE and CLIENT.EXE programs, which provided server and workstation services, respectively. NetWare Lite supported all access methods that worked with IPX, including Ethernet, token-ring, ARCNET, the Fiber Distributed Data Interface (FDDI), 100BASE-VG, and 100BASE-X.

NetWare Lite was installed by running the INSTALL utility on any machine that would be networked. Installation required designating a machine a client, a server, or both. If you chose server, you were prompted to enter a server name. NetWare Lite then configured the network and allowed you to edit changes made to the machine's CONFIG.SYS file and the LASTDRIVE= statement. You could then select and configure the machine's network adapter. When you rebooted the machine, a batch file called *STARTNET.BAT* executed that ran the network software and started the DOS utility SHARE.COM. SHARE.COM allowed file-sharing and file-locking under DOS. The installation utility also provided a way to verify network connections, which was similar to NetWare's COMCHECK utility.

Tip:
NetWare Lite v1.1 and later versions were easily integrated with NetWare client/server environments by adding the redirector NETX.EXE to the STARTNET.BAT file. You loaded the START-NET.BAT file after CLIENT.EXE and SERVER.EXE and modified the LASTDRIVE= statement in the CONFIG.SYS file. LAST-DRIVE= reflected the number of local drives on the machine and the number of NetWare Lite drives you planned. The NetWare login drive appeared as the next drive after the statement in the LASTDRIVE = command. For example, if you had three local drives, A, B, and C, and planned to have three NetWare Lite drives, D, E, and F, you wanted your LASTDRIVE statement to be drive F. G was the NetWare login drive.

NetWare Lite was accessed and administered with the NET utility. With NET, you could log into the network to share files and printers. From a client, you could use NET to display information about your user account, map drives, print, and send messages to other users. If you had supervisory rights to the machine, you could also use NET to manage the network. With NET you could configure network resources, share drives and printers, add users, and perform other supervisory functions.

To resolve NetWare Lite performance issues, Novell integrated its peer networking with DR-DOS, and introduced Novell DOS 7 and Personal NetWare.

Personal NetWare

Responding to criticisms of NetWare Lite, Novell created Personal NetWare, which installs on any version of DOS, but is tightly integrated with Novell DOS 7. One of the most dramatic changes was Personal NetWare's interoperability with NetWare.

Personal NetWare consists of desktop servers and client workstations. The client software is based on Novell's Universal NetWare Client and the Virtual Loadable Module (VLM) specification, which provides network redirection. When VLM.EXE loads, the Universal NetWare Client provides links to the NetWare v2.x and v3.x bindery, NetWare 4.x's NetWare Directory Services (NDS), and Personal NetWare workgroups. The desktop server uses a workgroup concept similar to the workgroups in Microsoft Windows for Workgroups and Windows NT. Because networking is built into Novell DOS, you must purchase a license for each network user. The design of Personal

NetWare is such that every user on your network can have a copy of the desktop server and Universal NetWare Client on his or her machine and share files within his or her workgroup.

SNMP Management

Personal NetWare has a built-in Simple Network Management Protocol (SNMP) agent and Management Information Base (MIB) that provides network information to a data collector and allows the MIB to control the system. Personal NetWare provides the following MIBs:

HRMIB—The Host Resource MIB collects information about any computer running Novell DOS.

PNWMIB—The Personal NetWare MIB collects information about a machine running the desktop server.

MIB II—MIB II is a standard SNMP MIB.

SNMP and MIB support is loaded by the VLM.EXE file and supports both IP and IPX.

User and Resource Administration

Personal NetWare is administered with the NET utility, a text-based, Windows, or DOS command line utility. With NET, you can log into the network and share files and printers. On workstation clients, you can use NET to join workgroups, display information about your user account; map drives, print, and send messages to users. If you have supervisory rights to the machine, you can use NET with the ADMIN command to manage the network. NET ADMIN lets you configure network resources, share drives and printers, add users, and perform other supervisory functions. The management functions of Personal NetWare's desktop server are more extensive than those of NetWare Lite. You may setup login scripts that automatically share drives on the desktop server you are logging into.

Security

The Personal NetWare security model is more extensive than that of NetWare Lite. Login security exists at the workgroup level and is similar to NetWare, with the exception that the maximum password length is limited to 15 characters. After you log into the workgroup, each server in the workgroup has share-level security on its drives and devices.

Tip:
Personal NetWare extends the concept of a workgroup further than Microsoft workgroups. Personal NetWare's security model has a login to the workgroup and does not allow users to cross workgroups. The workgroup bars access across the network.

Installation

Personal NetWare is installed via a Novell DOS 7 installation utility called *INSTALL*. The Novell DOS 7 installation utility is a text-based installation that is similar to that of NetWare. Installation requires you to set up network adapters, select the type of server the workstation is connecting to, and configure network management. Desktop Server installation requires you to enter the workgroup the workstation can enter and the disk drives and printers it shares. The installation utility then creates the required directories and start-up files for the network.

A welcome addition to Personal NetWare is a DOS- or Windows-based diagnostic utility called *PNWDIAGS*. With this utility, you can monitor a variety of network performance statistics and compare data across the workgroup with other machines. These reports allow you to compare the relative use of various machines and make some reasonable decisions about resource-sharing. The utility for testing network connections has been moved from the installation utility in NetWare Lite to the diagnostic utility.

MICROSOFT PEER NETWORKING

Microsoft introduced networking products in early 1987 with LAN Manager. LAN Manager was a peer network in concept and a client/server network in operation. Each workstation was able to share its devices with the rest of the network, but the network was managed through a server known as a domain controller. LAN Manager developed into an enterprise network system. However, it was not a large commercial success. Microsoft has recently revamped its networking services into peer-to-peer networks with Windows for Workgroups and Windows NT Workstation.

The domain concept remains with Windows NT 3.5 Server, a logical 32-bit LAN Manager extension. In recognition of the increase in workgroup-based peer-to-peer networks, Microsoft introduced the Windows

Open Systems Architecture (WOSA), a strategy to build workgroup-enabling features into Windows.

Windows for Workgroups

In 1992 Microsoft introduced Windows for Workgroups v3.11 (WFW), which extends the Windows interface to networked computers. WFW networks consist of workstation clients arranged into workgroups that share data ad printers. WFW installs as an upgrade to existing Windows workstations and adds network file- and printer-sharing components. Windows utilities such as the File Manager, Print Manager, and the Control Panel were also expanded to include drive- and printer-sharing. Microsoft also added Windows programs such as a workgroup-based Microsoft Mail, a fax manager, chat capabilities, and performance monitoring.

WFW supports WIN32S, which brings virtual mode operation to Windows. The virtual Cache Manager, VCACHE, replaces SMART-DRV.EXE in many situations and provides 32-bit memory control. 32-bit disk access was also installed. These functions allow WFW to take total control of machines and operate in a 32-bit environment. You must purchase a separate copy of WFW for each user.

WFW supports Network Driver Interface Specification (NDIS) and Open Data-Link Interface (ODI) drivers. (See Figure 6-2.)

NDIS 3.0, which allowed drivers and the Protocol Manager to operate in a 32-bit protected mode, extended network operations to 32-bit performance, increasing Windows and network speed. Drivers load from the SYSTEM.INI file when Windows loads. Protected-mode drivers include the following:

NETBEUI.386—This is the protected-mode NetBEUI network transport protocol support in WFW.

NDIS.386—This is the NDIS 3.0 Support Layer driver.

VNETBIOS—This driver represents the virtual NetBIOS protocol.

Driver	Specification	Loads from
NDIS 3.0	NDIS	SYSTEM.INI
NDIS 2.0	NDIS	AUTOEXEC.BAT
MLID	ODI	AUTOEXEC.BAT

Figure 6-2. *Windows for Workgroups driver support.*

VREDIR.386—This file is the protected-mode redirector.

NE2000.386—This is an NDIS 3.0 adapter driver for an Ethernet adapter.

VSERVER.386—VSERVER.386 is the protected-mode driver for WFW servers.

WFW drivers with the .386 extension are protected-mode drivers, which load in upper memory and operate in protected 32-bit mode. VNETBIOS is a virtual device driver that only loads in Windows sessions. It is not displayed if you view the memory contents.

Tip:
VSERVER.386 only operates when WFW loads in enhanced networking mode. It runs the Windows server, which allows file- and printer-sharing. If you are using an NDIS 2.0 driver, you must start the network with the NET START command when Windows loads. If you use the NET START WORKSTATION to start the workstation services under DOS, you cannot use server services under DOS. In addition, if you attempt to load the Windows network without first stopping the real-mode workstation service, VSERVER won't load and you won't be able to share the resources of that workstation.

To remain compatible with the large installed base of adapters using NDIS 2.0 drivers, WFW retains backward compatibility with NDIS 2.0 drivers. These drivers operate in 16-bit mode and load in lower memory with the NDIS 2.0 real-mode support layer NDISHLP.SYS. NDISHLP.SYS uses a wrapper called *NDIS2SUP.386* to link the driver into the 32-bit mode Virtual Protocol Manager. It slows down network operations, but lets you operate in WFW without difficulty. The driver loads from the AUTOEXEC.BAT file during execution of the NET START command.

While WFW uses NDIS 3.0 drivers as its primary adapter interface, it also uses ODI. To use ODI drivers, you must load the driver stack in the AUTOEXEC.BAT file. (See Figure 6-3 on page 71.)

In the figure, LSL represents the ODI Link Support Layer and TCTOKSH represents the LAN driver. ODI drivers must be loaded between the NET START command and the ODIHLP.EXE driver in the AUTOEXEC.BAT file. NWNBLINK makes NetBIOS services available to the IPX/SPX-compatible transport driver (ODI) as 32-bit protected mode virtual device drivers. This driver provides support for Windows NT when using IPX/SPX drivers. ODI drivers let you simultaneously

```
AUTOEXEC.BAT
c:\windows\net start
c:\windows\lsl
c:\windows\tctoksh
c:\windows\odihlp
```

Figure 6-3. *Loading ODI drivers in WFW.*

attach to a NetWare and WFW network. Because IPX is a routable protocol, you can route data over different physical networks. At present,
WFW supports two LAN adapters in a machine with two protocols
bound to one adapter and a single protocol bound to the other.

 Tip:
NetBIOS is not a routable protocol. If you use NetBIOS, WFW's
default network transport protocol, WFW stations must be on the
same physical network.

Windows NT

Windows NT ships with built in peer-to-peer networking, allowing NT
workstations to share files and printers with other network workstations. The peer networking in NT uses the workgroup organization of
WFW.

The difference between Windows NT and WFW is the security
model. NT provides login security, share, and local security. Unlike
WFW, users must have accounts on NT workstations to use network
services. The login to the local workstation generates a security token
that validates your rights through Windows NT's Security Access
Module (SAM). When a user accesses a remote machine, the security
token is generated based on the SAM at the remote machine. In addition, local security for files exists based on file attributes. NT File
System (NTFS) partitions use extended permission attributes that affect
file security rights.

In Windows NT, individual users must be created on each workstation through the user administration utility found in the Network
Group folder. Users can receive extended rights as individuals or members of a group. Although a series of predefined groups are created at
installation, you may customize groups as needed.

Tip:
Network users are responsible for their workstations. They must
create and grant rights to network users. Users can grant and
remove access as needed without waiting for IS to make changes.
Problems arise when peer networks grow. As more users join the
network, the time spent on network management grows proportionally and the need for centralized management increases. At
the point where the peer network becomes unwieldy, an NT
Server can be introduced.

Using NT Server, the network can be broken into logical
domains with domain controllers to centralize network management. (See *Chapter 4, "Microsoft Server-Based Networks."*)

Network Transport Protocols

The original version of Windows NT v3.1 used NetBIOS (NBF) as its
network transport protocol to allow backward compatibility with LAN
Manager. In addition to NetBIOS (NBF), NT uses IPX/SPX and TCP/IP
as network transport protocols. The introduction of Windows NT 3.5
changed the default transport protocol to IPX/SPX with TCP/IP as a
secondary transport protocol. NetBIOS (NBF) is still available. In addition, Microsoft added functionality to its TCP/IP transport on NT
Server 3.5 with the Dynamic Host Configuration Protocol (DHCP) and
the Windows Internet Naming Service (WINS). These services let NT
Servers autoconfigure and maintain IP addresses for workstation
clients.

NT Workstation supports multiple adapters and transport protocols.
While the network transport drivers consist of NetBIOS (NBF),
IPX/SPX, or TCP/IP, the adapter driver must be NDIS 3.0-compliant.
NT is a 32-bit operating system and cannot use 16-bit NDIS 2.0 or ODI
drivers. The lack of backward compatibility to NDIS 2.0 was a require-
ment of the move to the new operating system.

Network support is available in Windows NT 3.5 for WFW, NT
Server, and LAN Manager domains and NetWare. Under NT 3.1, only
Microsoft network support is available. Adding a 32-bit NetWare server driver and a requester provided NetWare support. These drivers
have a .LAN extension and were designed as drivers for NetWare

servers. The requester is added through the Network Icon and Control Panel.

 Tip:
If you have NT 3.1 network and want to make a NetWare connection, the installation of the NetWare requester is difficult and erratic at best. In addition, because the standard command prompt is not supported, you must use a special NetWare DOS prompt that ships with the requester. NT 3.5 has built-in NetWare support and uses NDIS 3.0 drivers that support NT utilities.

File- and Printer-Sharing

In Windows NT, files are shared and network drives attached through the Windows File Manager; network printers are shared and attached through the Print Manager. Users are maintained through the User Manager. WFW and Windows NT are interoperable.

WINDOWS 95 NETWORKING

Windows 95 is an extension of the Windows for Workgroups concept. It is a preemptive, multitasking 32-bit operating system that uses the Windows user interface. Windows 95 incorporates peer-to-peer networking and implements the Windows Open Systems Architecture (WOSA) networking model, which allows multiple networking software components to coexist in the operating system. WOSA uses the Service Provider interface (SPI) to call components of the operating system that process network data.

Windows 95 implements the 32-bit Virtual Network Services that operate in protected mode. Virtual Network Services are implemented by NDIS 3.0. Windows 95 also uses NDIS 2.0, although its use sacrifices system performance.

The network transport protocol in Windows 95 has changed from NetBEUI to IPX/SPX. This follows the Windows NT transport protocol implementation. Windows 95 also has built-in support for TCP/IP. If you are using IPX/SPX or TCP/IP, limited routing is available through the Multiple Provider Router, an extension of the WOSA model. Windows 95 supports any topology that provides an NDIS or ODI driver, including these:

- ARCNET
- Ethernet
- Token-ring
- Fiber Distributed Data Interface (FDDI)
- 100BASE-VG
- 100BASE-X

The adapter driver and media are independent of the upper layer NDIS support and transport protocols.

Client Network Connections

Windows 95 network support comprises several layers as defined by the WOSA model:

Application Program Interface (API)—The WIN32 API provides network-specific functionality.

Multiple Provider Router—The MPR is the routing component in Windows 95 that routes APIs to appropriate network components.

Network Provider—The Network Provider implements network services such as making and breaking network connections.

IFS Manager—The Installable File System Manager routes file system requests to the appropriate file system driver.

Network filesystem driver—The network filesystem driver is similar to the IFS, but provides file system support for remote network file systems.

Network Transport—The network transport protocol for Windows for Workgroups is currently NetBEUI. IPX/SPX and TCP/IP are also supported.

Network Driver Interface Specification (NDIS)—NDIS defines the interaction between the network transport protocol and the network adapter device driver.

Network adapter driver—The driver controls the adapter and is responsible for taking packets sent to the driver from NDIS and transporting them as frames on the physical medium.

The intent of WOSA is to provide 32-bit networking through a series of APIs and dynamic link libraries (DLLs) that provide a consistent user interface regardless of the network the user communicates through. The Universal Client is essential to WOSA. To fulfill this concept, Microsoft maintained the majority of the code for the user interface in common APIs and DLLs. The Network Provider is responsible for defining the network connection to the Multiple Provider Router using the common API structure and definition mechanism. The Network Provider is a .DRV file that loads when Windows 95 starts. The MPR loads each Network Provider according to the settings in the SYSTEM.INI file. Individual vendors are responsible for providing compatible DLLs for Windows 95. The following is a complete list of compatible network interfaces:

1. Microsoft MS-Net
2. Microsoft LAN Manager
3. Novell NetWare
4. Banyan VINES
5. TCS 10-Net
6. Sun Microsystems PC-NFS
7. Artisoft LANtastic
8. IBM AS/400 Network
9. FTP Software NFS
10. Digital Pathworks
11. Performance Technology POWERLan

The Universal Client allows multiple network support through the MPR.

Server-Based Support

Microsoft has not yet decided if server services will be implemented in Windows 95 or as a separate product. To date, every beta has included server services, which provide file- and print-sharing capabilities in almost the same manner as WFW. Server services run as 32-bit applications, making the network response as fast as possible.

The major component of the server is VSERVER, which runs as a multithreaded software component capable of allocating resources among several network requests. VSERVER controls printing, file-sharing, and security operations. It includes the peer-to-peer components of WFW.

The security model for Windows 95 has also changed from WFW. In WFW, security existed at the share level only. Windows 95 implements share-level security in the same manner as WFW, but extends security protection to the user level. In addition to using password protection to limit access to particular directories, you may now provide access to specific groups of users.

Other Peer Network Operating Systems

Peer-to-peer networks have been around for several years, offering low-cost alternatives to larger and more complex client/server network operating systems. Peer-to-peer networks typically are DOS-based and provide file-sharing and file-locking, network transport, redirector, management, and mail services. The transport protocol of most peer-to-peer systems is NetBIOS or Microsoft's NETBEUI. Peer-to-peer networks are useful for networks of 2–25 users. Among the better-known peer-to-peer networks are Artisoft's LANtastic, Performance Technology's POWERLan, and WebCorp's WEB.

Artisoft's LANtastic

LANtastic was the predominate peer-to-peer network during the 1980s and early 1990s. Currently, LANtastic version 6.0 has begun to approach a full-fledged network operating system for large networks. Until the introduction of LANtastic for OS/2 and LANtastic for Macintosh, LANtastic was a DOS-based peer-to-peer network operating system. LANtastic is sold in 5-, 10-, 25-, and 250-user versions.

LANtastic started as an Ethernet-based product running over NetBIOS. The introduction of Adapter-Independent LANtastic has developed a wide support base among manufacturers. It comes as a complete package with file- and printer-sharing services, and mail. Additions to the base system let you share modems and use voice mail. A chat mode is possible using the LANtastic sound board.

While LANtastic's network transport protocol is NetBIOS, additional support can be purchased for TCP/IP and IPX/SPX. Adapter drivers are LANtastic-specific. The primary user interface is DOS, but Artisoft supplies a menu user interface for managing network connections and network management.

LANtastic installs from a text-based dialog box that names your workstation and sets up the adapter driver, basic connections, and shares.

While LANtastic is a peer-to-peer network, it uses many of the concepts of a client/server network. Workstations may be workstations only, servers, or both servers and workstations. Workstations that share network resources are servers. Users log in to servers and are validated prior to accessing shared resources. Security is available at a share and user level for each resource. Password security is available both for the login and shares.

Performance Technology's POWERLan

Developed by Performance Technology of San Antonio, Texas, POWERLan is a peer-to-peer network similar to LANtastic. A workstation may be a workstation, a server and workstation, or a dedicated server. A server shares resources with the rest of the network. A dedicated server works similarly to a server in the client/server model and provides superior performance to workstations that act as both workstations and servers. Although POWERLan is primarily a DOS-based interface for server and workstation components, it also supports UNIX workstations. LANtastic is sold in 5-, 10- 25-, and 250-user versions.

POWERLan's default network transport protocol is NetBIOS. The UNIX version provides a gateway to DOS platforms. LANtastic uses proprietary LAN drivers, ODI drivers, or NDIS drivers. The large adapter driver support makes POWERLan a choice for many peer-to-peer users.

The PLAdmin utility provides the LANtastic user interface for users and network administrators. This utility lets you share network resources as well as administer users and change the settings for the adapter driver and NetBIOS. Resources are connected through the PLNavigate utility. POWERLan provides DOS, Windows, and Windows 95 versions of the utilities.

POWERLan security consists of share and login validation functions. Users must log in to the server with or without passwords. Each shared resource contains a user list users must be on before they can access shared resources.

WEB Networks

Originally developed by WebCorp, WEB networks are low-end peer-to-peer networks for no more than 25 users with file- and print-sharing and built-in e-mail. WEB is a DOS-based network.

Unlike many other peer-to-peer networks, WEB uses IPX/SPX as its network transport protocol. While the original design used IPX linkable drivers, the current version uses linkable or ODI drivers.

In a WEB network, each user maintains his or her own system user login security. Security is provided at the share level. Each user determines the files he or she will share and the access level of the file. Files may be shared in a batch file using a DOS command line message or via the Station Manager utility.

Network management is available for each user. The Station Manager utility is the primary means of sharing resources and connecting to resources of other users and changing network settings. Instead of connecting to resources, drives and printer resources are mapped as in NetWare. WEB provides DOS- and Windows-based versions of its Station Manager utility. Network support under Windows 3.11 is also provided to conform to existing specifications for network drivers. Windows 95 network client support is not currently available.

E-mail facilities are provided by the WEB ENotes application for DOS or Windows. One station acts as the post office for the network to handle the maintenance of the e-mail system. ENotes is accessed under DOS via the Station Manager utility. Windows provides a separate mail application for ENotes.

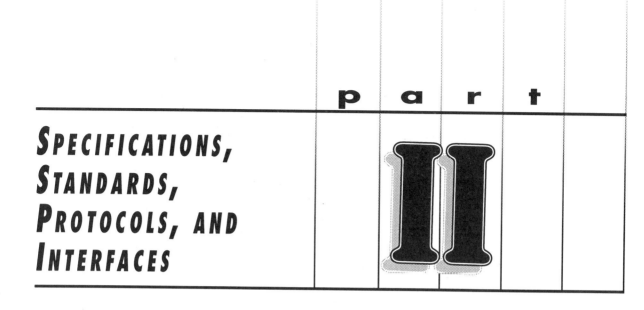

SPECIFICATIONS, STANDARDS, PROTOCOLS, AND INTERFACES

part II

The installation and operation of each network follows specifications, standards, protocols, and interfaces that define the manner in which network aspects take place. These rules define how network communications occurs and provide consistent definitions to follow when something on the network goes wrong.

Specifications we talk about in this book are those published by agencies such as the American National Standards Institute (ANSI), the International Telecommunications Union (ITU-T) or CCITT, the Federal Communications Commission (FCC), and the Electrical Industries Association/Telecommunications Industry Association (EIA/TIA).

Standards are defined for network communication and group similar features in reference platforms users can study to know how communication occurs. These standards, many of which are implemented in LANs, create a common platform for understanding and discussion. The standards we discuss in this book are the Institute of Electrical and Electronic Engineers (IEEE) LAN standards and the International Standards Organization's Open Systems Interconnection (OSI) Model.

Each LAN uses several protocols everyday to allow communication between network devices or specify how network technologies such as facsimile or document management interact. This section discusses network transport protocols such as IPX, NetBEUI, and NetBIOS or OSI Application, Presentation, and Session protocols such as the Sequenced Packet Exchange (SPX) protocol. It also describes the differences between token-passing and CSMA/CD protocols, which access methods implement.

Two interfaces are also important to networking. They are the Open Data-Link Interface (ODI) and the Network Driver Interface Specification (NDIS), one of which is used by each of the server-based network operating systems discussed in this book.

PROTOCOL AND DATA CONCEPTS

7

COMMUNICATION PARTNERS, PEERS, ADDRESSES, AND DATA

The intent of networking is to provide communication between devices such as printers, workstations, and file servers. Each of these *devices* is a partner to the communication process. When devices exchange messages consisting of *data*, they do so with *peer entities* built into each device. These peer entities have similar characteristics and functions. Thus, when a workstation requests a file, it does so of a *peer process*. The peer process answers the request or denies it. (See Figure 7-1 on page 82.)

Each network device also has several *addresses* by which it is known to other network devices. These addresses vary depending on the peer component. For example, each network adapter has an address assigned by the manufacturer that can often be changed by the user. Workstations containing adapters have other addresses associated with them. Addresses may be controlled by the IEEE, by the network installer, or by the device vendor. *Addresses* allow devices to recognize each other and allow other components to track the data exchange between communication partners.

The data transmitted across the network has a certain format or *syntax* consisting of headers and footers that define how the data is used or identify its type. As in language, these headers and footers modify the data, describing its meaning to other devices. Each set of data is

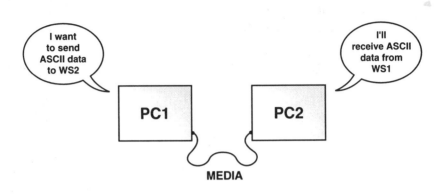

Figure 7-1. *Communication between peer partners.*

also *encoded* for transmission across the media. The forms of encoding are these:

Differential Manchester	Token-ring
4B/5B	FDDI
Sinusoidal dipulse	ARCNET
Manchester	Ethernet

These forms of encoding consist of specific voltage patterns. For example, in 4B/5B encoding, four bits of data are transmitted encodes as five bits of data. Individual bits are distinguished from each other by transitions in voltage.

PROTOCOLS AND LAYERING

Network devices use sets of rules or *protocols* to communicate with each other, so that no matter what type of machine they are or what access method or topology they use, they understand each other. Protocols specify the form of data and the methods used for transmitting data between devices. They control addressing of data packets and route data between networks. LANs use peer-to-peer protocols in which all workstations are equal in communications.

Protocols are often arranged in stacks. While protocols exist at all layers of the OSI Model, they operate independently of the other layers. For example, the network transport protocol of one workstation communicates with the network transport protocol of its peer partner. The stack consists of the layers data traverses to reach the peer partner. (See Figure 7-2.)

As packets move down through the protocol stack, they are enclosed in header and control information added by the protocol below. At the destination, each successive layer removes the header and control information. The user only receives data. In this process, called *encapsulation* and *decapsulation*, the packet's outermost layer consists of header, control, and address information added by the lowest layer protocol. (See Figure 7-3 on page 84.)

TOPOLOGY, MEDIA, AND ACCESS METHODS

LANs are arranged in physical shapes called *topologies,* and data passes in a manner according to the rules set by network access methods,

NetWare	OSI	TCP/IP
Applications	Applications	Application FTP, SMTP
Applications	Presentation	Application FTP, SMTP
NCP	Session	Application FTP, SMTP
NetBIOS NCP Acknowl.	Transport	Transport TCP, UDP
SPX/IPX	Network	Internet IP, RARP
Data Link	Data Link	Network Interface MAC
Physical	Physical	Network Interface MAC

Figure 7-2. *NetWare's protocol stack and the TCP/IP stack.*

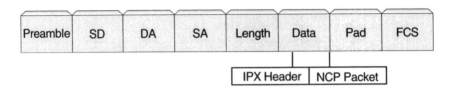

Figure 7-3. *Encapsulation and decapsulation.*

which control access to the medium. A number of topologies exist—bus, star, ring, and hybrid. Access methods include Ethernet, ARCNET, token-ring, and the Fiber Distributed Data Interface (FDDI). The medium corresponds to the physical or virtual connections among workstations, file servers, and printers.

FRAMES AND PACKETS

Data is sent across the LAN in frames, whose size depends on the access method being used. Frames are formed from packets used at higher-protocol layers. (See Figure 7-4 on page 85.) The content of a frame consists of the data being transported. Each frame contains header information, and source and destination addresses added by the network adapter firmware and software driver. The addresses indicate the source of the data and its destination.

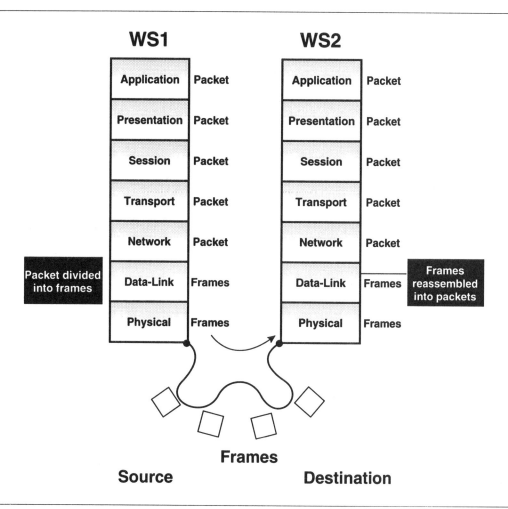

Figure 7-4. *Packets and frames.*

COMMON COMMUNICATION STANDARDS

8

S tandards organizations are the backbone of the LAN industry. These organizations, consisting of public and private companies, define the basic specifications for the development, operation, and installation of LAN cabling, access methods, and protocols. They form the framework for most commercial LANs and influence the buying decisions of most network administrators. Standards ensure that if you buy an Ethernet adapter, it will work with all other Ethernet adapters you have, and that when you install Category V cable, it will work with the adapters you purchase. And, when you attempt to install a network operating system, it will work flawlessly with your adapters and cabling. That is, almost.

In fact, most standards are not developed independently of the market, but in response to an existing product. Ethernet was only standardized after its development, and ARCNET only became an American National Standards Organization (ANSI) standard after years of work on the part of companies who had been selling ARCNET as a de facto standard for years.

The term standard also implies an all-seeing specification, protocol, or access method that defines the proper methodology for other technologies to follow. Many standards and standards organizations exist. Standards fall in three classes: *de jure*, *de facto*, and *proprietary*. *De jure* standards are those standards a recognized standards organization defines, such as IEEE 802.3. *De facto* standards grow from increasing or substantial use. Before ARCnet became a *de jure* standard, it was a *de facto* standard. *Proprietary* standards are devices by any company that decides its technology should be called a standard. Common LAN examples are Novell's Internetwork Packet Exchange (IPX) or Thomas-Conrad's TCNS. These standards are owned, defined, and controlled by the company, and while they have widespread use, a single company dictates the development and licensing of the standard technology. Proprietary standards may also evolve into *de jure* standards when the developer releases the specification to the market for further development. Each type of standard has a role to play in defining almost any development in the LAN industry, whether it is developed as a company-owned proprietary standard or developed as a standard at its inception by a standards organization.

Because standards need to meet so many expectations, most standards represent the least common denominator. A standard to which all vendors must develop products, can't have all the bells and whistles possible, or very few products would comply. As a result, standards often represent a baseline of required components, and vendors add features that give added value to their products.

In this chapter, we'll discuss those standards that have the largest impact on the access methods, protocols, and media networks use. They originate from organizations such as the American National Standards Institute (ANSI), the Consultative Committee for International Telegraph and Telephone (CCITT), the International Standards Organization (ISO), the Electronic Industries Association/Telecommunications Industry Association (EIA/TIA), the Federal Communications Commission (FCC), and the Government OSI Profile (GOSIP).

AMERICAN NATIONAL STANDARDS INSTITUTE (ANSI)

Founded in 1918, ANSI is a nonprofit organization of the U.S. government that controls encoding schemes and signaling definitions for data communications. It represents more than 1,000 businesses and other organizations. The organization is the U.S. representative to the

International Standards Organization (ISO), which developed the Open Systems Interconnect (OSI) model for networking. Also, ANSI is part of the Consultative Committee for International Telephone and Telegraph (CCITT), which itself is a committee of the United Nations International Telecommunications Union (ITU). Many ANSI standards dovetail with Institute of Electrical and Electronic Engineers (IEEE) standards for LANs, MANs, and WANs. ANSI also was responsible for developing the standards for COBOL and C, as well as the Small Computer System Interface (SCSI). Some of the standards you will need to know include these:

ANSI/ATI 878.1—The ARCNET specification.

ANSI 802.1-1985/IEEE 802.5—The specification for token-ring.

ANSI 802.3/IEEE 802.3—Defines Ethernet implementations including including 10BASE-2, 10BASE-5 and 10BASE-T.

ANSI X3.135—Defines the specifications for the Structured Query Language (SQL) for relational database queries.

ANSI X.392—Defines a standard for encryption algorithms for data security.

ANSI X3T9.5—Defines the specifications for the Fiber Distributed Data Interface (FDDI), the Copper Distributed Data Interface (CDDI), and FDDI II.

CONSULTATIVE COMMITTEE FOR INTERNATIONAL TELEPHONE AND TELEGRAPH (CCITT)

The CCITT is a committee of the United Nations International Telecommunications Union (ITU) (Comite Consultatif Internationale de Telephonie and Telegraphie) based in Geneva, Switzerland. The standards promulgated by the CCITT are also known as ITU standards. The U.S. is represented at the CCITT by the State Department. The CCITT is made up of 15 separate study groups that define standards for telecommunications services, maintenance, tariffs, and data transfer across international borders. Study groups are defined by categories that are labeled A–Z:

A–B—Terms, definitions, and procedures

D–E—Telecommunications tariffs

F—Mobile services

G–H—Transmission specifications

I—Integrated Services Digital Network (ISDN)

J—Television transmission standards

K–L—Protection of transmission facilities

M–N—Maintenance procedures

P—Telephone transmission

R–U—Telegraphy

V—Data communications over telephone services

X—Data communications and electronic mail networks

Two of these categories, V and X, are the most important for LAN management.

Data Transmission over Telephone Services

The V series defines standards for sending data over telephone wires through modems, including error detection and correction. For a long time, the Bell standard was the standard for the U.S. It was based upon proprietary telephone standards defined by Bell Telephone. However, the U.S. has replaced this standard with ITU standards. If you have purchased a modem recently, you have seen that it is labeled as being compatible with a variety of V standards. Versions of V standards are part of the standards name: bis indicates a second version; terbo indicates a third version. Here are some of the more important V standards to look for:

V.24—Defines the interface between modem and computer, equivalent of RS-232C

V.26bis—Defines 1,200 bit-per-second (bps) and 2,400bps full-duplex modems used on dial-up lines

V.28—Defines the specifications for RS-232 interfaces

V.32—Defines standards for asynchronous and synchronous communications at 4,800 to 9,600bps

V.32bis—Defines standards for communications rates of up to 14,400bps.

V.42—Defines standards for error-checking on high-speed modems

V.42bis—Defines standards for data compression on high-speed modems

V.terbo—Defines standards for communication rates of up to 19,200Kbps

V.34 (V.fast)—Defines standards for communication rates of 28Kbps

OSI Standards

The X series of LAN standards define the OSI telecommunications standards, including protocols, equipment, transmission speeds, and network interfaces. The X series standards include the following:

X.200/ISO 7498—Defines the OSI Model

X.25/ISO 7776—Defines the standards for terminal and public packet-switching networks, including error and link control and electrical connections

X.400/ISO 10021—Defines standards for public or private electronic mail networks

X.500/ISO 9594—Defines standards for directory services and messaging on LANs and WANs

X.700/ISO 9595—Defines standards for the Common Management Information Protocol (CMIP), which was defined to replace an interim standard, SNMP

GOSIP

The Government OSI Profile is a suite of standards, based on the OSI Model, that provides governmental purchasing guidelines.

CCITT Groups

Several groups exist that regulate facsimile transmission. Two of these, Groups 3 and 4, should be familiar. Group 3 defines digital facsimile at 9,600bps at standard image resolutions of 203 dots per inch (dpi) by 98dpi, or fine resolution at 203dpi by 198dpi. Group 4 is a high-speed standard for transmission of 400dpi images over ISDN.

ELECTRONIC INDUSTRY ASSOCIATION/ TELECOMMUNICATIONS INDUSTRIES ASSOCIATION (EIA/TIA)

The EIA/TIA develops wiring standards for all aspects of the communications and electronic industries, including the RS-232C specification. EIA/TIA defines the cabling standards for interoperation with LAN access methods. It also defines cable and device wiring standards to allow easy installation and data communication. If you want to wire a building with the latest Category V cable in a manner that operates with token-ring, Ethernet, and the latest standards, you should follow the EIA/TIA 568 Commercial Building Wiring Standard for unshielded twisted-pair (UTP) media.

UTP Cabling Standards

EIA/TIA defined five categories of UTP media:

Category I—Standard telephone cable
Category II—Data cable for transmission rates of up to 4 megabits per second (Mbps)
Category III—Data cable for transmission rates of up to 10Mbps
Category IV—Data cable for transmission rates of up to 16Mbps
Category V—Data cable for transmission rates of up to 100Mbps

In addition to the wiring standards, the EIA/TIA defined several standards for wiring connectors known as the 568A and 568B standards. Both standards are suitable for LAN wiring.

EIA/TIA Structured Wiring Systems

The largest part of the EIA/TIA standards is related to the structure and administration of the cable plant. The EIA/TIA has defined wiring systems structures for the following:

- The work area
- The horizontal wiring between work areas
- Backbone wiring between equipment rooms
- The telecommunications closet
- Main cross-connects between buildings
- Building wiring entrance requirements

You can write the EIA/TIA and receive copies of these standards and other material related to commercial building wiring. If you plan to install a cable plant, we recommend that you obtain these documents and read them.

FCC

The Federal Communications Commission (FCC) has a role in the networking as well as the more familiar consumer industry. FCC certification ensures that devices you purchase from United States companies or import from foreign manufacturers meet radio frequency interference (RFI) standards. FCC certification comes in two classes: Class A and Class B.

Class A devices are designed for commercial use in buildings that are at least 30 feet away from residential areas. Network adapters, hubs, and concentrators are most often Class A devices. Minicomputers and mainframes are typical Class A devices. PCs were originally Class A devices, as no one really expected them to be used outside of businesses.

Class B devices consist of electronic devices designed primarily for home use, including PCs and laptop computers. These devices must not interfere with radio or telephones within a 30-foot distance. Class B certification is more restrictive and expensive. Most PCs today have Class B certification.

Network devices that contain other FCC-certified devices assume the characteristics of the least restrictive specification. Thus, if you have a Class B PC that you install a Class A network adapter in, you effectively create a Class A PC.

THE IEEE

9

The Institute of Electrical and Electronic Engineers (IEEE) sets LAN, WAN, and MAN standards. It was founded in 1963 and includes engineers, students, and scientists as its members. IEEE standards are based on the Physical, Data Link, and Network Layers of the International Standards Organization's Open Systems Interconnect model. It is the world's largest professional society and makes recommendations to the American National Standards Institute that will be considered for national standards.

The IEEE has set a number of standards for networking and communications. They are 802.1, 802.2, 802.3, 802.4, 802.5, and several WAN and MAN standards.

IEEE 802.1

The IEEE 802.1 specification describes access to the media for bridges that link Ethernet, token-bus, or token-ring networks. This standard includes the spanning-tree algorithm used by Ethernet and token-ring hubs.

IEEE 802.2

The IEEE 802.2 standard encompasses the Logical Link Control Layer of the OSI Model, which controls the transfer of data to the Media Access Control Layer. IEEE 802.2 is part of the OSI Data Link Layer and creates packets that control error recovery, exchanges control signals to manage conversations, and organizes the flow of data. 802.2 transfers data from one layer to another and defines Service Access Points that link the LLC to higher-layer protocols. IEEE 802.2 is a connection-oriented service, which supplies addressing for LLC bridges.

IEEE 802.2 also interfaces with the MAC layer, which specifies mechanical connectors, signal encoding, the topology of the network, the medium the network uses, and the synchronization of data signals.

IEEE 802.3

The IEEE 802.3 standard was developed in the late 1970s by Digital, Intel, and Xerox, and was called Ethernet I. Ethernet II, which is the current version, has now replaced Ethernet I. The standard specifies a broad band or baseband Carrier Sense with Multiple Access and Collision Detection (CSMA/CD) protocol. It is a bus topology that has been adapted to a star topology with recent implementations such as 10BASE-T Ethernet for unshielded twisted-pair (UTP) media.

The Ethernet MAC layer is responsible for addressing, frame formatting, and error detection and control. There are presently several implementations of Ethernet.

Thin Ethernet (10BASE-2)

Thin Ethernet, also called *10BASE-2*, uses RG-58 coaxial cable and operates at 10 megabits per second (Mbps). It is a bus topology.

Thick Ethernet (10BASE-5)

Thick Ethernet, also called *10BASE-5*, is a 10Mbps access method that uses coaxial cable and is wired in a bus topology.

10BASE-T

10BASE-T Ethernet uses UTP media. It operates at 10Mbps and is wired in a star or distributed-star topology.

10BROAD36

10BROAD36 is a long-distance broadband 10Mbps Ethernet implementation with a maximum segment length of 3,600 meters.

10BASE-F

10BASE-F is a 10Mbps baseband Ethernet network that uses fiber-optic media and ST or SE connectors and is wired in a star or bus topology.

10BASEFP
10BASEFP is a passive fiber-optic network for fiber-to-the desktop use.

10BASEFL
10BASEFL is for moderate-sized workgroups. It uses 50/125, 62.5/125, or 100/125-micron multimode fiber-optic media and ST or SMA connectors. It operates at 10Mbps.

10BASEFB
10BASEFB is used as a fiber-optic backbone between buildings.

100BASE-VG
100BASE-VGis a 100Mbps technology that works with existing Ethernet hubs and media. It uses a Demand Priority architecture that allow nodes to handle high-speed, high-bandwidth applications.

100BASE-X
100BASE-X is a 100Mbps technology that operates over Category 5 UTP media.

IEEE 802.4

IEEE 802.4 is a token-passing protocol that operates at 10Mbps in a bus topology. It is rarely implemented in LANs, although the MAP/TOP access method General Motors uses derives from IEEE 802.4. Commonly called *token bus*, IEEE 802.4 defines an access method that uses possession of a token as permission to send data. Individual workstations receive a priority level that controls the passage of the token. IEEE 802.4 is designed for factory, industrial, and military environments.

IEEE 802.5

IEEE 802.5 is the designation for token-ring, an access method developed by IBM and codified by the IEEE. Token-ring is a token-passing protocol that operates at 4- or 16Mbps over UTP, STP, or fiber-optic media. Token-ring uses the Differential Manchester signal encoding.

IEEE 802.6

IEEE 802.6 is the Metropolitan Area Network standard for distributing voice, video, and data. It uses a Distributed Queue Dual Bus (DQDB) protocol across parallel fiber-optic cables. IEEE 802.6 will operate in excess of 100Mbps.

OTHER IEEE STANDARDS

Several other emerging standards exist. They are 802.7, 802.8, 802.9, 802.10, and 802.11. IEEE 802.7 is the product of the Broadband Technology Advisory Group, which studies broadband voice, data, and video technology. IEEE 802.8 is the progeny of the Optical Fiber Technology Advisory Group, which proposes standards for fiber-optic LANs. IEEE 802.9 is a proposed standard for integrated digital and video networking. IEEE 802.10 is a security standard for LAN interoperability. IEEE 802.11 is the proposed standard for wireless communications

10

THE OSI MODEL

WHAT IS OSI?

The Open Systems Interconnect Model (OSI), designed by the International Standards Organization (ISO), establishes standards for computer-to-computer and network system-to-system communication. An international agency, based in Geneva, Switzerland, the ISO is represented in the United States by the American National Standards Institute (ANSI).

The OSI reference model, or the seven-layer model as it is sometimes called, was conceived in 1978 and finally published in 1984. Its seven layers consist of a variety of interfaces that instruct how different protocols communicate with each other. In the ISO model, each layer builds on the functions of the layers below it. It was originally designed to spawn a series of open standards, but few companies have adopted the resulting ISO standards. However, as a framework for encouraging enabling communication between diverse devices with differing logic, the ISO works well. Most network protocols fit within the confines of the ISO model, and most hardware and software manufacturers have adopted its conceptual framework for their networking implementations. Although few OSI Model-specific protocols or specifications have been implemented, each network operating system has protocols that fill the individual layers of the model.

Each of the seven layers of the OSI model provides a standard means of communication between diverse systems, and like most network standards, in order to reach the largest audience, the layers address the lowest common denominator. The OSI Model diminishes the impact that vendor-specific implementations have on networking and encourages a method of interconnecting hardware and software without the attendant cost of acquiring proprietary, or closed, systems.

What Does OSI Consist of?

The OSI Model consists of seven layers with similar functions. Each layer has a limited number of functions to make manageability easier and keep overhead low. Although communications between devices may not use all seven layers, the OSI Model lets devices use certain protocols to establish connections with each other. Each layer is manageably small, but few enough layers exist to minimize overhead. Communication between peers may not use every layer of the OSI Model.

In OSI, each layer has a boundary between it and the next layer that minimizes the interaction of the layers. Each layer interacts with each other, receiving services from layers above it and providing services to the layers below it. The responsibilities and functions of the individual OSI layers do not overlap.

Layers 1-4 of the OSI Model regulate data transmission, while layers 5-7 handle applications and user interfaces. As data is encapsulated by the headers and addressing information of each succeeding layer, the data is passed to the next-lower OSI layer. For transmission across the network, the assembled data packets are broken into frames. On the opposite side of the transmission, data frames are reassembled, decapsulated, and passed to next layer.

The OSI Model consists of these layers: Application, Presentation, Session, Transport, Network, Data Link, and Physical. (See Figure 10-1 on page 101.)

The Application Layer

The Application Layer, the highest layer in the OSI Model, describes the manner in which applications communicate with the network. It controls the interaction between communication partners, determines that communication partners are available, and decides whether the

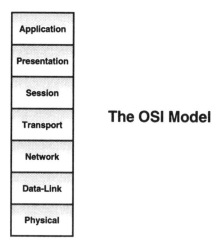

The OSI Model

Figure 10-1. *The OSI Model.*

quality of service is adequate. The Application Layer also provides communication security for individual application processes and is responsible for process error recovery. The Application Layer is represented by protocols such as the Windows NT Advanced Server file system or NetWare Loadable Modules (NLMs). When a user requests a file, resource, print job, or file transfer, the request is generated at the Application Layer.

THE PRESENTATION LAYER

The Presentation Layer of the OSI Model, sandwiched between the Application Layer and the Session Layer, converts data and data formats and handles the syntactical differences of data between nodes communicating with each other on the network. It defines the presentation, format, conversion activities, and encoding of data. The Presentation Layer also describes how applications such as electronic mail or database transactions interact with the network operating system. In NetWare, NetWare Loadable Modules (NLMs) span the Application and Presentation Layer.

THE SESSION LAYER

The Session Layer is responsible for establishing, controlling, and terminating logical connections, called *sessions*, between workstations. It keeps the connection secure, provides administrative functions, and synchronizes the flow of data.

Examples of Session Layer protocols are Novell's NetWare Core Protocol, the Windows NT Advanced Server's redirector, and VINES' socket interface.

THE TRANSPORT LAYER

The Transport Layer consists of protocols that structure data packets and monitor the validity of data transmission. They perform error checking, if necessary, and guarantee delivery of data. To ensure data delivery, Transport Layer protocols may require positive acknowledgments of data receipt, perform time-outs to measure the receipt of data, and resend data if necessary. Transport Layer protocols are also responsible for maintaining the flow of data across the communications link and provide the interface between the network portion of the OSI Model, consisting of the Physical, Data Link, and Network Layers, and the user portion of the OSI Model, which consists of the Session, Presentation, and Application Layers. These protocols isolate the user from the physical network aspects.

Common Transport Layer protocols are the Sequenced Packet Exchange (SPX) protocol and the Transmission Control Protocol (TCP).

Transport Layer communication may be connection-oriented or connectionless. In a connection-oriented transmission, a logical connection is established between partners before communication begins.

THE NETWORK LAYER

The Network Layer of the OSI Model is responsible for routing information between peer partners and between different networks. Its protocols provide a best-effort, nonguaranteed delivery system and seldom employ error control. Common Network Layer protocols are the Internetwork Packet Exchange (IPX) protocol and the Internet Protocol (IP), both of which are used by NetWare and Windows NT 3.5.

Between networks, the Network Layer monitors the number of hops and time between devices and specifies the conventions used for routing data. Within a single network, the routing features of the Network Layer are insignificant if only one path exists between communication partners.

THE DATA LINK LAYER

The Data Link Layer consists of two types of protocols, token-passing and CSMA/CD, which validate the integrity of data flow between communication partners and provide reliable transmission. Data Link protocols are implemented by access methods such as Ethernet, token-ring, and the Fiber Distributed Data Interface (FDDI), which accomplish their actions through LAN adapter hardware, firmware, and LAN driver software.

The Data Link Layer consists of two layers: the Logical Link Control (LLC) layer and the Media Access Control (MAC) Layer. The LLC, also called IEEE 802.2, is responsible for addressing, flow control, sequencing of data frames for transmission over the medium, and error recovery. It transfers data from the upper OSI layers to the MAC Layer. The LLC creates header information to transport data between different access methods.

The MAC maintains access to the Physical Layer medium. It is responsible for the manner in which data is placed on the medium. The access methods are part of the MAC Layer. MAC Layer functions are implemented in the LAN adapter and driver. The MAC Layer is also responsible for determining the logical topology the access method uses, the format of the individual frames that will be passed across the medium, and node addressing and error checking via the Frame Check Sequence (FCS). Simply put, the MAC Layer puts the packets it receives from the OSI upper layers into a format that can be sent across the medium.

The Data Link Layer represents the interface between the Network Layer protocols and the Physical Layer medium. It packages packets into frames for transmission across the network medium according to limitations imposed by the particular access method. The Data Link Layer is responsible for establishing the link between communication partners and determining whether partners are ready to exchange data. It checks for transmission errors, and it may require that communication partners acknowledge receipt of data and retransmit data if necessary.

THE PHYSICAL LAYER

The Physical Layer of the OSI models provides the communications means between the medium and the network hardware. It establishes, maintains, and terminates the physical connection between peer communication partners and ensures reliable delivery of data from one to another. The Physical Layer is responsible for the electrical and optical signals that pass over the medium and for specifying the type of medium used by a particular access method. Connectors such as BNC or fiber-optic ST connectors are defined by the Physical Layer. The Physical Layer is also responsible for determining the speed of transmission, for signal encoding.

Operations at the physical level also describe the speed in bits per second and for signal encoding. The 4B/5B encoding of FDDI is established at this layer, as is the Differential Manchester encoding token-ring uses. In all, the Physical Layer controls the physical aspects of communication, including the mechanical, electrical, procedural, and functional components. It defines grounds, voltage levels, capacitance, and resistance. While the Network Layer deals with packets and the Data Link Layer uses frames, the Physical Layer makes use of bits.

HOW DATA MOVES

The OSI Model is strictly a reference model that describes the movement of data between communication partners. On each end of the communication link, peer partners exist that have similar responsibilities. Data and headers from the upper layers of the OSI Model are encapsulated in Data Link protocol data units (PDUs), also called *frames*. The frames pass across the medium at the Physical Level. At the receiving end, the recipient views the header information and determines what it will do next. Successive layers remove the header its peer partner placed on the data, and passes the data to the next layer.

LAN PROTOCOL TYPES

11

In a local-area network or internetwork, two types of protocols determine how data is transferred on the network and how it gets from the source node to the destination node. These protocols are based on different operational principles and are represented by different access methods, media, and topologies. Part of the Data-Link and Physical Layers of the Open Systems Interconnect (OSI) Model, these protocols are the Carrier Sense Multiple Access with Collision Detection (CSMA/CD) protocol and the token-passing protocol. They are responsible for packaging, formatting, and error-checking information so that it is placed properly on the medium.

CSMA/CD

The Carrier Sense Multiple Access and Collision Detection is a contention-based protocol. In it all workstations on the medium hear every signal passed, and only the node the frame is destined for receives it. CSMA/CD is a nondeterministic access method. Each workstation vies to communicate on the network. High-traffic nodes may dominate CSMA/CD transmission. It operates like a telephone party line. As a result, nodes are not guaranteed equal access to the medium and receive access to the medium only after determining that data does not exist.

Before a node transmits data, it listens to the transmission medium for the presence of a carrier that indicates data being sent. If the node does not sense a carrier for 9.6 microseconds, it will transmit data and then listen for collisions, which interfere with network traffic. If it hears data being transmitted, it defers until it senses that the wire is free. Because of the distance between nodes and the propagation delay of the signal across the medium, an individual node may not sense that data is being sent and may send data of its own. When this occurs, the two data packets clash, causing a collision. Collisions increase as the number of nodes on the network and the length of the network increases.

Each node on a CSMA/CD network can monitor and transmit data at the same time. Data is heard by all network nodes, but only the node the frame is intended for receives it. The receiving node, also called the destination node, reads the address of the data frame, checks for fragments and errors, and if there are none, reads and processes the data. Data may be broadcast to all nodes on the network, multicast to a group of nodes, or sent to individual nodes.

When a collision occurs and the sending workstations recognize it, they send a signal called *jam* to notify the rest of the network that a collision has occurred. Collisions interrupt all traffic on the network. The workstations then back off for a random amount of time determined by the binary exponential backoff algorithm. This algorithm is computed for each node and creates random backoff times that are different for each node. Backoff lessens the chance of the two workstations attempting to transmit at the same time and again colliding. Workstations can attempt to retransmit data up to 16 times before aborting transmission.

CSMA/CD networks may be implemented in bus, star, or distributed-star topologies and use a variety of different media ranging from thick Ethernet to fiber-optic cable. They also use a variety of frame types.

The protocol is implemented by the Institute of Electrical and Electronic Engineers (IEEE) 802.3 model, and by the Ethernet access method developed at Xerox Palo Alto Research Center (PARC) by Robert Metcalfe. It also includes the refinement of Ethernet refined by Digital, Intel, and Xerox (DIX) called Ethernet I or DIX Ethernet. A variation of CSMA/CD called CSMA/CA (Collision Avoidance) is characterized by 230 bit per second AppleTalk used by Macintosh computers.

Advantages

CSMA/CD implementations have several advantages over their token-passing partners. Because the implementation of CSMA/CD is relatively simple, it requires very little overhead to administer it. In small networks where traffic is low, data throughput is high.

Disadvantages

As the amount of traffic increases on a CSMA/CD network, the number of collisions increases, diminishing performance. Because access to a CSMA/CD network is random, deterministic performance is not possible.

TOKEN-PASSING

Token-passing networks use a token to grant permission to transmit data on the network. Because the token grants each station an equal chance to transmit, token-passing networks are called *deterministic*. Of the token-passing access methods, token-ring, ARCNET, and the Fiber Data Distributed Data Interface (FDDI) are the most popular. Token-passing network are wired as physical stars or bus networks.

In token-ring, the primary implementation of a token-passing protocol, each node connects in a ring fashion to two other nodes. The node it receives data from is called the *nearest active upstream neighbor*; the node it passes data to is called its *downstream neighbor*. When data is transmitted, each node repeats the data to its downstream neighbor. The destination workstation receives and processes the data.

A token, consisting of a special frame, grants station access to the media. Although an individual node can place priority on the data it passes, thus ensuring greater access to the ring, priority has until recently not been implemented in LAN environments, although it has always been present. FDDI commonly uses priority. The token passes sequentially from one physical node to its downstream neighbor.

Advantages

Token-passing networks are deterministic—each station has a probable expectation of passing data on the network. As traffic increases on token-passing networks, throughput will increase and then remain stable.

Disadvantages

Token-passing protocols are more complex than CSMA/CD implementations, necessitating higher overhead for administration and error control.

chapter

NetBIOS and NetBEUI

12

A number of network operating systems use NetBIOS (the Network Basic Input and Output System) or NetBEUI as their OSI Session Layer protocols for communicating data between devices. Among these network operating systems are LAN Manager, LAN Server, Windows NT Advanced Server, Windows for Workgroups, Banyan VINES, and LANtastic.

NetBIOS

NetBIOS (Network Basic Input/Output System) is a protocol that was developed by Sytek for the IBM PC LAN Adapter, as a networked BIOS that resided on the adapter and interoperated with the PC BIOS. The protocol was adapted by IBM in 1984 for use in developing networked applications. NetBIOS provides peer-to-peer networking services, gives applications access to network resources, and provides file- and record-locking capability for DOS- and OS/2-based networked PCs. It makes sure that files opened by one user can't be opened and overwritten by another at the same time, jeopardizing the integrity of the data. NetBIOS also has three additional functions—establishing connections, data transfer, and addressing.

NetBIOS is used by IBM LAN Server, Banyan VINES, and LANtastic. NetWare workstations in IBM environments may use

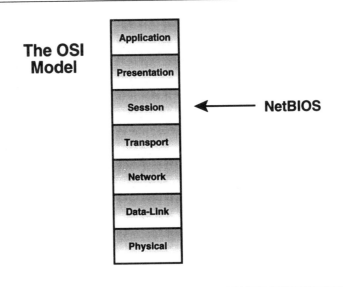

Figure 12-1. *NetBIOS' relation to the OSI Model.*

NetBIOS at the OSI Session Layer and IPX at the Network Layer to emulate IBM PC Network workstations by passing IPX data to the NETBIOS.EXE program loaded on the workstation, which creates NetBIOS packets for presentation to NetBIOS applications. (See Figure 12-1.)

NetBEUI and NBF

NetBEUI (the NetBIOS Extended User Interface) was developed by IBM Corp. in 1985 to provide a nonroutable OSI Session Layer protocol for use in small to midsized LANs. It extends NetBIOS functions by adding network file and printer redirection. Microsoft adopted NetBEUI for its networking implementations. NetBEUI allows error and flow control and supports performance tuning. It is Microsoft LAN Manager's default protocol.

In Windows NT, the original NetBEUI is replaced by a three-component protocol driver. The driver consists of the NetBIOS application

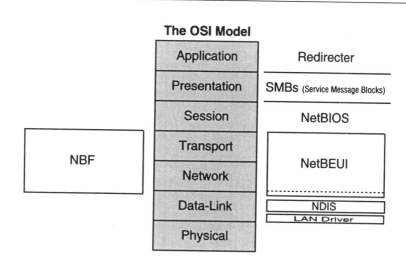

Figure 12-2. *NetBIOS', NetBEUI's, and NBF's relation to the OSI Model.*

program interface (API), incorporates Server Message Blocks (they provide added network functionality), and supplies a transport protocol, called the *NetBIOS Frame* (*NBF*). Communicating devices use SMBs to perform a variety of network functions such as logging in, security, printing, and file and directory manipulation.

NBF provides Windows NT's Network and Transport Layer services by encapsulating SMB data for transport via the access method across the network. Like NetBIOS and NetBEUI, it is not routable. (See Figure 12-2.)

DRIVER SPECIFICATIONS: ODI AND NDIS

13

WHAT ARE ODI AND NDIS?

Turn on the Wayback Machine for a trip to the yesteryear of computer networking when networks were monolithic. (Don't turn the dial too far—we're only going to 1988.) If you had multiple interconnected networks, they each used the same access method. To reach two different network transport protocols from a single workstation, you had to install two network adapters or two different LAN drivers for each network transport protocol. Your only choice was to reboot your machine and load the new driver each time you wanted to use the other protocol. When protocol stacks changed or when Novell changed the NetWare shell, and when Microsoft, Banyan, or IBM changed their client software, manufacturers had to write new LAN drivers and users needed to update their workstations with the newest driver.

In 1988-1989, networking changed. Single networks used multiple access methods, client operating systems, and network transport protocols. Integrating these networks, clients, and protocols became a daunting task, as did the task of writing new drivers for each network operating system version and each transport protocol.

These problems led to the development of two separate interface specifications that handle multiple protocols from a single LAN adapter and driver. Novell and Apple Computer developed the first specification, called the *Open Data-Link Interface (ODI)*. Microsoft introduced the second, called the *Network Driver Interface Specification (NDIS)*.

With the introduction of these interfaces, multiple protocol support from a single driver was allowed and users could use a single LAN adapter to address these protocols. NDIS and ODI also standardized development procedures for LAN drivers and ensured standardized access to protocol stacks such as NetWare's Internetwork Packet Exchange (IPX), the Internet Protocol (IP), Sun's Network File System (NFS), or AppleTalk.

THE OPEN DATA-LINK INTERFACE

In NetWare networks, the network manager used a utility called *WSGEN* to link a binary driver file supplied with each adapter to NetWare's network transport protocol, IPX. The utility generated the IPX.COM file that opened the adapter and provided network transport protocol support. This technique required you to know each adapter's settings and relink the driver with IPX each time you changed the adapter's settings.

ODI separates the device driver and the IPX driver allowing for simultaneous support for different network transport protocols. Network drivers attach themselves to the Link Support Layer (LSL), an interface between the driver and the protocol stack that acts as a traffic cop. (See Figure 13-1 on page 115.)

ODI standardized the development of network adapter drivers. Vendors no longer needed to write a driver for each protocol stack. Instead, they now write drivers to attach to the LSL. ODI handles the mechanics of interfacing with multiple protocols.

A Layered Approach

ODI consists of layers that are implemented on each workstation by a series of commands. The lowest layer is the *Multiple Link Interface (MLI)*. This layer is the interface with the adapter's device driver, which is known as a *Multiple Link Interface Driver (MLID)* and the LSL. Above the LSL, the *Multiple Protocol Interface (MPI)* provides a link to the available protocol stacks. Finally, the LSL provides the link between the MLID and the protocol stack, directing packets between the two as necessary based on a look-up table it keeps that tells it which drivers

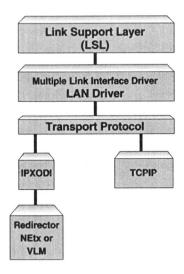

Figure 13-1. *Novell's Open Data-Link Interface specification viewed from the client.*

are bound to each protocol and which workstations contain each driver. (See Figure 13-2 on page 116.)

In DOS, workstation drivers are implemented in order:

LSL.COM—The file loads the Link Support Layer. LSL keeps a database that tells it which adapter is bound to each protocol, and which driver belongs to which workstation.

NE2000.COM—This file is the name of the Multiple Link Interface Driver for a common Ethernet adapter.

IPXODI.COM—This file represents the IPX protocol. TCPIP.COM could also be loaded.

The server in NetWare 4.0 is set up differently than client workstations. Server drivers are divided as follows:

MSM.NLM—This file represents the Media Support Module (MSM).

Topology Support Module (TSM)—The TSM consists of several NLMs for different access methods. Examples are ETHERTSM.NLM, TOKENTSM.NLM, and RXNETTSM.NLM for

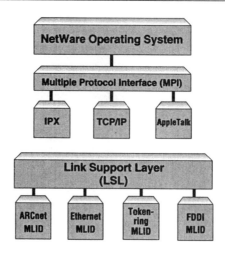

Figure 13-2. *ODI components and interaction.*

Ethernet, token-ring, and ARCNET LANs. These NLMs link the
driver to a specific topology module.

HSM.NLM—The Hardware-Specific Module (HSM) is represented by the MLID, which has the extension .LAN. An example is
NE2000.LAN. The adapter vendor writes this NLM to specifications Novell supplies.

Novell provides the MSM and TSM NLMs as part of NetWare. The
adapter vendor provides the HSM as its server driver for the adapter.
In the server, the transport protocols are bound to the drivers. NetWare
currently supports IPX/SPX, TCP/IP, NFS, and AppleTalk.
The ODI specification from the server view is as shown in Figure 13-3
on page 117.

Tip:
In NetWare v3.x, you must implement an additional NLM called
LSLENH.NLM that patches additional functionality into the LSL.
You must also load an MSM NLM that is specific to NetWare v3.x,
called *MSM31X.NLM*.

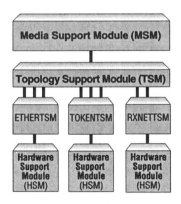

Figure 13-3. *A view of the ODI specification from the server.*

Each access method, with the exception of ARCNET, supports multiple frame types. Each frame type operates with a specific transport protocol. The frame types for Ethernet, token-ring, and ARCNET are these:

ETHERNET_802.3—This frame is for IPX/SPX networks and represents the NetWare v3.x default frame type.

ETHERNET_802.2—This frame is for IPX/SPX networks and represents the NetWare 4.x default frame type.

ETHERNET_II—This Ethernet frame support TCP/IP communications.

ETHERNET_SNAP—The ETHERNET_SNAP frame supports TCP/IP and AppleTalk communications.

TOKEN-RING—This token-ring frame is NetWare's default.

TOKEN-RING_SNAP—This is the default frame type for TCP/IP and AppleTalk.

NOVELL_RX-NET—This ARCNET frame is the default frame for IPX/SPX, TCP/IP, and AppleTalk.

The ODI specification also coexists with NDIS. When you must join an NDIS-based client to a NetWare LAN, you add a shim (a specific program that joins different protocol types) that makes ODI look like

NDIS. The shim is accomplished by an additional driver called *ODIN-SUP.COM*.

THE NETWORK DRIVER INTERFACE SPECIFICATION (NDIS)

Microsoft's approach to multiprotocol networking is the Network Driver Interface Specification (NDIS). The design of NDIS frees the adapter vendor from writing protocol-specific drivers. Instead, vendors write drivers known as MAC drivers, which operate at and below the Media Access Control (MAC) layer of the OSI model. (See Figure 13-4.)

Any NDIS-compliant network transport protocol can pass data to any MAC driver. The drivers connect to the protocols through a process called *binding*. The Protocol Manager controls this process and is responsible for binding the transport protocol to the MAC Layer driver.

In NDIS v2.0, as many as four network adapters could be placed in a single computer. Each adapter can bind up to a maximum of eight protocols. The Protocol Manager routes network requests to the MAC Layer driver. An innovation provided in NDIS v2.0.1 provides for dynamic unloading of transport protocols from the computer's RAM.

NDIS v2.0 operates equally well in OS/2 or DOS environments. In the DOS environment, the Protocol Manager, PROTMAN.DOS, loads

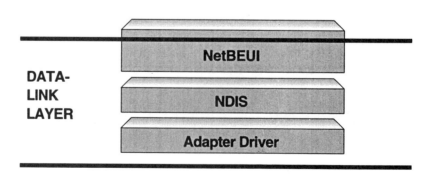

Figure 13-4. *OSI Model and the NDIS protocol.*

through the CONFIG.SYS file along with the MAC Layer driver. The transport protocol, such as NetBEUI, loads and binds to the MAC Layer driver after running NETBIND.EXE prior to logging into the network. Versions of the MAC drivers, Protocol Manager, and binding utility for OS/2 are loaded by the OS/2 CONFIG.SYS file and have .OS2 extensions. Configuration information related to the transport protocol and MAC Layer driver is maintained in a configuration file, PROTOCOL.INI. This text file may be modified manually, if necessary.

NDIS presently supports NetBEUI, TCP/IP, and IPX/SPX. NetBEUI has, until recently, been the transport protocol of choice for NDIS-compliant network operating systems.However, starting with Windows NT v3.5, IPX/SPX is the default protocol. NDIS supports any access method and adapter that provides an NDIS-compliant driver. NDIS-compliant network operating systems include the following:

- Microsoft MS-NET (NDIS 2.0)
- Microsoft LAN Manager (NDIS 2.0)
- Microsoft Windows for Workgroups (NDIS 3.0)
- Microsoft NT Advanced Server v3.1 (NDIS 3.0)
- Windows NT 3.5 (NDIS 3.0)
- IBM LAN Server (NDIS 2.0)
- 3Com 3+ Open (NDIS 2.0)
- Banyan VINES (NDIS 2.0)
- DCA 10-NET (NDIS 3.0)

In addition to direct support, many peer-to-peer network operating systems use NDIS drivers, including Artisoft's LANtastic and Performance Technologies' POWERLan.

Windows for Workgroups v3.11 provides direct support for ODI- or NDIS- compliant DOS drivers. This, along with support for the IPX/SPX transport protocol, allows you to use NDIS and ODI-compliant drivers.

Tip:
Currently under DOS, the ODI driver support provides for only one transport protocol to be bound to the driver. Thus, an NDIS-compliant operating system that provides support for IPX/SPX such as NT or WFW will operate. However, an operating system that provides support for only NetBEUI and TCP/IP only will not operate. WFW, which uses NDIS 3.0 compliant drivers, allows you

to bind IPX/SPX as well as NetBEUI to provide simultaneous support to older NDIS 2.0 operating systems such as LAN Manager.

NDIS 3.0: The Wave of the Future?

With Windows for Workgroups v3.11, Microsoft introduced NDIS 3.0 standards. NDIS 3.0 has also been fully implemented in NT and Windows 95. NDIS 3.0 utilizes a 32-bit C language application programming interface (API) to access the network adapter. NDIS 2.0 was limited to a 16-bit implementation. In DOS environments, NDIS 3.0 drivers run in protected mode and reside in extended memory, while NDIS 2.0 drivers run in real mode and reside in conventional memory.

In WFW the NDIS support layer and the NetBEUI transport protocol are implemented as a series of virtual device drivers:

VNETBIOS—NetBIOS interface

VSERVER.386—Virtual server services

VREDIR.386—Virtual redirector services

NETBEUI.386—NetBEUI interface

NDIS.386—NDIS 3.0 support layer

?????.386—NDIS 3.0–compliant adapter driver provided by the adapter vendor

Virtual or protected mode support is also provided for IPX/SPX and TCP/IP. NDIS 3.0 is supported in a similar manner in Windows 95. Protected mode IPX/SPX and TCP/IP support is also provided. Under NT, the NDIS interface is provided as a protected subsystem.

A Map to the Past with NDIS 2.0

NDIS 3.0 support of protected mode networking services provides a cleaner and faster interface than NDIS 2.0. With the network support provided in a 32-bit protected mode interface, frames can be processed much faster than they can in a 16-bit interface. The only drawback is that an adapter supplied only with an NDIS 3.0 driver will not work in an operating system designed for NDIS 2.0 drivers.

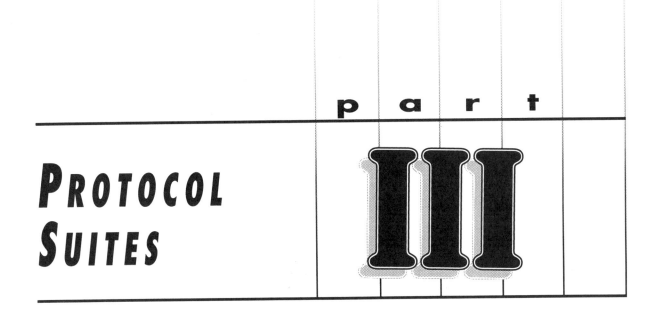

PROTOCOL SUITES

p a r t

III

Most protocols travel in suites. Three of the most common, the Sequenced Packet Exchange/Internetwork Packet Exchange (SPX/IPX), the Transmission Control Protocol/Internet Protocol (TCP/IP) and AppleTalk, consist of a variety of protocols, each with its own function. Protocols within suites work with each other to ensure that messages can be sent and delivered to their destination over the network.

IPX AND SPX

E ach network device and network operating system makes use of protocols that allow nodes to transmit data across the network. These protocols, which are access-method and data-link–independent, provide reliable, high-performance network transport. Several of the protocols in the IPX/SPX suite were designed by Novell programmers based on the Xerox Network Services (XNS) protocols. IPX has recently been adopted by Windows NT 3.5 as a default transport protocol.

NetWare Core Protocol (NCP)

The first of the protocols in the IPX/SPX suite is the NetWare Core Protocol (NCP). NCP is a service protocol that carries requests between DOS, Windows, and OS/2 workstations and NetWare servers. It redirects requests for information and responses to the workstation's local drives or to network drives. A file, NETx.COM or NETx.EXE, depending on the version of NetWare you are using, represents the NetWare shell and performs the redirection function. In a client, the shell is loaded as a terminate-and-stay-resident (TSR) program that captures data and requests from the workstation and converts them to NCP packets that may be encapsulated in Internetwork Packet Exchange

(IPX) protocol packets and data-link information for transmission across the network. When a workstation loads the NetWare shell, requester, or redirector, it establishes a connection with the server using a Create Service Connection Request, which provides a source and destination address for further NCP packets.

NCP corresponds in the OSI Model to the Session Layer, which also contains the Network File System (NFS) used by Sun Microsystems' networks; the AppleTalk Filing Protocol (AFP) from Apple Computer, which provides an extensible file system for Apple, Macintosh and PowerPC machines; and OSI's File Transfer Access Method (FTAM).

In NetWare, the most common type of information packet is an NCP packet that contains function calls or data. Function calls, which operate at the OSI Presentation Layer, instruct the destination node to perform a function; data is enclosed which the function call acts on. Each NCP packet also contains a sequence number, which is used to order the packet into complete messages at its destination. Acknowledgments to NCP requests take place at the Transport Layer.

NCP packets are encapsulated in IPX packets for transport across the network, and if necessary, are broken into frames according to the access method being used. NCP is often called a "Ping-Pong" protocol—one NCP request elicits one NCP reply.

NCP Packet Structure

NCP packets have two formats: one for requests, the other for responses. The format of the NCP Request Packet consists of five fields:

Request type—The request type represents whether the request is to create a service connection, to terminate a connection, for service, or for a burst mode transfer of data.

Sequence number—The sequence follows communication between the client and the server to determine if messages are received in the proper order.

Connection number low—This field consists of the connection number the client is assigned when it logs in to the network. You can see this connection number when you use the NetWare utility USERLIST.

Task number—This field indicates the number of the client task making the request.

Connection number high—This field is only used in 1,000-user NetWare.

NCP Reply packets consist of eight fields:

Header—When the server answers a client request, the header indicates that the request was received and if the connection is still in place.

Reply type—This field indicates the type of reply packet. Three types can exist: service replies that answer most requests, request being processed, and burst-mode connection.

Sequence number—The sequence follows communication between the server and the client to determine if messages are received in the proper order.

Connection number low—This field consists of the connection number the client is assigned when it logs in to the network. You can see this connection number when you use the NetWare utility USERLIST.

Task number—This field indicates the number of the client task making the request.

Connection number high—This field is only used in 1,000-user NetWare.

Completion code—This field indicates whether the request was received successfully.

Connection status—This field indicates whether the connection between the client and server is still active.

Each NCP request or response contains function and subfunction codes that indicate the type of requested service or response. In NetWare, for example, the function code 2222 is used to request a file open; when a backup of the network needs to be performed, a function code of 23 and a subfunction code of 68 direct the server to close the bindery.

Other NCP Packets

In addition to NCP requests and replies, three other NCP packets are available: watchdog, serialization, and message. The server issues watchdog packets to confirm active workstations. When a connection does not issue communications for a long time, the watchdog packet notifies NetWare that the connection can be terminated. NetWare also issues serialization packets that ensure that no more than one server contains the same license to NetWare. If the serialization packet detects a copyright violation, it issues a message. Message packets let users broadcast messages to users or groups without the server's intervention.

How NCP Works

When a workstation loads NETx.COM or NETx.EXE, the workstation sends a Create Service Connection NCP packet, which requests a connection with the NetWare server. An equivalent NCP layer in NetWare responds to NCP requests. The server checks to determine if an available connection exists before granting the connection. After granting the connection, the client and the server negotiate the maximum packet size they will use for communications. This maximum packet size is also called the buffer size. When buffer size negotiations are complete, the client sends a Logout NCP packet to close any previous connections.

Next, the client issues a Get Nearest Server NCP packet. The server responds, and the client and server exchange routing information. Once this is done, the server grants the client a connection to the network.

When a workstation logs out from the network, the server sends a copy of the LOGOUT.EXE file to the client. The client issues a Close File NCP packet, and the server terminates its connection. To open an application, a series of NCP requests and responses take place. The client requests a file to be opened. The server asks the client for the directory path to the file. The client request the server to search for the file, and when the server finds it, the client issues a request to open the file, which the server answers with an open file reply.

IPX

The Internetwork Packet Exchange (IPX) protocol, which corresponds to the OSI Model Transport Layer, guides and routes packets from their origin to their destination over the same or different networks. It is a connectionless, nonguaranteed form of delivery that corresponds to the Internet Protocol and AppleTalk. IPX is a native NetWare protocol and also available as a default protocol in Windows NT 3.5. Other protocols such as NCP use IPX for transporting messages across the network. IPX routing is based on the least number of hops, in which one hop equals the distance between a node and a router or between two routers. In NetWare DOS and Windows workstations, the LAN driver is linked to IPX when a workstation runs its AUTOEXEC.BAT file. In OS/2, a daemon consisting of the IPX protocol interacts with the OS/2 shell, which redirects NCP calls to the file server. UNIX and AppleTalk machines use built-in shell software to communicate with IPX.

IPX appends information fields containing a header to identify LANs. It uses the network and node address of the packet to determine the packet's location.

IPX Packet Structure

The IPX packet consists of several fields:

Checksum—The checksum is not used by NetWare. It is a remnant of XNS. In NetWare, the LAN adapter performs the checksum.

Length—This field indicates the length of packet in bytes and includes a minimum of 30 bytes of header and data. The maximum length of an IPX packet is 576 bytes, although new LAN drivers and technologies like the Burst Mode Protocol can handle larger maximum packet sizes.

Transport control—This field includes the hop count routers use to find the total number of routers a packet traverses between the source and destination node. In NetWare, the 16th router discards the packet.

Packet type—This field indicates the type of IPX packet. Upper-layer protocols such as NCP or the Service Advertising Protocol (SAP) use this information to identify themselves. For example, a packet type of 17 indicates a NCP packet and 5 indicates an SPX packet.

Destination network—The destination network field indicates whether a packet is for a local or remote network. If the packet is for a node on the same network, this field contains a zero.

Destination node—This field indicates the physical address of the destination node.

Destination socket—This field indicates the socket number of the communication assigned to the destination. Sockets are assigned by packet type. 452h indicates a Service Advertising Protocol packet.

Source network—This field indicates the address of the packet's source network.

Source node—This field indicates the address of the source node.

Source socket—This field indicates the socket number assigned to the source of the communication.

Data—This field contains the NCP request or response, an SPX packet, a Routing Information Protocol (RIP) packet, or a SAP.

How IPX Works

After a workstation loads IPX and the NetWare shell (NETx.EXE or NETx.COM), the server grants the client a connection. The client logs into the network. The shell views every request the workstation makes to determine if it is for the workstation operating system or for the network operating system and redirects it as appropriate. Each NCP request or reply to the network operating system is encapsulated in an IPX packet. The IPX packet is further encapsulated by information required by the access method for transport across the medium.

SEQUENCED PACKET EXCHANGE (SPX)

The Sequenced Packet Exchange (SPX) protocol is an OSI Model Transport Layer protocol that is responsible for flow control. It is a guaranteed, connection-oriented delivery service, which requires packet acknowledgment and validation.

When an SPX call is made, it is enclosed in an IPX packet with a checksum. SPX on the destination node checks the packet contents and sends a positive acknowledgment if the packet passes the checksum. If the packet fails the checksum, the destination node issues a negative acknowledgment. The source node sends a duplicate IPX packet.

In NetWare, SPX is used rarely because of the excessive overhead it takes in setting up, maintaining, and terminating connections. Two NetWare utilities that use SPX are PSERVER, NetWare's print server utility, and RCONSOLE, a remote console management facility.

There are two versions of SPX: one for NetWare v2.x and v3.x and one for v4.x. SPX I has a maximum packet size of 576 bytes, which includes a 42-byte header. If, for example, you want to send 4,000 bytes of data, you will need to enclose it in approximately eight frames. An acknowledgment at the destination will be generated for each frame, and only one frame may be sent at a time without acknowledgment.

SPX II was introduced in 1991. It allows larger packet sizes and implements a sliding-window protocol. SPX II also has a 42-byte header and a maximum length of 64 kilobytes. In SPX II, multiple frames can be sent without acknowledgment, depending on the maximum frame size supported by the access method. Ethernet supports a maximum frame size of 1,518 bytes; token-ring allows over 17,000 bytes. The SPX connection control field indicates the negotiated maximum frame size.

SPX Packet Structure

SPX packets contain many of the same fields as IPX packets. In addition, SPX uses several additional bytes in its header. These additional bytes are positioned after the source socket field:

Connection control—This field is responsible for the data flow between peer nodes.

Data stream type—This field indicates the type of data in the packet.

Source connection ID—This filed is the connection number assigned at the packet's source node.

Destination connection ID—This field, which is assigned at the destination node, allows packets that arrive from different connections on the same socket to be separated.

Sequence number—This field contains the number of packets exchanged at one time.

Acknowledge number—This field indicates the sequence number so packets may be ordered.

Allocation number—This field indicates the number of listen buffers available at the destination.

SERVICE ADVERTISING PROTOCOL

In NetWare, servers advertise their services every 60 seconds. These notification packets are called Service Advertising Protocol (SAP) packets. SAPping is not limited to file servers, but occurs also on print, gateway, communication, and fax servers. SAP allows the dynamic reconfiguration of the network. Information from SAPs is stored in the

NetWare bindery in NetWare v2.x and v3.x and in a dynamic bindery partition in NetWare 4.x. NetWare clients receive information about the network services available and their location from the SAPping process. Network routers copy SAP information into Server Information Tables, which they use for transporting data between networks. SAP packets are transported within IPX.

Three types of SAPs exist: information broadcasts, service queries, and service responses. Information broadcasts allow an up-to-date view of the network resources available. If, for example, a router doesn't hear a SAP from a server after three minutes, the router assumes the server is no longer active on the network and removes it from its tables. SAP service queries are used by nodes to locate available servers. Service responses consist of General Service and Nearest Services packets. The General Service SAP consists of the service information broadcast; the Nearest Service SAP is sent when a node requests Nearest Service.

In NetWare 4.x, the network manager can adjust the 60-second SAP default. Some SAPs can be observed by using NetWare's console utility, TRACK ON.

SAPs in Internetworks

While SAPs are acceptable in local area networks, their overhead causes delays and congestion in wide-area links. In X.25 or Frame Relay networks, SAP traffic can be reduced by filtering in which only changes are broadcast every several minutes. SAPs can also be filtered via third-party routers or by Novell's MultiProtocol Router.

ROUTING INFORMATION PROTOCOL

In NetWare, servers exchange information with other servers and routers on the network to inform each other of available network paths. This information is contained in a routing table on each router, which represents the router's view of the network. It contains only the networks a router can communicate with.

Like IPX, the Routing Information Protocol (RIP) is based on the Xerox Network Service (XNS). It includes an additional field that allows a client or server to select the fastest route from the source to the destination. The fastest route is indicated by the number of ticks (units of time equivalent to 1/18th of a second.)

RIP packets are encapsulated in IPX for transport. In NetWare v2.x and v3.x, RIPs occur every 60 seconds. NetWare 4.x allows the network manager to change the time between RIPs. Like SAPs, TRACK ON displays RIP traffic.

PROTOCOLS FOR WIDE-AREA NETWORKING

To increase the efficiency and performance of IPX over wide-area links, Novell designed several new protocols, which are available in NetWare v3.12 and NetWare 4.x. These protocols are the NetWare Link Services Protocol (NLSP), IPXWAN, the Large Internet Packet (LIP), and the Packet Burst Protocol.

NetWare Link Services Protocol

NetWare Link Services Protocol (NLSP) is a link-state routing protocol designed to enhance performance, scalability, and manageability of internetworks. NLSP replaces RIP and SAP with a link-state algorithm similar to IETF's OSPF (open shortest path first) and IS-IS (intermediate system to intermediate system routing).

It reduces the amount of traffic caused by RIP and SAP by broadcasting information only when the network's configuration changes, and hence supports larger networks. In NLSP, data is routed over the optimal path based on the link's delay, speed, and cost. NLSP is implemented by a NetWare Loadable Module called IPXRTR.NLM.

NLSP increases the number of hops possible between source and destination nodes to 127 hops, eight times more than RIP supports. In addition, NLSP is a manageable protocol that is backward-compatible to RIP.

IPXWAN

IPXWAN extends IPX for use in Point-to-Point, X.25, Frame Relay, and Integrated Services Digital Network (ISDN) networks. It allows connections to be quickly identified and provides services similar to connection-oriented services without degrading the performance or efficiency of IPX. Novell is presently working with router vendors to incorporate IPXWAN into their routers; the IETF, which oversees the Internet, has accepted IPXWAN as an alternate transport protocol.

Packet Burst and Large Internet Packet

Two additional protocols have been introduced that increase network efficiency over routes and diminish the effect of the Ping-Pong characteristics of NCP. They are Packet Burst and the Large Internet Packet (LIP).

In the fall of 1992, Novell released a client shell that supported LIP. Previous to this, the maximum packet size allowed was 576 bytes, which consisted of 512 bytes of data and 64 bytes of header. LIP is implemented by the BURST NLM and allows peer communication partners to negotiate the maximum packet size they will use to communicate. For PBURST to work, all routers and servers on the network must support it. The negotiated maximum packet size becomes the smallest maximum packet size supported. For example, if a client can only support 1,518 bytes and a router can support 4,202 bytes, 1,518 will become the maximum packet size used.

PBURST also allows multiple packets to be sent between acknowledgments, speeding the transfer of NCP requests and responses. Because fewer acknowledgments are necessary, performance increases. Up to 64KB of data can be transmitted without acknowledgment. In burst mode, the BNETx or Virtual Loadable Module client requests a file and may receive up to 64KB of data in the response. VLMs support a maximum of 16 outstanding read packets and 10 outstanding write packets.

PROTOCOL SUITES: TCP/IP

15

F rom its beginnings as a protocol designed for the U.S. Department of Defense (DOD) to join different computer systems of government agencies, defense contractors, and universities together, TCP/IP (the Transmission Control Protocol/Internet Protocol suite) has become the most pervasive protocol suite in the world. TCP and IP are the network transport protocols used for the largest TCP/IP computer network, the Internet. According to Vinton Cerf, considered by many to be the father of the Internet, in 1994, a total of 26,000 networks were part of the Internet and another 52,000 private networks used TCP/IP.

History of the Internet and TCP/IP

TCP/IP was developed to allow a multitude of different multivendor systems to interoperate in a configuration that appeared to be a single, very large, internetwork. In 1969, the DOD Advanced Research Projects Agency (DARPA) released the first contract requesting a protocol suite that would allow the exchange of information between physically separate and different systems. DOD needed a communications network that could survive the failure of any individual station and communicate at high data rates with many varying systems.

Bolt, Beranek, and Newman (BBN) conducted the original research, and contracts for the software were released to research and educational institutions. By the early 1970s, a demonstration network using a host-to-host protocol called the *Transmission Control Protocol (TCP)* was established.

By 1973, Bob Kahn, who was associated with DARPA, and Vinton Cerf of Stanford University had created the TCP portion of the protocol suite. By 1978, the protocol had evolved via the efforts of Denny Cohen at the University of Southern California, into the sequenced, connection-oriented TCP and the best-effort connectionless IP. Cohen argued that the best-effort delivery system of IP was more appropriate for many of the internetworking features of a network than were the guaranteed delivery features of TCP. According to Cohen, the overhead required for a connection-oriented service was too costly on a large internetwork and could be left to upper-layer protocols in the TCP/IP suite, which would provide error-checking and control retransmission of the data. Of these upper-layer protocols, the User Datagram Protocol (UDP) was developed as a way for applications to access the connectionless features of IP.

As early as 1975, the result of this work, the ARPANET (Advanced Research Projects Network), had left the experimental stages and had become a fully functioning internetwork. At that time, control was transferred to the DOD Defense Communications Agency (DCA), and the DCA began administering the network. In 1985, DCA turned over control and funding to the National Science Foundation (NFS), and the NFSnet was born. (See Figure 15-1.)

Features

The evolution of TCP/IP closely follows the evolution of the Internet. TCP started as a low-level experimental packet-switching protocol and evolved to a connection-oriented protocol with an added connection-

1969	First used as the ARPANET
1974	TCP/IP first proposed
1975	Control of ARPANET transferred to DOD Defense Communications Agency (DCA)
1984	ARPANET split into ARPANET and MILNET. Internet coined as the name for both.
1985	Control and funding turned over to National Science Foundation. NFSnet born.

Figure 15-1. *A chronology of TCP/IP and the Internet.*

less end-to-end layer. TCP has a media-specific frame and addressing scheme. IP was specifically designed to be easy to introduce into groups of switching nodes as a media-independent network transport protocol.

TCP/IP consists of three components: hosts, networks, and routers. Hosts are any computer, whether a mainframe, minicomputer, graphics workstation, or PC workstation, that connects to the TCP/IP internetwork. Networks consist of collections of at least two interconnected hosts. Routers were developed to transfer data from one network to another and handle the packet-switching needs of a wide-ranging, media-independent internetwork.

In TCP/IP, the address of the gateway encapsulates the message. An upper-layer protocol such as the File Transfer Protocol (FTP) or TEL-NET passes information in the form of datagrams to IP for transmission. The host's IP stack examines the network address (also called the *IP address*) of the datagram and determines if the destination node in the datagram is on the local network or on a remote network. If the destination of the datagram is on a remote network, the datagram is relayed to a locally attached IP router. IP hands datagrams to the Data Link protocol for segmenting into frames according to the requirements of the access method being used. The router looks up the address enclosed in the datagram in its routing table and relays the datagram to another IP router or to the local network host. Each datagram is routed individually based on the table lookup in each router. The intelligence in the router allows it to examine the datagram's address, even if the datagram is sent by a different router, and send the datagram on its way. In this manner, the datagram can travel through many routers to its final destination.

Tip:
On an IP network, the host is any computer running TCP/IP software. Each host maintains a list of other known hosts on the internetwork.

With the development of the packet-switched network, the Internet took its basic shape. However, the equipment to maintain an Internet connection was still expensive and TCP/IP was not widely used, except on the Internet. Simultaneous to the development of TCP/IP was the development of the UNIX operating system. When AT&T UNIX was developed as Berkeley UNIX, it included TCP/IP as its transport protocol for LANs. TCP/IP changed to accommodate the needs of LANs and became the default network transport protocol for

UNIX environments. As LANs grew and moved into non–UNIX based operating environments, TCP/IP moved into these areas as well.

TCP/IP has evolved because of the work of hundreds of persons. Researchers wishing to make changes to TCP/IP publish Requests for Comment (RFCs). RFCs are debated and criticized prior to implementation and reviewed by the Internet Engineering Task Force (IETF). Standards are developed over a long period of testing. Final standards are promulgated from meetings of engineers who are members of the Internet Engineering Task Force (IETF), who meet on a regular basis to finalize standards and publish the results.

In addition to basic packet switching, additional functionality in TCP/IP was developed for remote login, file transfer, and electronic mail. These functions are described by a series of protocols added to the TCP/IP protocol suite:

> **ARP**—The Address Resolution Protocol provides IP address-to-physical adapter address resolution. It is defined in RFC 826.
>
> **RARP**—The Reverse Address Resolution Protocol provides physical adapter-to-IP address resolution. It is defined by RFC 903.
>
> **ICMP**—The Internet Control Message Protocol provides diagnostic features. It is defined by RFC 792.
>
> **SNMP**—The Simple Network Management Protocol provides management features. It is defined by RFC 1065.
>
> **SMTP**—The Simple Mail Transfer Protocol is the Internet mail protocol. It is defined by RFC 821.
>
> **TELNET**—TELNET is the TCP/IP remote login protocol. It is defined by RFC 854.

TCP/IP Services

The TCP/IP protocol suite includes a number of services such as file transfer between hosts, terminal emulation to remote hosts, electronic mail, remote command execution, and remote printing.

In file transfer, TCP/IP uses FTP, which lets users access the directories of remote hosts and perform file transfers. In terminal emulation with TELNET, hosts can emulate (act as) VT100 or VT220 terminals to access applications on other hosts. Electronic mail lets uses exchange messages via the local system or the Internet, using IP as the transport protocol. Remote command execution allows user to create and execute batch processes and edit files on remote hosts. Remote printing lets users print data to printers attached to remote hosts.

TCP/IP LAYERS

Conceptually, the TCP/IP protocol suite consists of four layers: Application, Transport, Internet, and Network Interface. These layers each have specific functions. The Application Layer is responsible for the appearance of messages, defines the interaction of processes, and contains application protocols such as FTP, the Simple Mail Transfer Protocol (SMTP), and TELNET.

The Transport Layer contains transport protocols and provides reliable, connection-oriented services. It handles frame sequencing, detects duplicate frames, and handles flow control. The connection-oriented TCP and UDP reside at the Transport Layer.

The Internet Layer sizes, fragments, and reassembles IP datagrams. It consists of connectionless datagram services such as IP, ARP, and RARP and performs IP routing.

The Network Interface Layer is similar to the MAC Layer—it works with network-specific frames, controls access to the medium, specifies the frame format, frame size, and bit rate. It uses Data Link protocol implementations such as Ethernet, ARCNET, and token-ring on Serial Line IP (SLIP) or the Point-to-Point (PPP) protocol.

THE INTERNET PROTOCOL (IP)

Whether you are using connection-based TCP or the connectionless UDP for the transmission of data, the primary network transport protocol in TCP/IP is IP. IP is the connectionless protocol that provides datagram services. In a datagram service, there is no flow control, acknowledgment, error-checking or sequencing of datagrams passed across the internetwork. Since routing is performed by the IP router, each datagram may take a different route to its destination. The destination host resequences datagrams it receives. If an IP network becomes congested, datagrams are discarded. As a result, IP networks are extremely efficient.

Datagrams are encapsulated within IEEE 802.3, 802.4, or 802.5 headers and footers as described in RFC 1042 for transport across the media.

They can also be encapsulated in ARCnet frames, as defined by RFC 1051. The encapsulation of IP datagrams in 802.x Media Access Control (MAC) Layer frames is defined by extensions required in the 802.2 Logical Link Control (LLC) Layer for the Subnetwork Access Protocol (SNAP). These extensions provide the protocol ID for IP frames. (See Figures 15-2 and 15-3.)

The datagram is encapsulated in an 802.x or ARCNET frame. The first field within the frame is the local header. The next subfield is the IP header. (See Figure 15-2.) The minimum length of the IP header is 20 octets and consists of these fields:

Version—The IP version number consists of four bits.

Internet Header Length—This four-bit field designates the length of the header in 32-bit words.

Type of Service—This 8-bit field contains flags that specify reliability, precedence, delay, and throughput parameters.

Total Length—This 16-bit describes in octets the total length of the IP datagram.

Identification—This 16-bit field provides a unique identification for the datagram.

Flags—This 3-bit field indicates that fragmentation is used.

Fragment offset—This 13-bit field indicates the location in the completed datagram where the particular fragment belongs.

Time to Live—This 8-bit field contains the amount of time before the datagram should be removed from the internetwork. Time to Live is measured in the number of hops or seconds.

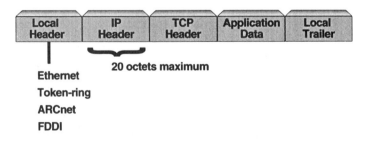

Figure 15-2. A TCP/IP header in data frame.

SNAP Data Frame

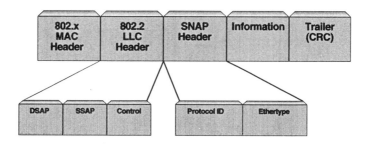

Figure 15-3. *A SNAP frame.*

Protocol—This 8-bit field identifies the next protocol that follows this header, such as TCP.

Header Checksum—This 16-bit field represents the checksum for the IP header.

Source Address—This 32-bit field indicates the Internet address of the originating host.

Destination Address—This 32-bit field indicates the Internet address of the destination host.

Options—This variable-length field includes options from the sender such as a route specification.

Padding—This variable length field is used to end the IP header on a 32-bit boundary.

Data—This variable length field consists of multiples of eight bits and doesn't exceed 65,535 octets for IP header and data.

The maximum size of an IP datagram is 65,535 octets; the minimum size is 576 octets. (See Figure 15-4 on page 140.)

IP Addressing

TCP/IP was designed as an internetwork that would not depend upon any particular hardware. As a result, its addressing scheme allows for a large number of hosts and is independent of any other addressing method. The Internet address consists of a 32-bit (four-byte) address that identifies the network and the local host. In a host joining the

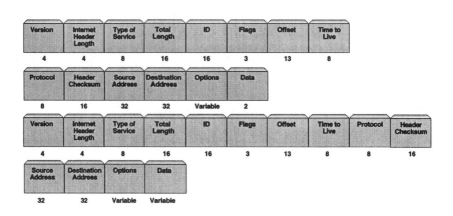

Figure 15-4. *The IP datagram.*

Internet, the network portion of the address is provided by the Defense Data Network (DDN) Information Center. The host portion of the address is provided by the local network administrator.

The IP address is written as a series of four decimal numbers separated by periods (192.124.119.33). Each of the four address fields represents eight bits and can have a value from 0 to 255. The range of IP addresses is split into five classes, labeled A through E:

> **Class A**—In a Class A address, bit zero (0) is always zero. A Class A address can range from 1 to 127. Eight bits of the network field and 24 bits of the host ID contain this address.
>
> **Class B**—In a Class B address, the first octet begins with 10. A Class B address can range from 128 to 191. Sixteen bits of the network field and 16 bits of the host ID contain this address.
>
> **Class C**—In a Class C address, the first octet begins with 110. A Class C address can range from 192 to 254. Twenty-four bits of the network field and eight bits of the host ID contain this address.
>
> **Class D**—Class D addressees are used for IP multicast addressing. The first octet begins with 1110.
>
> **Class E**—A Class E address is used for experimental purposes. Its first octet begins with 1111.

For all classes, addresses 0 and 255 are reserved. (See Figure 15-5 on page 141.)

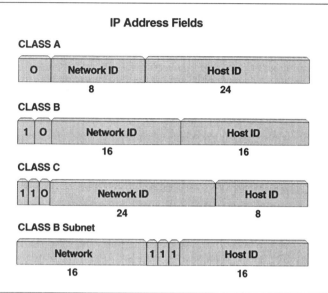

Figure 15-5. *IP address fields.*

As you can see, the number of host addresses available for your network depends on the class of the IP address. Class A addresses support 16 million hosts, but only 127 networks. Class B addresses support 65,000 hosts and 16,000 networks. Class C addresses support two million networks, but only 254 hosts.

However, many computers can share the same host number as long as their network numbers are different. Thus, the actual number of hosts that can attach to the Internet is immense. However, even with such a large number of hosts and networks supported, Internet addresses are limited. To solve the problem of address shortages, a new protocol called the *Simple Internet Protocol (SIP)* has been proposed. SIP uses a 64-bit address rather than IP's 32-bit address, effectively doubling the size of the potential address base. SIP will be fully compatible with IP.

Subnetworking Your Net

Once you've obtained Internet addresses, it is necessary to fit them to the available hosts on your system. If your network is divided into smaller subnetworks, you must also subnet your IP address. To do this, take a portion of the IP address reserved for hosts and give it to the network address. You generally take between 1 and 3 bits of your host address and assign it to your network address. The remainder of the host address is then divided among the subnets, depending on the number of bits used to make the subnetwork. The bits used to create the subnet are called the *subnet mask*. While the bits used to define a subnet are often taken from the most significant bits and are contiguous, they don't need to be. However, if you decide to use noncontiguous bits, you run the risk of a strange configuration of host addresses. Also, the addresses that coincide with the bits 00 and 11 are unavailable, effectively reducing the number of hosts available.

Let's assume you have a network with Class C address 192.124.119. You have to divide your network into six subnetworks. A subnetwork represents a piece of medium that forms a network. You take the three most significant bits of the Class C address as your subnet. This gives you a subnet mask of 224. Since a subnet cannot use the binary equivalent of 11 or 00, you have effectively divided your network into six subnets with subnet 1 using hosts between 32 and 63; subnet 2 using hosts between 65 and 95; subnet 3 using hosts between 97 and 127; subnet 4 using hosts between 129 and 160; subnet 5 using hosts between 161 and 191; and subnet 6 using hosts between 192 and 223. Hosts 0–31 and 225–255 are illegal.

 Tip:
The subnet mask is the decimal representation of the binary number you create with the bits you plan to use as your mask. To find the subnet mask, take the decimal number and "and" it to the proposed host address. (To "and" two numbers together, convert both numbers to binary, then match each of the bits in both binary numbers. Where both bits are one, the corresponding bit in the result is also one. For every other bit, the result is zero.) The result is the number the subnet is on. You can use this formula to arrive at the subnet for any host address you want to use.

THE TRANSMISSION CONTROL PROTOCOL (TCP)

TCP provides a virtual circuit connection-oriented end-to-end transmission between end-user applications. Additionally, TCP provides support for end-to-end connections for host processes. It has reliability features not found in IP such as flow control, sequencing, checksum, acknowledgment, and retransmission.

To establish a TCP connection, an upper-layer protocol such as FTP must be identified to a TCP socket. A socket represents the end point of a communications link between two applications. In a network application such as TCP, the socket is the connection between two or more applications running on two separate computers attached to the network. Sockets provide a full-duplex communication link between the two systems. In TCP, a stream socket is used, which consists of two separate addresses. The first address is the address of the specific application or process running on the computer. The second address is the IP address of the workstation on the network. Common sockets include the following:

- FTP 21
- TELNET 23
- SMTP 25

Through sockets, upper-layer protocols are identified by the port address and the IP address. The process continues operation with error control and out-of-sequence packet detection enabled. Flow control ensures that the sender of data does not overwhelm the receiver and is accomplished by cooperation between the two end systems to establish a sliding window of data. The sender increases the data stream until the recipient asks for retransmissions. At that point, the speed of transmission is reduced. In TCP, connection control features are also responsible for establishing, terminating, and interrupting connections.

In TCP, data transmission from the upper-layer protocol is a continuous stream. TCP divides this stream into 65 kilobyte octet segments. Each octet is assigned a sequence number for reassembly. The segment then passes to the IP layer which creates and passes the datagram to the lower Network Interface Layer for header information and transmission.

The TCP header contains a minimum of 20 octets:

Source Port—This 16-bit segment contains the port address of the application process using the TCP service.

Destination Port—This 16-bit segment contains the port address of the called port.

Sequence Number—This 16-bit segment assures reliable reassembly. It represents the byte sequence number of the first octet in the

TCP block and is increased by one for each octet transmitted in the TCP segment.

Acknowledgment Number—This 32-bit segment provides an indication of receipt so retransmission can be completed if necessary.

Data Offset—This 4-bit segment indicates the size of the header in 32-bit words.

Reserved—This 6-bit segment is set to all zeros.

Flags—This 6-bit segment provides control functions such as setup and termination of sessions. Flags include the urgent pointer (URG), acknowledgment (ACK), push function (PSH), reset connection (RSC), synchronize sequence numbers (SYN), and data transmission completed (FIN).

Window—This 16-bit segment indicates the receive window size (the number of octets the receiver can accept).

Checksum—This 16-bit segment is a checksum based upon the IP fields plus the TCP header information.

Urgent Pointer—This 16-bit segment points to the first octets that follows the urgent data so the receiver can determine how much urgent data is coming.

Options—This variable-size segment is set aside for future options. At present only one option has a defined maximum. It is the TCP segment size.

While TCP provides a reliable end-to-end connection ID, it does so at the expense of higher overhead.

THE USER DATAGRAM PROTOCOL (UDP)

When TCP was split into TCP and IP, a new protocol was developed to provide a transport protocol for applications that did not need extensive error checking. The protocol is known as UDP. The Simple Network Management Protocol (SNMP) uses UDP because UDP is the best choice for transmitting data.

The UDP header contains only four fields:

Source Port—This 16-bit field represents the address of the calling port.

Destination Port—This 16-bit field represents the address of the port being called.

Length—This 16-bit field represents the length of the UDP datagram.

Checksum—This 16-bit field is the checksum for the UDP header.

As you can see from the UDP header information, UDP does not guarantee delivery system as TCP does. UDP uses best-effort delivery. Any error checking and calls for retransmission must be done by upper-layer protocols.

THE APPLETALK PROTOCOL SUITE

16

When Apple Computer designed its computers, it included a feature previously found only on UNIX-based systems—built-in networking. To implement this network, Apple designed a network architecture called *AppleTalk*. AppleTalk represents a suite of protocols that describe how Apple and Macintosh computers communicate over networks.

Originally, AppleTalk was designed to use only the LocalTalk access method, which was built into every Apple or Macintosh computer and peripheral device that could be attached to the network. LocalTalk is slow—it operates at 2,040 kilobits per second (2.004Mbps), which is slower than other common LAN access methods. As a result, AppleTalk began to support Ethernet and token-ring adapters through additional access methods called *EtherTalk* and *TokenTalk*. ARCNET was also supported by encapsulating Ethernet packets into ARCNET frames.

As originally developed, AppleTalk only supported AppleShare, Apple Computer's network operating system, which uses a Macintosh as server. The server running AppleShare software provides file- and print-sharing as well as electronic mail services. Network users run AppleShare client software on their machines to access the network. The client software integrates with the Macintosh Operating System. With System 7.5, the latest release of the Macintosh Operating System, Macintosh systems could share files with other Macintoshes on the network without a dedicated AppleShare server. The user simply sets up shared files on his or her system that can be viewed by other network users.

Appletalk Basics

To make network setup as simple as possible, AppleTalk uses the standard Apple graphical user interface. When a new device is introduced into the network, it automatically assigns itself a randomly generated node ID. When the new device enters the network, it verifies that its node ID is unique on the network.

In AppleTalk Phase 1, there were only 254 possible node IDs possible. AppleTalk Phase 2, which was introduced in 1989, provided extended addressing. The node ID for Phase 1 consisted of 8 bits; the extended addressing features of Phase 2 uses a 16-bit address, providing up to 16 million possible addresses. However, extended addressing is only available with EtherTalk and TokenTalk implementations. LocalTalk is still limited to 254 nodes.

Tip:
You will soon realize that there are 255 possible combinations of node IDs in AppleTalk Phase I. The node ID 255 is restricted for use as the LocalTalk broadcast ID, resulting in an effective maximum 254 nodes.

Once the node ID is generated and verified, it is mapped to a device name the user picks. This device name identifies the node on the network and makes finding and using the node's resources much easier.

As the number of devices on a network increases, the ability to easily find a device decreases. The inverse relationship between the size of the network and the ability to find nodes was not acceptable to users that thrived on the Macintosh' ease-of-use. To alleviate this problem, Apple developed the *zone concept*. A zone is a logical group of devices on the network. Multiple grouped zones form internetworks.

Zones operate as a way to organize groups. For example, all sales nodes may be in a zone called SALES. When you use the Apple Chooser to access the network, you will find a group of zone names. Picking the proper zone will show you a list of the devices in that zone.

The Appletalk Protocol Suite

As we previously told you, AppleTalk is a series of protocols that are layered on one another to form a coherent networking system. An extremely complicated system of smaller specific protocols form the overall network architecture, and it is best to describe how the protocols work by comparing them to the protocols in NetWare or the OSI Model. (See Figure 16-1.)

The Physical Layer

For TokenTalk and EtherTalk networks, the network topology is the same as token-ring or Ethernet access methods. LocalTalk uses unshielded twisted-pair (UTP) cable and RS-422A synchronous data

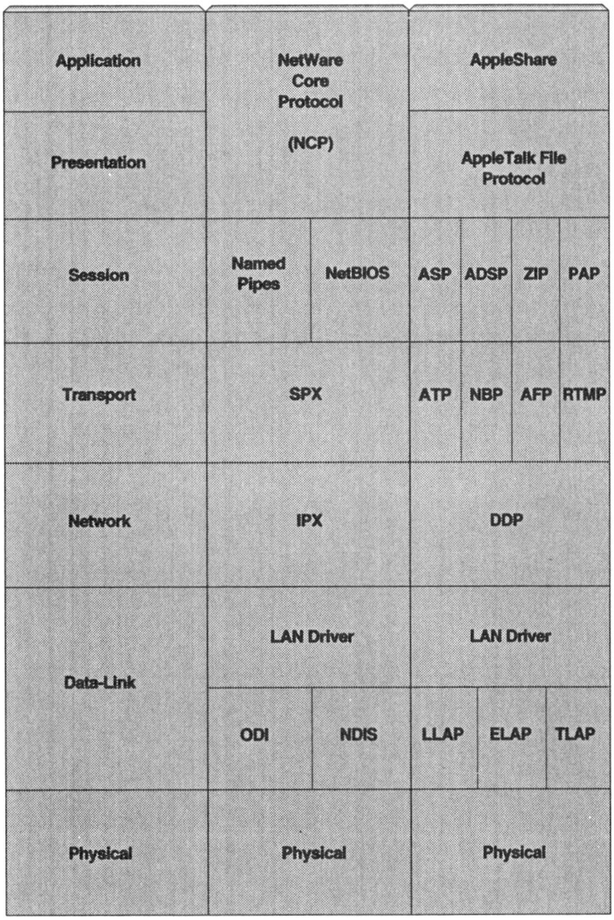

OSI	NetWare		AppleTalk			
Application	NetWare Core Protocol (NCP)		AppleShare			
Presentation			AppleTalk File Protocol			
Session	Named Pipes	NetBIOS	ASP	ADSP	ZIP	PAP
Transport	SPX		ATP	NBP	AFP	RTMP
Network	IPX		DDP			
Data-Link	LAN Driver		LAN Driver			
	ODI	NDIS	LLAP	ELAP	TLAP	
Physical	Physical		Physical			

Figure 16-1. *An AppleTalk comparison with the NetWare and OSI Models.*

communications. RS-422A is also known as EIA-422-A, a frequency modulated (FM) analog signal.

The Data-Link Layer

The Data-Link Layer is divided into a series of Link Access Protocols (LAPs). The LAPs are EtherTalk (ELAP), TokenTalk (TLAP), and LocalTalk (LLAP). LocalTalk is a combination of the Ethernet Protocol and the High-Level Data Link Control (HDLC) Link Layer Protocol. One function of these protocols is to bind with the LAN driver to link the Link Access Protocol to the network adapter. The other function of the Link Access Protocol is to hide the access method from upper-layer protocols and from the user interface. LAP takes packets from upper-layer protocols and converts them to frames that are placed on the network medium. The mechanics and specifications for specific access methods are described in Part IV of this book.

The Network Layer

The Network Layer is straightforward. It consists of the Datagram Delivery Protocol (DDP). DDP is a connectionless best-effort delivery method similar to the Internet Protocol (IP) or NetWare's Internetwork Package Exchange (IPX) protocol. DDP's main function is to provide the logic for bridging and routing functions in Appletalk networks. It communicates directly with the Routing Table Maintenance Protocol (RTMP) and divides packets sent from the upper-layer protocols into 586-byte datagrams. DDP then attaches address and other header information and sends the datagram to the Data-Link Layer protocols, which divide the datagrams into frames for transmission across the medium.

The Transport Layer

The Transport Layer is divided into four protocols, which are responsible for specific Transport Layer functions. While these protocols are independent functions, they work together to provide a coherent package. Among these protocols are the Routing Table Maintenance Protocol (RTMP), the AppleTalk Echo Protocol (AEP), the AppleTalk Transaction Protocol (ATP), and the Name Binding Protocol (NBP).

The Routing Table Maintenance Protocol (RTMP)

This protocol creates and maintains the address table and uses DDP to communicate with other routers and maintain their routing tables. RTMP has been the sore spot in most large AppleTalk networks. With RTMP, the entire routing table was sent across the LAN every 10 seconds. This very large file could take up lots of network bandwidth. In small AppleTalk networks, routing table updating was not a big problem, but as small networks grew into larger, it became an issue quickly. In response, Apple introduced the AppleTalk Update Routing Protocol in 1992 as an additional protocol to complement RTMP. With AURP, as long as the network is stable, almost no routing information is exchanged. When the network changes, only the changes to the routing tables are sent across the network. In addition to an improved routing mechanism, AURP provided a means to encapsulate AppleTalk into a TCP/IP or OSI packets.

AppleTalk Echo Protocol (AEP)

The Appletalk Echo Protocol determines whether destination nodes are capable of receiving data from sending nodes. Prior to a communications session, the sending node sends an echo datagram. The destination node sends back the echo datagram with a positive or a negative response. If the sending node receives a negative response, it retransmits the echo packet.

AppleTalk Transaction Protocol (ATP)

The ATP creates and maintains connection-oriented transactions similar to TCP or NetWare's Sequenced Packet Exchange (SPX). It uses three types of transactions. The Transaction Request (TREQ) determines if a transaction is possible and opens the transaction. TREQ works with the Transaction Response (TRESP) to open the transaction with another node. The Transaction Release (TREL) closes a completed transaction. TREQ and TRESP determine sequences and verify communications during transactions.

Name Binding Protocol (NBP)

The NBP translates the generated node ID to the node name provided by the user. NBP sends broadcast packets across the internetwork to locate network node IDs that correspond to network names. The device matching the network name responds, and the responses are kept in a list maintained in a table for each device on the network.

The Session Layer

The Session Layer contains protocols that maintain communications between nodes and are similar to TCP/IP utilities such as the File Transfer Protocol (FTP), TELNET, or the Simple Mail Transport Protocol (SMTP). These protocols work in conjunction with the Transport Layer protocols to maintain connection-oriented communications.

AppleTalk Data Stream Protocol (ADSP)
The ADSP provides data transmission management between two sockets on separate machines. A socket is an area of memory on the machine that holds the machine's address and the port address of an application that is using ADSP services. ADSP provides full-duplex byte-stream communications, if required. Once the lower-layer protocols establish the communication link, ADSP manages the flow of data across the network.

AppleTalk Session Protocol (ASP)
ASP opens, maintains, and closes communications sessions between nodes. It uses the NBP and ATP to provide node addresses and to obtain the information about the ability of the destination node to establish communications.

Printer Access Protocol (PAP)
The PAP establishes and maintains the link between a user and a printer on the network. It uses the NBP and ATP to find and establish the link between two nodes and manages the link once it is established.

Zone Information Protocol (ZIP)
The ZIP uses the RTMP and AURP to maintain device mappings on the network. It also creates and maintains the Zone Information Tables and transmits the information on the network zones to routers and bridges.

The Presentation and Application Layers

The Presentation and Application layers provide the interface to the user. The protocols in these layers are responsible for file translation and formatting, data encryption, and data compression.

AppleTalk Filing Protocol (AFP)

The AFP provides the user with access to the AppleShare file server. It sets up the local environment so that remote files appear as local files. When the user selects a file on a remote system, AFP redirects the call to the other layers of the AppleTalk protocol suite to establish the connection with the remote machine and access the file. AFP also is responsible for the security of remote and local files.

AppleShare

AppleShare uses AFP to provide centralized file- and print-sharing services. It is the server-based solution for AppleTalk networks. For print services, AppleShare provides print queue facilities and job definitions. It also provides the administrative functionality for maintaining the network as well as security and mail functions.

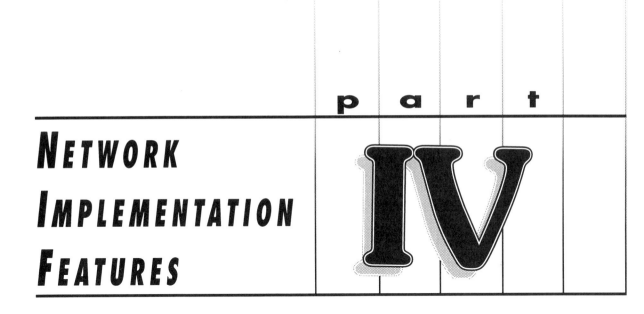

NETWORK IMPLEMENTATION FEATURES

p a r t

IV

In installing or upgrading a LAN, two features have primary importance. They are the topology of the network and the medium used to connect devices.

The next two chapters describe the advantages and disadvantages of different network topologies, and the implementation characteristics and benefits of using certain media.

Network cabling is the largest cause of network problems. If you learn to implement and manage cable for your network correctly, you will avoid a large number of problems from the start.

NETWORK TOPOLOGIES

17

The topology refers to the physical or logical shape of the hardware and cabling. Topologies can be logical or physical. The physical topology describes the physical arrangement of the LAN and the type of cabling it uses. The logical topology describes how data flows throughout the physical topology from node to node. For example, 10BASE-T Ethernet networks are wired as star topologies, even though their electrical signals flow to all nodes as they would in a bus topology. Logical topologies operate as rings or buses. In logical ring topologies such as token-ring, data passes from node to node. In a logical bus topology, all nodes on the network hear the data, but only the node the data is destined for receives it.

The topology represents the lowest layer of the OSI Model, the Physical Layer. The physical structure of the cabling depends on the media access method you are using. Also, the cable you use many times determines the topology you will use for your network.

There are three basic topologies: bus, star, and ring. There are also variations of each of these topologies called *hybrids* that incorporate more than one topology. Hybrids include the star-wired bus and the distributed-star topology.

BUS TOPOLOGY

The most common network topology is the bus, also called a *linear bus*. In the bus, a single cable runs around the office, attaching to individual

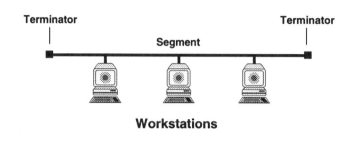

Figure 17-1. *A bus-topology network.*

workstations via drop cables. The main trunk, the piece of cable that forms the main line that other stations are connected to, is terminated at either end with appropriate terminators. (See Figure 17-1.)

The bus topology is easy to install and uses very little cable. However, the small amount of cable it uses is often outweighed by maintenance problems. A single break along a bus may brings down the network, making troubleshooting a nightmare.

Tip:
If you have ever had a problem with a string of Christmas tree lights, you'll understand the problems associated with finding bad adapters in bus topologies.

Star Topology

The star topology uses a central wiring device called a *hub, repeater, multistation access unit,* or *concentrator* to connect workstations to the LAN. Individual cables attach each node to the hub, radiating out in a star fashion. When problems occur, they can be easily isolated. Single adapter failures rarely bring the entire network down. Data transfers from the node through the hub to its destination. (See Figure 17-2 on page 159.)

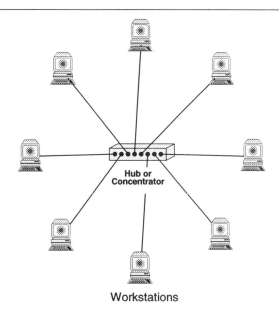

Hub or
Concentrator

Workstations

Figure 17-2. *A star topology network.*

Star topologies are simple to plan and install. The main disadvantages of the star topology are that it uses a lot more cable than bus topologies and if a hub fails, a large portion of the network may become isolated.

RING TOPOLOGY

Ring topologies are often associated with access methods that use token-passing protocols. In a ring topology, the network consists of a closed loop with devices connected to it. The signal travels from node to node until it returns to its source. Data signals on ring topologies are normally transmitted over two pairs of wires—transmit and receive. If a break occurs in the wire, the ring repairs itself. The major advantage of the ring topology is its ability to self-heal if a cable break appears. Also, because each node regenerates the signal before passing it to the next node, very little signal attenuation occurs. The major disadvantages of ring topologies are the amount of cable required and the short wiring distances allowed between nodes. (See Figure 17-3 on page 160.)

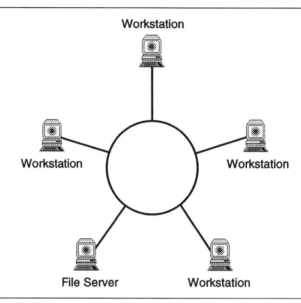

Figure 17-3. *A ring topology network.*

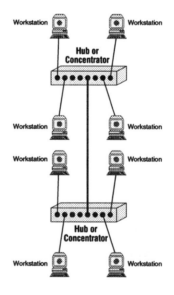

Figure 17-4. *A distributed-star topology.*

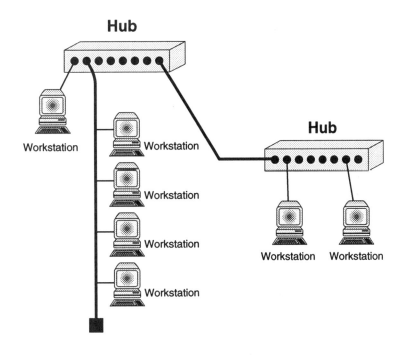

Figure 17-5. *Other hybrid topologies.*

HYBRID NETWORKS

Hybrid networks combine one or more topologies. If you connect more than one hub to a network, the network becomes a distributed-star topology, in which hubs connect to the bus directly and nodes radiate from the hub. (See Figure 17-4 on page 160.)

Star networks may also connect to buses, as shown in Figure 17-5.

ACCESS METHOD CHARACTERISTICS

The following tables show the topologies and the access methods and media they support.

Topology	Access Method	Media
Bus	ARCNET, Ethernet 10BASE-5, and Ethernet 10BASE-2	Coax
Star	ARCNET Ethernet	Twisted-pair
Ring	Token-ring and FDDI	Twisted-pair and fiber-optic
Hybrid	ARCNET, Ethernet, and token-ring	Coax, twisted-pair, and fiber-optic

Access Method	Physical Topology	Logical Topology
ARCNET	Bus, star, and hybrid	Bus
Ethernet	Bus, star, and hybrid	Bus
Token-ring	Star and hybrid	Ring
FDDI	Ring	Ring

18

MEDIA AND CONNECTORS

The old Western truism "A carriage is only as fast as the slowest horse" has a lot to say about life—it also has a lot to say about network media. Your network is only as good as the medium that connects network devices. The medium is the network's physical heart—a good cabling job results in healthy network performance; a faulty or bad cabling job leads to endless problems.

In many instances, media installation is the single most expensive item in a network installation. Because of this, people often make compromises in price and quality. Few network managers are able to have their cable plants installed solely by people that know what they are doing—those that do are lucky.

If you understand a few cabling concepts and follow basic rules, you can have a well-designed and easily maintained cabling system.

WHAT IS THE MEDIUM?

Network devices use medium to deliver electrical signals from one device to another. Media almost always consists of physical cable such as fiber-optic, coaxial, or twisted-pair, but nontraditional media like wireless, microwave, and satellite media are being used more often.

No matter which media you choose for your network, you'll need to avoid certain problems and pitfalls. In this book, we divide media according to the type of cable, and try to explain the intricacies of each type.

CHARACTERISTICS

Cabling has several characteristics and responds to certain environmental factors that affect its transmission of network data. Among these characteristics and factors are attenuation, interference, noise, crosstalk, dispersion, capacitance, impedance, and bend ratio. The meanings of these terms may differ between media types, but for now, these are general definitions. In addition, for proper operation, electrical cable requires grounding.

Attenuation

An electrical signal only travels so far without losing signal strength, also called *amplitude*. Decreases in amplitude as the signal traverses the medium are called *attenuation*. Attenuation is measured in decibels. Fiber-optic media have the lowest attenuation; unshielded twisted-pair (UTP) media have the highest. Most attenuation problems are caused by cable runs that exceed the recommended distance or by damaged coaxial cable. Repeaters minimize attenuation by boosting signals to their original amplitude.

Noise, Interference, and Crosstalk

Electrical signals are also subject to interference from other electrical signal sources such intercoms, electric motors, or transmitters. This results in signal mixing or *distortion* of the transmitted signal. This interference or noise takes the form of *electromagnetic interference (EMI)* or *radio frequency interference (RFI)*. EMI is generated by motors; RFI is generated by transmitters. To reduce noise, make sure the devices you use are FCC-certified or shielded, that cable and devices are properly grounded, and that your computer equipment and media are shielded from radio transmitters.

When cables or channels are placed next to each other, interference between their magnetic fields results in crosstalk. To reduce crosstalk, don't run cables across fluorescent lights, bundle them with other power cables such as traditional electric lines, or bundle the medium itself too tightly. UTP cable is graded according to the amount of signal crosstalk between the pairs near the connector ends. This form of signal crosstalk is called *Near-End Crosstalk (NEXT)*.

Dispersion

Digital signals in fiber-optic media are represented by the presence or absence of light, which indicates voltage variations. Optical signals are subject to attenuation as well as light-source spreading, called *dispersion*, as they travel down the medium.

Capacitance

Capacitance is the measure of energy or charge a cable stores. The outer covering of wires and adjoining wires in wire bundles contribute to capacitance. Capacitance increases signal distortion.

Impedance

Impedance is the resistance of a wire, which changes at different frequencies, causing frequency components of a signal to arrive out of step at the receiver. As the frequency or length of the cable increases, impedance worsens. Impedance is measured in ohms.

Bend Ratio

Each medium type has a ratio that controls the maximum angle a piece of medium can bend. It is called the *bend ratio*. If the angle exceeds the bend ratio, data transmission can be interrupted or faults introduced. Bend ratio is a significant concern in fiber-optic cable.

Balanced vs. Unbalanced Lines

Nonfiber cabling that conducts electrical signals uses *balanced* or *unbalanced* lines. Twisted-pair cable uses a balanced line—it requires two wires individually surrounded by an insulating sheath. Each wire in the pair has an equal current that flows in opposite directions, so that one wire provides a signal return that balances the circuit of the transmitting wire. The twisting of the wire pairs helps reduce noise.

Coaxial cable is an example of an unbalanced line. In an unbalanced line, current flows through the signal conductor and returns on the ground line. In coaxial cable, the shielding that surrounds the central conducting core serves as both the ground wire for the return signal and a shield against EMI and RFI.

Grounding

Another discussed, but little-understood, installation issue of copper-based media is proper *grounding*. An electrical ground is a reference point for an electrical signal. This reference point may be an earth ground, a metal ground such as a machine chassis, or a person. Three objectives need to be met in grounding media—they are human safety, electronic signal reference, and electrostatic discharge.

Earth serves as the ground reference for safe distribution of electricity to power workstations and gives the electricity coming into the building the same reference point the machine has. Electricity chooses the path of lowest flow resistance. This path can be through media or a person. A low-resistance earth ground gives the electricity a better path. In this book, a good earth ground is required because you want a good signal reference for your cable.

Electronic signal reference is different from an earth ground. It gives the digital signal a solid point of reference from which to distinguish the difference between logical zeroes and logical ones. In your computer, a logical 1 is represented by a +5-volt pulse and a logical 0 is represented by a 0-volt nonpulse. There must be a reference point from which to determine 5 volts. The reference point is established through the ground—it is 5 volts above the ground voltage. The ground shorts all electrical signals except the reference ground voltage.

Electronic signal reference is the most important objective to remember. Data travels between two points in a computer network. Ungrounded equipment can cause signal distortion. In networks, different devices in different areas have different ground references. In addition, the ground potential, or the earth ground reference voltage is different in different areas. In a single building, the building is tied to the same earth ground, but adjacent buildings are not. As a result, signal distortion can occur as data travels from building to building.

Static discharge is the final objective of a good ground system. Static is introduced anywhere—people accumulate static energy walking across carpets; low-humidity environments become charged with static electricity. Because static build-up can be harmful to computer components, it is important to avoid it. For this reason, adapters and other network components are shipped in antistatic material. To avoid static discharge, you need to have the same electrical resistance as the machine you are working with. By wearing a grounding appliance or touching the computer's chassis prior to picking up an adapter, you can dissipate static buildup and return your body to the same resistance as the machine you are installing.

Tip:

Never use copper media to connect networks together in different buildings. The EIA/TIA specification requires fiber-optic media between buildings.

CABLE STANDARDS

While there are several standards for wiring, the most often-used standard is the EIA/TIA 568 Commercial Building Standard. This standard applies to wiring guided media in commercial buildings. The National Electrical Manufacturer's Association (NEMA), AT&T, the Underwriter's Laboratories, and the USOC have similar cabling standards.

Fire Codes

Another standard you have to observe is the local fire code. Cables, whether copper-, twisted-pair-, or fiber-optic-based, that are installed in the plenum of a building must meet certain fire code requirements. Plenum space is the air space between the suspended ceiling and the next floor or the roof. Standard wiring is insulated with a polyvinyl chloride (PVC) outer sheath. Plenum wiring is insulated with fluoropolymer sheathing such as Du Pont Teflon.

CABLE TYPES AND CONNECTORS

Individual access methods such as Ethernet and token-ring impose cable implementation and type requirements. Well laid-out Category 3 UTP media for 2.5 megabit per second (Mbps) ARCNET is worthless in an environment that must sustain high speeds as is a high-speed medium in environments that don't need it.

The types of media we discuss in this chapter are coaxial, twisted-pair, shielded twisted-pair, and fiber-optic cable.

The preferred cable method of the future in commercial buildings is data-grade UTP. Although the EIA/TIA standards do not consider coaxial cable for future use, that does not mean you can't use coaxial cable. The wiring standards define methods of running cable that reduce the chance of interference. In many installations such as manufacturing environments, coaxial cable is still the preferred method.

Despite the type of media you use, it relies on many of the characteristics described earlier in this chapter. These characteristics are attenuation, background noise, capacitance, and impedance.

COAXIAL

Coaxial cable consists of a solid or stranded copper core surrounded by insulating material, a metal shield, a ground wire, and an outer protective jacket. Coaxial cable is used most often in bus topologies such as Ethernet 10BASE-2 or 10BASE-5, and ARCNET. Coaxial cable is also used in star-wired ARCNET. It is a common medium for connecting IBM terminals to System Network Architecture (SNA) networks. As a result of the dominance of mainframe computer system, coaxial cable is often found in buildings.(See Figure 18-1.)

Stranded

Solid Core

Figure 18-1. *Varieties of coaxial cable.*

Most coaxial cable is designated by an RG number. (10BASE-5 is the exception.) This number represents the size of the inner copper cable. Thin Ethernet uses RG-58 cable; ARCNET uses RG-62 cable, which is slightly larger in diameter. Coaxial cable, with the exception of thick Ethernet, is easy to work with, flexible, and strong enough to withstand wear and tear. Coaxial cable is reasonably resistant to EMI and RFI.

Tip:
When you install cable, you "pull" it. This term is derived from the amount of time you spend tugging on the cable to get it into position. In many buildings, you pull cable through special polyvinyl pipes in the walls called *conduit*. If you are in a relatively new building, you may have special areas in the ceiling or floors called *cable trays* you can lay the cable in. If you have conduit or cable trays, consider yourself lucky. We have spent many hours pulling cable through open ceilings and walls without conduit. After a weekend of working with fiberglass insulation, you'll appreciate the term "pulling cable."

Connectors

Coaxial cable uses BNC connectors with male ends. The male end of the BNC connector slips over the female connector of a T or barrel connector and locks with a twist motion, providing a solid connection. Adapters and hubs have female BNC receptacles.

A T-connector consists of one male BNC and two female BNC connectors shaped to form a T. The male end fits onto the female BNC receptacle on the adapter, and the two female ends act as a barrel connectors to connect ends of the cable that are terminated by male connectors. (See Figure 18-2 on page 170.) Barrel connectors are used in bus-topology networks to continue cable runs.

Tip:
There are three types of BNC connectors sold—twist-on connectors, crimp-on connectors, and solder-style connectors. Twist-on connectors are fast and easy to apply to cable ends and provide reasonably good connections. To use them, you cut the cable according to manufacturer's specifications and twist the connector onto the cable. Because connectors are not reusable, make sure you do it right the first time. Crimp-on connectors have either a

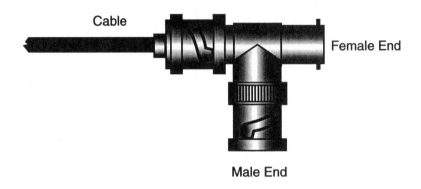

Figure 18-2. *Cable with a BNC and T-connector.*

metal slip, a crimp ring, or a crimping sleeve attached to the connector. After putting the connector on the cable end, you must use a crimping tool to crimp the slip, crimp ring, or sleeve around the outer jacket of the cable to provide a solid connection. Like twist-on connectors, the crimp-on connector is a single-use method. Solder-type connectors must be soldered to the end of the cable and have the benefit of being permanent connections. To replace solder-type connectors, you need to cut the connector off and use a new connector.

Most cable installers use twist-on connectors. We recommend crimp-on connectors because they provide the greatest combination of reliability and ease-of-use. (Besides, we like the way it feels when we pinch ourselves with the crimping tool.)

ARCNET

ARCNET uses RG-62 coaxial cable, which is similar to the cable used in cable TV and older broadband DCA 10Net networks. RG-62 cable uses male bayonet connectors (BNC) on its ends with a twist-lock feature that keeps the cable in place when attached to a female BNC connector.

In star-topology ARCNET networks, the cable runs between the workstation's network adapter and the active or passive hub. (See Figure 18-3.)

If you are using ARCNET in a bus topology, the cable runs from computer to computer. At each computer, a T connector attaches the cable to the adapter. The beginning and end of the cable segment use 93-ohm terminators, which consist of a male BNC connector with a 93-ohm resistor soldered to it that completes the circuit. (See Figure 18-4 on page 172.)

If you are laying bus cable, you should do one of two things. You either need to lay a single cable around the area and cut it at the appropriate point for each workstation, or you start at one end of the bus and custom-cut each length of cable to fit. The distances between workstations, from workstation to hub, and overall network distance are discussed in Chapter 21.

Ethernet

Ethernet coaxial cabling was designed for two types of Ethernet networks: 10BASE-2, which uses RG-58 cable, and 10BASE-5, which uses a

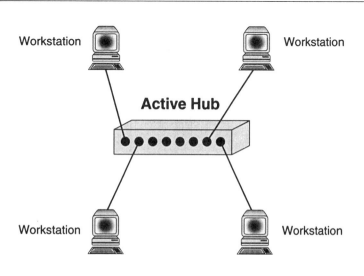

Figure 18-3. *Cabling for an ARCNET star-topology network.*

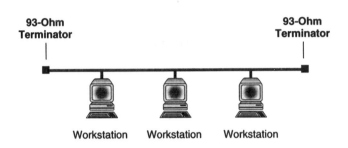

93-Ohm Terminator   **93-Ohm Terminator**

Workstation   Workstation   Workstation

Figure 18-4. *Cabling for an ARCNET bus-topology network.*

0.4 inch 50-ohm coaxial cable. RG-58 50-ohm cable is similar to the RG-62 cable used in ARCNET, though smaller in diameter. It is sometimes called *thin Ethernet*. 10BASE-5, or *thick Ethernet*, is large bulky 50-ohm cable.

Thin Ethernet (10BASE-2)
As in ARCNET bus networks, 10BASE-2 adapters connect to the cable with T-connectors. The T-connector consists of three parts, one male and two female. The male connector forms the leg of the T-connector and attaches to the adapter. The female ends form the top of the T and attach to the medium. If the connector ends a cable run, it connects to a terminator instead of another cable. One terminator must connect to the computer's chassis to ground the cable. (See Figure 18-5 on page 173.)

The cabling requirements for thin Ethernet are discussed in Chapter 19.

Thick Ethernet (10BASE-5)
10BASE-5 uses 50-ohm 0.4-inch diameter coaxial cable. In 10BASE-5, transceivers connect network adapters to the network cable using vampire taps. A vampire tap pierces the cable to make the electrical connection without the need to cut the cable and splice a connector in place. Vampire taps are less costly to install than traditional cable splices. The

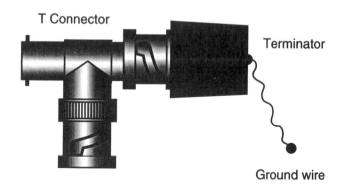

Figure 18-5. *A T-connector with a grounding terminator attached.*

connector on the transceiver and the network adapter is a DB-15 (DIX) connector. Transceivers often ship with their own 50-ohm cable.

10BASE-5 cable is difficult to work with and is the most expensive cable to install. As a result, it is now rarely installed. However, a large installed base of thick Ethernet networks exists, which makes a working knowledge of this type of cable essential.

The basic cabling requirements are discussed in Chapter 19.

TWISTED-PAIR CABLING AND CONNECTORS

Twisted-pair cabling consists of UTP and STP. It is the most successful of all cabling methods and has been codified in the EIA/TIA Commercial Building Specifications 568 standard. UTP requirements have been defined for ARCNET, Ethernet, token-ring, 100BASE-T, 100BASE-VG, and FDDI access methods. STP cable requirements have been defined for token-ring and 100BASE-VG.

Tip:
While it is not necessary to memorize the EIA/TIA 568 standards, you should at least have them available, and require that any UTP cable installation is certified according to the standards.

UTP

UTP is the single most popular LAN cabling method currently in use and, with the codification of EIA/TIA specifications, should continue to remain the best-selling cable. The UTP wiring scheme listed in the 568 standard is for ARCNET, Ethernet, 100BASE-T, 100BASE-VG, and FDDI networks. UTP cable consists of a pair of 110-Ohm cables that twist around each other. The cables, which are normally a solid and a striped color such as blue and blue/white, are graded according to their attenuation, capacitance, impedance, and Near-End Crosstalk (NEXT).

Tip:
As the frequency of the transmitted signal increases, NEXT problems increase. UTP cable designed to carry 100Mbps data rates must present very low NEXT characteristics.

UTP uses mostly RJ-45 eight-wire connectors, although some earlier ARCNET products used RJ-11 four-wire ends. These connectors are similar to the connectors on telephone handsets. In UTP, pin one on one cable end must match pin one on the other end. Although there are occasions when following this rule is not possible, such as point-to-point 10BASE-T or interconnecting older concentrators without MDI/MDIX ports, you should not vary from it.

UTP standards
The predominant standard for UTP cable is the EIA/TIA 568 Commercial Building Standard. It proposes two wiring standards for UTP cables—568A and 568B. 568A pin assignments are the primary telecommunications standard. 568B is an optional standard that is equivalent to the AT&T 258A wiring specification.

The 568 standards are described in Figures 18-6 and 18-7 on page 175.

In 568A and 568B, the pair assignments are different. Pairs are color-coded as follows:

Pair 1—Blue and blue/white

Pair 2—Orange and orange/white

Pair 3—Green and green/white

Pair 4—Brown and brown/white

Pin	Color
1	White/Green
2	Green/White
3	White/Orange
4	Blue/White
5	White/Blue
6	Orange/White
7	White/Brown
8	Brown/White

Figure 18-6. *The EIA/TIA 568A wiring standard.*

Pin	Color
1	White/Orange
2	Orange/White
3	White/Green
4	Blue/White
5	White/Blue
6	Green/White
7	White/Brown
8	Brown/White

Figure 18-7. *The EIA/TIA 568B wiring standard.*

 Tip:
In addition to the EIA/TIA 568 standards, you might want to become familiar with the following documents and Technical Service Bulletins (TSBs) available from the EIA/TIA for a fee:

- TSB-36 defines additional cable specifications for UTP.
- TSB-40 provides additional transmission specifications.
- TSB-53 describes the extended specifications for 150-ohm STP cable.

- EIA/TIA-606 describes the standard for the telecommunications infrastructure of commercial buildings.
- EIA/TIA-569 describes the Commercial Building Standard for telecommunications pathways and spaces.

The EIA/TIA defines five grades of UTP cabling according to impedance, attenuation, and NEXT:

- Category 1 cable is standard telephone cable installed before 1983.
- Category 2 cable is for up to 4Mbps data transmission.
- Category 3 supports up to 10Mbps transmission and is required for 4Mbps token-ring and 10BASE-T networks.
- Category 4 is certified for 16Mbps transmission and is the minimum category required for 16Mbps token-ring.
- Category 5 is certified for transmission of up to 100Mbps.

 Tip:
In Category 5 installations, the quality of the cable installation is only as good as the hardware used. If you use Category 3 or 4 cable connectors, connection boxes, or punch-down blocks, your installation no longer qualifies as a Category 5 installation. Many vendors who supply 100Mbps Category 5 solutions won't support products using Category 3 or 4 connections.

Several other organizations and companies, including NEMA, UL, AT&T, and USOC, have developed their own grading and certification standards. The UL, in particular, defines cable according to five levels:

- Level I is for basic communications and power-limited circuits. It does not specify performance characteristics.
- Level II is a performance criterion similar to IBM Type III or EIA/TIA Category 2 cable. It describes cable consisting of 25 twisted-pair bundles.
- Level III complies with EIA/TIA Category 3 cable. It describes UTP and STP.
- Level IV complies with NEMA standards for low-loss premises telecommunications cable and is similar to EIA/TIA Category 4 cable. It applies to both UTP and STP.

- Level V complies with NEMA standards for proposed low-loss extended frequency premises telecommunications cable. It is similar to the EIA/TIA Category 5 standard.

Phone Wire

Much of the telephone wire sold in the United States is called *flat* or *silver satin cable*, which is UTP cable with a braided cable core. Most adapter vendors don't support silver satin cable. It falls into Category 1 of the EIA/TIA 568 standard and is not suitable for LAN connections.

The problem with installations that use Category 1 cable is that most access methods will operate with almost any grade cable for short distances and only a few users. When you start with a small network of three nodes using silver satin, the network works fine. By the time you added the fourth and fifth nodes to the network, problems may become intermittent. As you add more nodes, persistent problems will make you wish you had used Category 3, 4, or 5 cable to start with.

ARCNET

Most ARCNET adapter manufacturers recommend Category 3 cable with RJ-45 connectors, used in a star or bus configuration. Each ARCNET adapter ships with two connectors and a terminator that consists of an 110-ohm RJ-45 connector. In a star configuration, only one connector is used, and the terminator is placed in the unused connector. Both RJ-45 connectors are used in bus configurations: one for the cable coming to the adapter; the other for the cable continuing to the next adapter on the bus. Terminators are used at each end of the bus.

The cabling length requirements for ARCNET UTP cabling are discussed in Chapter 21.

10BASE-T UTP

Because of its ease-of-use, 10BASE-T is the fastest growing Ethernet market segment. 10BASE-T cable consists of Category 3, 4, or 5 and uses a star-wired topology, making the connections easier to install and troubleshoot. Users changing from UTP-based ARCNET or token-ring networks find that few cabling changes are required. 10BASE-T uses RJ-45 connectors at each cable end. Four wires make up the connection. The RJ-45 connector uses pins 1 and 2, and pins 3 and 6. The EIA/TIA 568B pin-outs for 10BASE-T are shown in Figure 18-8 on page 178.

Pin	Color	Signal
1	White/Orange	Transmit Positive
2	Orange/White	Transmit Negative
3	White/Green	Receive Positive
4	Blue/White	Not Used
5	White/Blue	Not Used
6	Green/White	Receive Negative
7	White/Brown	Not Used
8	Brown/White	Not Used

Figure 18-8. *10BASE-T pinouts.*

10BASE-T UTP cable has a straight-through wiring scheme. For some connections, UTP cables may need to be wired in reverse polarity, so that the transmit positive pin 1 goes to the receive positive pin 3, and the transmit negative pin 2 goes to the receive negative pin 6. If you are using concentrators that have MDI/MDIX ports, you must use cables with crossover connections. Also, point-to-point connections between two 10BASE-T Ethernet adapters must use a crossover cable.

100BASE-T

100BASE-T uses Category 5 media and has a distance limit of 100 meters from adapter to hub. Concentrators are daisy-chained in a hierarchy. The pin configurations for 100BASE-T are the same as 10BASE-T. They are shown in Figure 18-9.

Pin	Color	Signal
1	White/Orange	Transmit Positive
2	Orange/White	Transmit Negative
3	White/Green	Receive Positive
4	Blue/White	Not Used
5	White/Blue	Not Used
6	Green/White	Receive Negative
7	White/Brown	Not Used
8	Brown/White	Not Used

Figure 18-9. *100BASE-T pinouts.*

100BASE-VG

100BASE-VG operates on STP, fiber-optic, or Category 3, 4, or 5 four-pair 100-Ohm UTP. The specifications for these categories are given in Figure 18-10 on page 180.

The 100BASE-VG standard is still evolving. As it currently exists, each cable runs point-to-point from adapter to hub. The topology is similar to that of 10BASE-T, without the restrictions of the 5, 4, 3 rule.

The difference between Category 3 and 5 100BASE-X cable is the distance restrictions per cable segment. Category 3 cable supports lengths up to 100 meters; Category 5 supports lengths up to 150 meters. In addition, you can use cabling devices such as punch-down blocks, patch panels, and wall plates that are consistent with the category you are installing.

100BASE-VG cable uses RJ-45 connectors. At present, the pinouts follow the EIA/TIA 568 standard and fit into any certified cable plant. Cables are wired straight-through according to the EIA/TIA 568B standard. (See Figure 18-11 on page 180.)

To transmit information, all four pairs are used in a single direction. 100BASE-VG's Demand Priority Protocol controls signals between the node and the hub that are sent on pairs 1 and 4, and control signals from the hub to the node are transmitted on pairs 2 and 3.

Token-Ring

Token-ring specifications follow the IBM Cabling Plan, which classifies cable by type. Type I is STP wiring; Type III is UTP wiring. Type III media uses an eight-position RJ-45 jack at both cable ends and corresponds to EIA/TIA Category 3, designed for 4Mbps token-ring with up to 72 stations. A minimum of Category 4 cable is required for 16Mbps token ring.

Token-ring uses RJ-45 or RJ-11 connectors. The Type III RJ-45 connector follows the EIA/TIA 568 standard and uses pins 3 and 4 for one pair and pins 5 and 6 for the other. Pins 1, 2, 7, and 8 are not used. If you are using a six-pin RJ-11 connector, the pinouts are 2, 3, 4, and 5. (See Figure 18-12 on page 180.)

IBM has developed a standard formula for computing overall network length and individual node lengths. The rules are listed in Chapter 20.

STP Cable and Connectors

STP cabling was originally designed for token-ring LANs as an inexpensive replacement for existing coaxial cable. It consists of two solid

Category	Bandwidth	Grade	Pairs Required
Category 3	15MHz	Voice	4 pairs
Category 4	20MHz	Data Grade	4 pairs
Category 5	100MHz	Data Grade	2 or 4 pairs

Figure 18-10. *Specifications for 100 Base-VG Category 3, 4, or 5 cable.*

Pin	Color	Pair
1	White/Orange	2
2	Orange/White	2
3	White/Green	3
4	Blue/White	1
5	White/Blue	1
6	Green/White	3
7	White/Brown	4
8	Brown/White	4

Figure 18-11. *100BASE-VG UTP cable pinouts.*

Pin	Color	Signal
1	White/Orange	Not Used
2	Orange/White	Not Used
3	**White/Green**	**Transmit Positive**
4	**Blue/White**	**Receive Positive**
5	**White/Blue**	**Receive Negative**
6	**Green/White**	**Transmit Negative**
7	White/Brown	Not Used
8	Brown/White	Not Used

Figure 18-12. *Token-ring UTP pinouts.*

or braided pairs of 22AWG 150-ohm copper wire. Each pair twists around the other. Both sets of wire are surrounded by metal foil and an outer jacket. Depending on the type of wire, STP may be bundled with UTP cable and surrounded by another jacket. STP wire is not subject to background noise or NEXT, and it easily allows data transmission rates ranging from 10 to 100Mbps, depending on distance. Token-ring, 100BASE-VG, FDDI, and Thomas-Conrad's TCNS operate on STP cable.

While STP's ease of installation is superior to that of coaxial cable, it is difficult to pull. STP takes careful handling and is not as flexible as UTP or as resilient as coax to bending. However, with a little care and the use of proper patch and under-carpet cables, STP provides an excellent network medium.

STP Standards

EIA/TIA TSB-53 corresponds to the IBM Cabling Plan. The IBM cable requirements for STP cable are based on use:

Type I is an STP cable that contains two 22AWG twisted-pair cables shielded by a metal foil. This is the token-ring medium.

Type II is a shielded 22AWG twisted-pair voice/data cable enclosed in a foil wrapper for data. It contains four 26AWG UTP cables for voice.

Type VI is a flexible 22AWG STP used for connecting PCs with a wall outlet or for short distances between MAUs.

Type VIII is a 26AWG shielded twisted-pair cable for use under carpets. It allows only one-half the distance of Type I cable.

Type IX consists of two 26AWG STP fire-safe cables for plenum use. It can be run two-thirds the distance of Type I cable.

STP Connectors

The standard for STP networks calls for one DB-9 connector and a self-sealing data connector called a *hermaphroditic* connector. The hermaphroditic connector is defined by the IEEE 802.5. (See Figure 18-13 on page 182.)

The pinouts for the cable connected to the hermaphroditic connector and DB-9 connector are shown in Figure 18-14 on page 182.

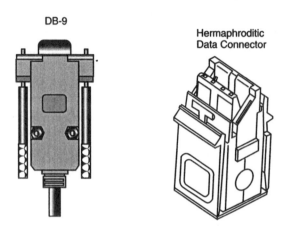

DB-9

Hermaphroditic
Data Connector

Figure 18-13. *A DB-9 connector and a hermaphroditic data connector.*

Wire Color	Hermaphroditic Connector	DB-9 Pin	Signal
Red	Red	1	Receive +
Green	Green	6	Receive −
Orange	Orange	9	Transmit −
Black	Black	5	Transmit +

Figure 18-14. *The pinouts for an STP cable that uses DB-9 and hermaphroditic connectors.*

Patch cables for connecting MAUs or wiring bridges have hermaphroditic connectors on each end.

Although the majority of STP networks use hermaphroditic connectors and DB-9 connectors, some vendors have developed products that only use DB-9 connectors. One of these products is Thomas-Conrad's proprietary TCNS.

Token-Ring
One of the first implementations of STP cabling was for IBM token-ring networks. Token-passing protocols such as token-ring are excellent

choices for STP because they provide a transmit and receive path. The noise immunity and attenuation characteristics of STP cable provide good overall network length.

The basic cabling formula for STP cable is listed in Chapter 20.

 Tip:

Cabling for IBM Token-Ring networks is an art. Its distance and use depends on the number of wiring closets, the distance between wiring closets, the quality of cable, and the phase of the moon. Books and classes have been devoted to the subject. The distance formulas presented in Chapter 20, while not the ultimate formula, are designed for the majority of token-ring LANs. However, if you adhere to the IBM Cabling Plan, it will keep you out of trouble when you attach the boss's node to the network and he or she can't find the file server.

Token-ring operates as a physical star and an electrical ring. Multistation Access Units (MAUs) provide a dual-path device for the electrical signal, which provides a measure of protection against cable breaks. When a break is detected, the relays on either side of the break close. MAUs contain self-sealing connections that complete the ring and keep the network up. The hermaphroditic connector is a result of token-ring's self-sealing requirements.

100BASE-VG

100BASE-VG was developed as a direct medium replacement for token-ring. It uses a DB-9 connector to attach the medium to the adapter and a Type I hermaphroditic connector to attach the adapter to the hub.

100BASE-VG uses both pairs of wire for transmitting and receiving data. The pin assignments for STP cable follow the token-ring assignments. (See Figure 18-15.)

Hermaphroditic Connector	Cable Color Code	DB-9 Pin Assignment	Transmission From Node	Transmission From Hub
Pair 1	Red	1	RX +	TX +
	Green	6	RX –	TX –
Pair 2	Orange	9	TX –	RX –
	Black	5	TX +	RX +

Figure 18-15. *100BASE-VG STP pinouts.*

Fiber-Optic Cable

The promise of fiber-optic cable was access to high-speed, high-bandwidth data networks. As newer technologies introduced implementations on copper cable and as signal multiplexing and switching networks became popular, fiber was delegated to the background and prevented from wide acceptance as the solution for high-speed desktop connections. However, applications still exist for which fiber is the best solution. These include electrically noisy environments and areas that need high security.

Fiber-optic cable relies on light as its transmission medium. As such, fiber is immune to background noise, EMI, and RFI. These characteristics make fiber ideal for areas such as manufacturing environments that are susceptible to EMI. Because fiber transmission does not radiate signals, it is often used where data security is a must. Fiber can also be spliced without noticeable drops in signal strength.

Fiber-optic cable is defined in the EIA/TIA 568 Commercial Building Standard as the cable of choice for connections between buildings and as the interconnection between wiring closets within buildings. The industry's acceptance of fiber as the cable for long-distance premises wiring has been due mainly to its strengths and problems with copper-based media over long distances or areas where high interference is present.

Cable Construction

Fiber-optic cable consists of several layers. The inner portion, which is responsible for light transmission, consists of glass or plastic called the *core*. The *cladding* surrounds the core and is made of a reflective glass sheath. The dimensions of the core and cladding determine the size of the fiber-optic medium. Surrounding the core and cladding is a plastic buffer of Kevlar or other material that gives the cable strength and flexibility. Finally, the cable is surrounded by an outer protective jacket. (See Figure 18-16 on page 185.)

Light passes through the core and reflects off the cladding on its trip through the cable. Fiber is classified by the refractive index of the core and its light propagation capabilities, called *mode*. There are three modes of fiber-optic cable:

- Single index monomode fiber, which is used for long-distance applications that use laser transmission.

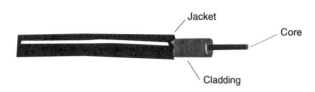

Figure 18-16. *Fiber-optic cable construction.*

- Step index multimode, which has a large-diameter core with high dispersion characteristics. It is used for LAN applications.
- Graded Index Multimode, which uses multiple layers of glass to contain dispersion of the signal.

Characteristics

Fiber has characteristics that affect signal transmission. A working knowledge of these characteristics is essential to designing and planning a good fiber-optic cable installation. These characteristics include dispersion, attenuation, microbend loss, fiber strength, and bend radius.

Dispersion

Dispersion is the spreading of the light pulse as it travels down the optical core. As frequency increases, the chances of overlapping signals increases, which limits the bandwidth or data-carrying capacity of the cable. Three types of dispersion exist:

- Modal dispersion occurs only in multimode fiber-optic cable. It results when the rays of light follow different paths through the fiber and arrive at the other end at different times.

- Material dispersion results when different wavelengths of light travel at different speeds in the same mode.
- Waveguide dispersion occurs because the optical signal travels in both the core and cladding, which have slightly different refractive indices. Thus, the signals travel at different velocities in the core and cladding. This problem occurs most often in single-mode fiber-optic cable.

Attenuation

Attenuation is the loss of optical signal as light travels through the fiber and is analogous to the attenuation that takes place in copper cables. Attenuation in fiber-optic media is measured in decibels (dB) per kilometer. The range is over 300dB/km for plastic fiber and 21dB/km for single-mode fiber. Unlike copper-based media, attenuation in optical cable is not frequency-dependent. It is constant through the frequency range. Attenuation of a fiber signal has two causes:

- Scattering is caused by the loss of optical energy due to imperfections in the fiber and the structure of the fiber. Light scatters in all directions and is no longer directed down the length of the fiber.
- Absorption is the process by which impurities in the fiber absorb optical energy and dissipate the signal as heat. As manufacturing techniques improve, absorption problems diminish.

Microbend Loss

Microbend loss results from small imperfections in the cable, caused by bumps or bend imperfections in the core-to-cladding interface.

Fiber Strength

Fiber strength represents the ability of the fiber to withstand stress. Tensile strength is the ability of the fiber to be stretched or pulled without breaking and exceeds that of steel filaments the same diameter or copper cable of twice the diameter. The main cause of weakness in fiber-optic cable is microscopic cracks or flaws on the surface of the fiber.

Bend Radius

The bend radius is the angle of the bend that can be applied to a fiber cable before it breaks. In addition to breaking, bends in fiber-optic cable affect attenuation and tensile strength. As the bend in the fiber-optic cable increases, the angle of incidence and reflection changes enough that higher-order modes are lost. This is similar to the problem of microbend. If pull is exerted across a bend, the fiber fails at a lower tensile strength.

Connectors

The access method determines the fiber-optic connectors used. For most LAN applications other than FDDI, you use SMA or ST connectors. An SMA connector screws on; an ST connector is similar to a BNC connector for copper connections. The preferred method is the ST connector because it provides proper alignment of the fiber cable under stress conditions, lessening slippage and data loss.

ARCNET

ARCNET uses multimode fiber-optic cable as a transmission medium. Adapters have two ports—one for transmitting, the other for receiving. Fiber-optic ARCNET is wired in a star topology using a fiber hub. Two adapters can also be used point-to-point. The cable connection must be reversed in ARCNET—the transmitting fiber of one adapter goes to the receiving port on the other adapter or hub.

Fiber-optic cable is designated by the size of the cable in microns. ARCNET uses 62.5/125-, 50/125-, or 100/140-micron fiber. Most ARCNET manufacturers recommend 62.5/125-micron fiber, which yields a distance of 8,000 feet between active devices.

FDDI

FDDI cabling is available as single-mode or multimode fiber. Each type uses two separate cables—one for transmitting and one for receiving. Special receptacles are used depending on the type of connection made.

Single-mode fiber is based on the X3.194 standard and is intended for campus-wide or Metropolitan Area Network (MAN) use. It uses lasers as a light source and supports a distance of up to 60 kilometers between stations. Multimode fiber is designed for standard FDDI installations. It allows distances of up to two kilometers between stations. FDDI supports 62.5/125-, 50/125-, 85/125-, and 100/140-micron cable.

Connectors

FDDI cable ends must be terminated with special keyed connectors, which can be inserted only into a matching receptacle. The keyed connector is called a *Media Interface Connector (MIC)*. Four types of MICs exist:

- MIC A is a primary/secondary out for joining DAS to FDDI main rings.
- MIC B is a secondary in/primary out for joining DAS to FDDI main rings.
- MIC M is a master connector that fits into any connection receptacle.
- MIC S is the connector for SAS stations.

Token-Ring

Fiber-optic connections in token-ring are used for repeaters, which regenerate and retime signals to allow them to travel longer distances. Fiber-optic media is also used in pairs to daisy-chain MAUs or along the lobe length of a single station. In a fiber-optic token-ring implementation, a repeater is placed at each end of the cable run.

100BASE-VG

The proposed standard for 100BASE-VG over fiber-optic cable follows the EIA/TIA 568 standard and uses ST connectors. The fiber-optic link uses single-pair multimode fiber-optic 62.5/125-micron glass cable.

WIRELESS LANs

Wireless transmission for both local and remote connections is becoming more common. Local wireless LANs use transmission facilities located within a company's physical facilities. Mobile wireless LANs involve telephone or public communications services when users are away from the company's physical premises.

The typical wireless LAN consists of a central transceiver and separate transceivers connected to each workstation or server. Wireless LANs use three types of transmission. They are infrared light transmission, narrow-band radio, and spread-spectrum radio.

Infrared

Infrared light transmission offers the advantages of wide bandwidth and high signal rates. However, it only operates in a line-of-sight transmission mode between a transmitter and a receiver. Equipment that blocks or reflects light can interfere with transmission. Infrared uses mirrors to bend light from the transmitter around corners to the receiver. It is not subject to government restriction and supports transmission speeds up to 10Mbps.

Narrow-Band Radio

Narrow-band radio is similar to standard radio broadcasts. Transceivers are tuned to a tight frequency band. Unlike infrared transmission, narrow-band radio can transmit through walls and obstructions. Narrow-band transmission is subject to ghosting and signal reflection. Because it is a radio transmission, it is subject to FCC regulation. Narrow-band transmitters must be tightly tuned and regularly maintained. Transmission speeds up to 4,800 kilobits per second (Kbps) are available.

Spread-Spectrum Radio

To avoid problems associated with narrow-band transmission, companies developed spread-spectrum radio. In spread-spectrum, a coded signal is transmitted over a wide spectrum of frequencies. The signal must be decoded by the receiver. Coded signals allow transmission over a wide frequency range even in the presence of other signals. The low-output strength of spread-spectrum inhibits interference with other broadcast media. Transmission speeds of up to 2Mbps are available.

Microwave and Satellite

In addition to wireless transmissions within a single building, microwave wireless transmitters are available for limited areas between buildings in a campus or metropolitan area. For long-distance transmission, satellite, microwave, and broadcast technologies are available.

chapter

ETHERNET

19

The Ethernet access method was originally described in 1973—by Bob Metcalfe of the Xerox Palo Alto Research Center—to connect Alto computers together. (The microprocessor-based Alto preceded the Xerox star, which was the first computer to use a graphical user interface.) Based on the Aloha System radio network developed at the University of Hawaii, Xerox renamed Ethernet The Xerox Wire when it developed a 2 megabit per second (Mbps) version in 1976. In 1979, Xerox, Digital, and Intel developed, implemented, and standardized Ethernet (sometimes called Digital–Intel–Xerox Ethernet). The DIX Ethernet standard was modified by the Institute of Electrical and Electronic Engineers (IEEE) into the 802.3 Ethernet standard. The IEEE promulgated the 802.3 standard to codify the basic structure of 10BASE-2 thick and 10BASE-5 thin Ethernet. Presently, according to Metcalfe, there are 50,000,000 Ethernet-connected computers and a total of 5,000,000 Ethernet networks.

Ethernet and its implementations have become the most widely used network access method. The Ethernet standard defines the electrical and frame formats of the access method that comprise the Physical and Data Link Layers of the Open Systems Interconnect (OSI) Model.

Ethernet is a carrier-sense, multiple access with collision detection–based (CSMA/CD) protocol in which nodes contend to communicate data on the medium. Definitions have been codified for one megabit per second (Mbps), 10Mbps, and 100Mbps Ethernet and gathered under a consistent naming convention. Very few 1Mbps Ethernet networks exist, and 100Mbps Ethernet is just now making its way into the market.

In Ethernet implementations, the numerical series at the beginning of the name defines the access method's transmission speed in megabits per second. The alphabetic portion defines either baseband or broadband transmission. The final number in Ethernet implementations represents the maximum meters of medium per segment, multiplied by 100. For example, the third most common Ethernet implementation, 10BASE-5, designates a 10Mbps baseband access method that allows an overall distance of 500 meters per segment.

 Tip:
The standard naming convention the IEEE originally intended does not carry over into 10BASE-T, 10BASE-F, 100BASE-T (called Fast Ethernet), or 100VG-AnyLAN Ethernet implementations.

The IEEE defines the following Ethernet implementations:

- 10BASE-2 Ethernet, also called *thin Ethernet* or *Thinnet,* uses RG-58 A/U coaxial media. It is a baseband access method that operates at 10Mbps.
- 10BASE-5 Ethernet, also called thick Ethernet, is a baseband access method that operates at 10Mbps.
- 10BASE-F Ethernet uses fiber-optic media and operates at 10Mbps.
- 1BASE-5 Ethernet has a maximum segment length of 500 meters and a transmission speed of 1Mbps. 1BASE-5 networks are rarely seen.
- 10BROAD-36 is broadband Ethernet at 10Mbps.
- 10BASE-T is unshielded twisted-pair (UTP) Ethernet operating at 10Mbps.
- 100BASE-T is a proposed 100Mbps Ethernet that requires new Ethernet adapters and hubs or concentrators. 100BASE-T runs over two- or four-pair UTP or fiber-optic media.
- 100VG-AnyLAN is a proposed 100Mbps Ethernet standard that operates on variable grade twisted-pair media and uses the Demand Priority Protocol (DPP) access method.

OPERATIONS

Ethernet is a nonrooted, branching bus topology—each adapter attaches to a cable segment that contains other devices. Cable segments can be connected with medium attachment units (MAUs), repeaters, or concentrators to form longer segments or branch existing segments.

Each device connects to the medium via a transceiver, concentrator, or hub. Bus segments follow a wiring rule known as the 5, 4, 3 rule, in which no more than five segments separate any two workstations, no more than four repeaters or concentrators exist between any two workstations, and no more than three segments contain nodes. (See Figure 19-1.) The 5, 4, 3 rule is based on the propagation delay of the signal (the amount of time the signal takes to propagate along the length of the segment) and is absolute—if you violate the rule, trouble will occur. Problems caused by propagation delay are insidious and difficult to diagnose without dismantling the network and starting over.

 Tip:
The most common Ethernet implementation, 10BASE-T, is electronically a bus configuration. Although physically the network

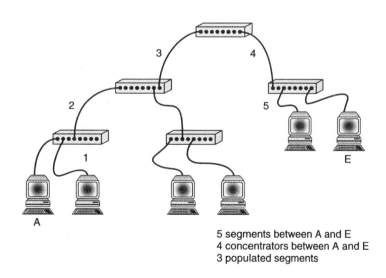

5 segments between A and E
4 concentrators between A and E
3 populated segments

Figure 19-1. *The 5, 4, 3 rule.*

appears as a star topology, the communications operate as a bus—each active node on the bus hears every transmission. 10BASE-T also is subject to the 5, 4, 3 rule. Because a segment is defined as the medium from the network adapter to the hub, the rule that no more than three populated segments may exist does not apply. If you mix 10BASE-T networks with 10BASE-2 or 10BASE-5 networks, you can also ignore this part of the 5, 4, 3 rule.

In Ethernet, only one station may transmit on the network at a time. Each adapter listens on the network for a carrier signal, which indicates that traffic exists on the network. If the node doesn't detect traffic within a certain time, it begins to transmit. Problems occur when workstations try to transmit simultaneously. When this occurs, the signals from the stations collide, network traffic halts, and the colliding packets are destroyed. When stations that sent messages do not receive acknowledgments of frame receipt, they assume a collision has occurred, transmit jamming signals indicating a collision has occurred, and back off a random amount of time before transmitting again. An algorithm randomizes the adapter's waiting periods to prevent adapters from backing off the same amount of time. The stations then listen for free periods on the wire and attempt to transmit again. This contention-based mechanism makes Ethernet efficient for smaller networks. However, as the number of nodes increases, the protocol becomes more inefficient. This decreased performance is a result of the rising number of collisions as traffic increases.

Departmental and enterprise hubs used in 10BASE-T networks make performance problems less noticeable because they are more easily recognized, but delays still occur. Managed hubs allow large numbers of attached devices to be manually or automatically segmented into smaller groups of stations or disabled when problems occur to balance traffic. Managed hubs can be controlled locally from the hub or by management software that uses the Simple Network Management Protocol (SNMP).

An additional method of segmentation, and hence traffic control, is achieved by adding bridges or routers to the network. In NetWare, this can be accomplished by adding another adapter in the server. The resulting goal is to limit the number of stations attached to an individual network. Realistically, no more than 40 workstations should exist per segment.

ETHERNET IMPLEMENTATIONS

There are a variety of implementations of Ethernet. Most operate at 10Mbps and vary by the type of medium they use. Two newer implementations of Ethernet, 100BASE-T and 100VG-AnyLAN, operate at 100Mbps. Of the 10Mbps varieties, 10BASE-T is most common, followed by 10BASE-2 and 10BASE-5.

10BASE-2 Thin Ethernet

10BASE-2 Ethernet, also known as *thin Ethernet* or *Thinnet*, is a linear bus topology that uses RG-58 A/U coaxial medium, which is thinner, less expensive, and easier to work with than thick coaxial 10BASE-5 medium. Thin Ethernet media uses BNC connectors to attach to adapters. (See Figure 19-2.)

Components
A variety of components are used in 10BASE-2 media:

> **Adapters**—Most 10BASE-2 Ethernet adapters have two connectors: a BNC connector and an AUI, also called a *DB-15 connector*. The AUI connector allows the adapter to attach to a variety of

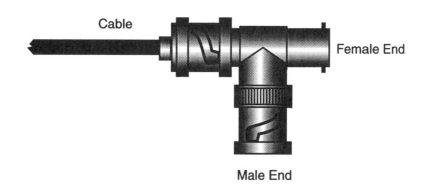

Figure 19-2. *A thin Ethernet segment.*

media. Some adapters have three connectors, one each for 10BASE-2, 10BASE-T, and 10BASE-5.

Repeaters—The repeater regenerates and retimes signals to increase the distance of cable segments. Repeaters can be managed and used to connect dissimilar segments together.

RG-58 A/U cable—RG-58 A/U cable is 50-ohm shielded coaxial media.

BNC connectors—BNC connectors connect adapters to the media and vice versa.

BNC T-connectors—T-connectors connect lengths of media to each other.

BNC terminators—The BNC terminator terminates the end of the Ethernet bus. A 50-ohm resistor connects the center pin of the BNC connector to the end of the shielding.

The maximum segment length in 10BASE-2 Ethernet is 185 meters. Up to five segments may be joined using repeaters. Only three of the segments may be populated with nodes. A maximum of 30 nodes is allowed per segment. Nodes include repeaters, bridges, routers, and workstations. The number of nodes on a thin Ethernet network cannot exceed 1,024.

Tip:
You can combine thin and thick Ethernet nodes on the same segment by using the following formula to determine the length of the segment:

$$(1{,}640 \text{ feet} - l) \text{ divided by } 3.28 = t,$$

in which l is the length of the trunk segment desired, and t is the maximum amount of thin Ethernet medium.

10BASE-5 Thick Ethernet

10BASE-5 was the original Ethernet implementation. Currently, it is seldom installed, but there is still a large base of installed nodes. Thick Ethernet is installed in a linear bus topology, in which each node attaches to a single cable. Workstations attach to the trunk segment using transceivers, small devices that provide electrical isolation for the device attached to the medium. (See Figure 19-3.) The transceiver may be attached to the main trunk segment with an N-series connector or with a vampire tap, a device that pierces the cable's shielding to make its attachment. Vampire taps eliminate the need to cut the cable and attach connectors. A third connector on the transceiver attaches to another cable using a DB-15 connector. A similar connector exists on the network adapter. The DB-15 connector on the adapter also is known as an *Attachment Unit Interface*.

Components

10BASE-5 Ethernet consists of a number of components:

Adapter with DB-15 (DIX) connector—The 10BASE-5 adapter has a DB-15 connector on the edge bracket. Some newer adapters also have a connector for 10BASE-T or 10BASE-2 Ethernet.

Repeater—The repeater regenerates and retimes the signal to increase the distance of a cable segment. Repeaters can be managed and used to connect dissimilar segments together.

Transceiver and transceiver cable—The transceiver and its cable join the network adapter to the media.

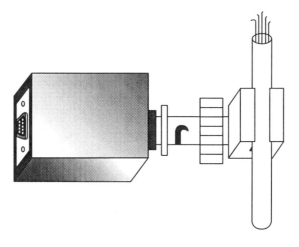

Figure 19-3. *A 10BASE-5 transceiver.*

Thick Ethernet medium—10BASE-5 Ethernet uses 0.4-inch coaxial medium.

N-series connectors—The N series connector joins the transceiver to the Ethernet bus.

N-series terminators—N-series terminators terminate each end of the bus.

10BASE-5 is installed as a linear bus topology along a trunk segment of thick Ethernet. The maximum segment length is 500 meters. The maximum distance between the transceiver attached to the segment and the node is 50 feet. Five trunk segments may be joined together using repeaters. No more than three of the five segments may be populated with nodes. A node is a workstation, repeater, router, or bridge. Up to 100 nodes may be placed on a segment. The number of nodes on a 10BASE-5 network cannot exceed 1,024. (See Figure 19-4.)

10BASE-T Unshielded Twisted-Pair Ethernet

10BASE-T Ethernet uses UTP medium in a star-wired configuration in which adapters connect to the network via a concentrator or hub. Although the physical configuration is star-wired, the electrical configuration is a linear bus. Each length of medium from an adapter to a

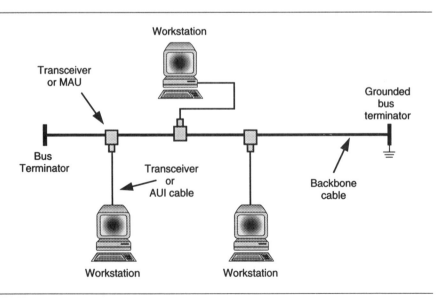

Figure 19-4. *A thick Ethernet configuration.*

concentrator is a populated segment that is not limited by the 5, 4, 3 rule. The medium uses twisted-pair wiring that supports 10Mbps transmission. At a minimum, Category 4 UTP should be used. All devices use RJ-45 connectors. 10BASE-T wiring, consistent with the EIA/TIA 568A standard, uses pins 1 and 2 and 3 and 6. (See Figure 19-5.)
10BASE-T Ethernet consists of several components:

Adapter—10BASE-T adapters normally have an RJ-45 receptacle on the end bracket and a DB-15 AUI connector for attaching to other media. Some adapters have three connectors on the end bracket, allowing use of 10BASE-T, 10BASE-2, or 10BASE-5 networks.

Concentrator or hub—The concentrator or hub is a centralized wiring device that connects adapters to the network.

Repeater—The repeater regenerates and retimes signals to increase the length of a cable segment. Repeaters can be managed and used to connect dissimilar segments together.

Transceivers—The transceiver joins the network adapter to the media. It is most commonly used to connect a 10BASE-T adapter to a different medium.

UTP medium—The UTP cable used for 10BASE-T networks uses RJ-45 connectors. UTP medium is susceptible to radio and electromagnetic interference and may be used only over short distances.

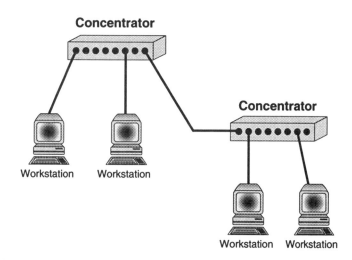

Figure 19-5. *A 10BASE-T network.*

⊘ Tip:
Many users try to use voice grade (Category 3) medium for
10BASE-T. While Category 2 medium works, you are inviting
trouble that is difficult to isolate and solve.

The maximum length for a cable segment, the cable between the
workstation and the concentrator, is 100 meters. Concentrators may be
connected using 10BASE-5 or 10BASE-2 medium and repeaters in the
form of a backbone cable. (See Figure 19-6.) You can connect adapters
that have AUI ports by using an transceiver. Any two workstations can
be separated by only four concentrators and five cable segments. Up to
1,024 nodes may be attached to the network.

100VG-AnyLAN Ethernet

Although Ethernet is the most-used access method, its 10Mbps transmission speed and topology limit its effectiveness with new traffic- and

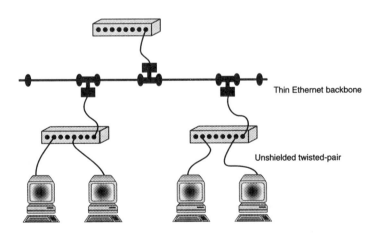

Figure 19-6. *A UTP network showing a 10BASE-2 backbone with repeaters.*

data-intensive applications such as multimedia. To increase the speed of Ethernet and add additional features that let it work well in multimedia environments, AT&T and Hewlett-Packard designed 100VG-AnyLAN. This Ethernet implementation is a 100Mbps Ethernet- or token-ring-compatible access method that uses Category 3, 4, or 5 UTP or fiber-optic medium. In the twisted-pair medium, all four pairs are used. The medium is compatible with the EIA/TIA 568B standard and uses RJ-45 connectors. Nodes attach to a wiring hub in the same way as 10BASE-T nodes. Hubs also can be attached together using a port called an *Up-link port*.

100VG-AnyLAN consists of a number of components:

Adapter—100VG-AnyLAN adapters use UTP, STP, or fiber-optic media.

Hub—The hub or concentrator in 100VG-AnyLAN supports 10- and 100Mbps transmission. It uses the Demand Priority Protocol (DPP) to determine the processing order of data.

In 100VG-AnyLAN, which can operate at 10- or 100Mbps, the frame can be either an Ethernet or token-ring MAC frame. Instead of using the CSMA/CD or token-passing protocol to determine access to the network, 100VG-AnyLAN requests are assigned a priority called *demand priority*, which allows greater access to requests such as real-time video that require more bandwidth. The 100VG-AnyLAN arbitrates the incoming frames by polling the devices on the network. Higher-priority requests are serviced prior to normal-priority requests. A normal priority request automatically rises in priority if it is not serviced in 200–300 milliseconds.

A mechanism called *link training* is used to verify cable connections and provide additional information about attached nodes. The hub polls each node attached to it and transmits data across the link. The hub's initial transmission verifies the cable link. If the cable link is valid, the node transmits data to the hub telling it the type of workstation it is, its operational mode (either private or promiscuous), and its address.

100VG-AnyLAN media varies from voice-grade Category 3 to high-speed, data-grade Category 5 media. As a result, it is suitable for many environments and will also interconnect existing Ethernet networks at the MAC layer. The Demand Priority Protocol (DPP) and variable media grade use makes 100VG-AnyLAN ideal for next-generation network applications.

100BASE-T Ethernet

The "other" approach to 100Mbps Ethernet is 100BASE-T, also called Fast Ethernet, which was developed by a consortium of companies including Grand Junction Networks, 3Com, Bay Networks (formerly SynOptics), Intel, Standard Microsystems, Corp., and approximately 35 other vendors. 100BASE-T modifies the existing CSMA/CD protocol. To allow 100Mbps transmission, the developers of 100BASE-T shortened the allowable cable distances of the technology. (See Figure 19-7.)
100BASE-T networks consist of numerous components:

Adapter—The 100BASE-T adapter has an RJ-45 or fiber-optic connector on the end bracket and operates at 10 or 100Mbps.

Concentrator—The topology is similar to 10BASE-T, in that each adapter connects to a hub or concentrator in a star-wired configuration. The concentrators are then wired together in a hierarchy.

Category 5 UTP medium—100BASE-T uses Category 5 medium that has a maximum length of 100 meters, unless it uses fiber-optic medium.

62.5/125-micron fiber-optic cable—100BASE-FX uses this type of fiber-optic medium.

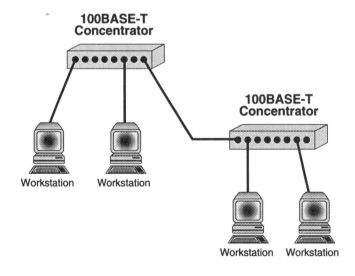

Figure 19-7. *A 100BASE-T configuration.*

The advantage of 100BASE-T is its compatibility with established Ethernet. Many vendors are manufacturing 100BASE-T adapters that perform at 10Mbs and are designed to ease the transition to 100Mbps access methods. 100BASE-T has the added advantage of using the existing CSMA/CD protocol and supporting the IEEE Media Access Control (MAC) sublayer so it can be bridged with existing Ethernet networks. However, any bridge between Ethernet and token-ring needs to be speed-matched to make it compatible. Finally, 100BASE-T has the advantage of being supported by a majority of existing Ethernet manufacturers.

Packet-Switched Ethernet

Manufacturers such as Kalpana (now a subsidiary of Cisco Systems) have developed a method for increasing the throughput of current Ethernet. Switched Ethernet is introduced at the 10BASE-T concentrator. The switch creates a connection-oriented link between the transmitting and receiving nodes. This gives the two nodes a direct communications line and access to the full bandwidth of the wire for a short period of time. By isolating traffic, collisions can be eliminated. With switching, the transmitting station does not have to compete as often for the right to transmit, so stations that have a large amount of data can transmit in a shorter period of time. If switching is used in combination with full-duplex Ethernet, another proposed specification, the bandwidth can be used efficiently and provide greater overall network throughput. Full-duplex Ethernet gives nodes the ability to transmit and receive at the same time.

Adapters

A wide variety of Ethernet adapters and chip sets exists. Manufacturers include 3Com, Eagle Technology (now a subsidiary of Artisoft), IBM, Microdyne, Olicom, Proteon, Standard Microsystems Corp., and Thomas-Conrad. The Novell NE-2000 adapter, manufactured by Artisoft, and the various NE-2000 clones are based on the National Semiconductor ATLANTIC chip and are among the most popular Ethernet adapters on the market. The ATLANTIC chip combines numerous components to allow manufacturers to make less expensive adapters. Although the ATLANTIC chip supports higher IRQs, it has a limited number of interrupt (IRQ) settings available. However, for workstation use, the adapter is ideal.

File servers need higher performance than workstations. Manufacturers have developed a large number of adapters that operate at 10Mbps, but transfer data on and off the CPU bus more quickly. These adapters include EISA and bus-mastering ISA adapters. Bus-mastering EISA and ISA adapters increase total network throughput dramatically.

One of the most-used features of 10BASE-T networks is link integrity. Each adapter and concentrator transmits a signal along the transmit pair and monitors the cable on the receive pair. Link integrity LEDs light on the adapter or concentrator if the unit monitoring the receive pair detects the signal. For Ethernet troubleshooting, you can use the LEDs to verify cable integrity.

Concentrators

Concentrators are the heart of the 10BASE-T network. All nodes connect to the concentrator via medium to transmit signals. Concentrators have unique wiring diagnostics that allow you to perform reverse polarity tests of the medium and the integrity of the link. A LED on the concentrator lights up or changes color if a reverse polarity cable is plugged into the concentrator. The link integrity LED is lit when the connection between the adapter and the concentrator is functioning correctly. In 10BASE-T, adapters and concentrators monitor the receive pair of the wire for electrical signals present on the wire. If the concentrator detects a signal, it assumes a good pair of wires exists and lights the link polarity LED that corresponds to the attached port.

10BASE-T networks also are susceptible to jabber, in which a corrupted signal on the wire that is out of specification corrupts network traffic. Jabber can be caused by a bad adapter or medium. If the concentrator detects a segment that is jabbering, it automatically removes that node from the network and informs you by lighting its auto-removal or partition LED.

Switching Hubs

A recent development in Ethernet is the switching hub, which implements a matrix switch to provide the entire 10Mbps bandwidth to an individual network connection. With a switching hub in place, two nodes are directly connected via a virtual circuit for a short period of time, allowing the nodes to communicate across the entire bandwidth of the wire. The workstations connected to switching hubs exhibit increased throughput. Switching hubs can be added to existing networks.

Full-Duplex Ethernet

Another proposal for increasing Ethernet bandwidth is full-duplex capability, which allows devices to transmit and receive data at the same time. This development dovetails with the introduction of the switching hubs and requires new hubs. Full-duplex technology effectively doubles the capabilities of the adapter in a transmission cycle. It was implemented only in 1994.

The Ethernet Frame

The Ethernet frame is up to 1,524 bytes in length and is divided into the following fields (See Figure 19-8 on page 206):

Preamble—The first field, the preamble, consists of eight octets of alternating ones and zeros. It ends in 1 (10101011).

Destination Address—This six-octet field indicates whether the adapter is using the burned-in physical layer address or a locally administered address for the destination address. Additionally, this field indicates whether the frame is for a group or individual station.

Source Address—The source address field is six octets in length and indicates the Physical Layer address of the source Ethernet adapter. This field has the same format as the destination address.

Type Field—Consisting of two octets, the type field indicates the higher-layer protocol used in the data field, including IP, XNS, and DECnet.

Data Field—The data field has a minimum length of 46 octets and a maximum of 1,500 octets. This field includes the packet data and 802.3 Data Link layer information.

Frame Check Sequence (FCS)—The FCS consists of four octets and indicates the sequence of bits used for error checking.

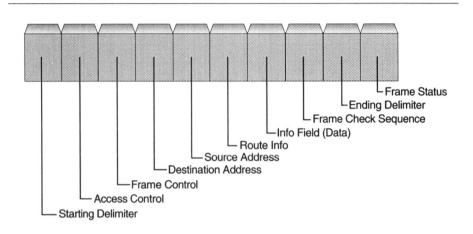

Figure 19-8. *Ethernet frame format.*

In addition to these fields that all Ethernet frames use, 100VG-AnyLAN also includes an IEEE 802.1 Training Frame, which indicates the adapter's configuration and its location on the bus. (See Figure 19-9 on page 207.) This frame consists of these fields:

Destination Address—The six-octet destination address field indicates whether the adapter uses the burned-in Physical Layer address or a locally administered destination address. Additionally, this field indicates if the address corresponds to a group or individual address.

Source Address—The source address consists of six octets that indicate the Physical Layer address of the source Ethernet adapter. This field has the same format as the destination address.

Configuration—This 16-bit field indicates whether a node is a cascade, promiscuous, or bridge, its format, and whether it uses an 802.3 or 802.5 frame.

Data Field—This 46- to 1,500-octet field includes the packet data. If the frame type is 802.5, this field also includes Data Link layer information.

Frame Check Sequence (FCS)—This four-octet field is used to determine the integrity of the transmitted data.

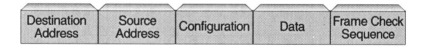

Figure 19-9. *A 100VG-AnyLAN Training Frame.*

MEDIA

Before discussing the physical attributes of each medium specification, you should familiarize yourself with three terms that are not specific to Ethernet cabling but are of value in any cabling situation.

The first, *attenuation*, is the amount of signal strength or power the electrical signal loses as it travels over a length of wire. The longer the cable segment, the greater the loss and the greater the attenuation. If the signal loss or attenuation is too great, the device at the end of the cable will not be able to decode incoming signals accurately, and data will be lost.

The second term, *impedance*, is the amount of resistance measured in ohms the media produces at a given transmission frequency. The cable's impedance should be, within the specified range for the type of signal being transmitted.

The last term, *crosstalk*, applies specifically to UTP media and represents the interference of a signal on one pair of wires from an adjacent pair in the same bundle. Crosstalk is measured in decibels (dB) at a particular frequency measured in megahertz (MHz). The lower the decibel level over the frequencies used by the media the better. Before purchasing any medium look for these specifications and verify with your adapter manufacturer that the medium is proper to install.

10BASE-2 Media

10BASE-2 uses RG-58 A/U cable, which is similar to the RG-62 A/U cable used in ARCNET but smaller in diameter. The maximum cable segment for RG-58 A/U medium is 185 meters (or 607 feet) per segment. An additional standard increases the maximum segment length by 20 percent and requires that all nodes, including transceivers, on the segment support the extended distance. The maximum cable length of extended-distance 10BASE-2 Ethernet is 925 meters.

In 10BASE-2 Ethernet, a maximum of 30 nodes can exist on a segment and a maximum of 1,024 nodes is available per network. The medium used must have a 50-ohm terminator at the end of the bus, and one end should be grounded. The minimum distance between adapters is .5 meters. Adapters and T-connectors use a BNC-style connector. Transceivers can be separated from adapters by a maximum cable distance of 50 meters, or 164 feet. (See Figure 19-10 on page 209.)

10BASE-5 Media

10BASE-5 Ethernet uses 50-ohm 0.4-inch diameter coaxial cable with a maximum length of 500 meters (1,640 feet). The ends of the cable terminate with 50-ohm terminators, and one end of the cable must be grounded. A transceiver must connect the adapter or device to the main network cable or trunk segment. Transceivers must be placed a minimum of 2.5 meters (8 feet) apart. (See Figure 19-11 on page 209.)

The maximum network distance is 1,500 meters (4,920 feet). A total of 100 transceivers can be placed on any segment.

Transceivers connect to the network media using vampire taps, which pierce the medium and make the electrical connection without the need to cut the medium and splice a connector in place. Vampire taps are less expensive and faster to install than splicing cable. (See Figure 19-12 on page 210.)

The 10BASE-5 transceiver and adapter use DB-15 connectors. The vampire tap cable is 50-ohm cable, but more flexible than the main trunk segment. The maximum cable length for vampire tap cables is 50 feet. (See Figure 19-13 on page 210.)

Fifty-ohm 10BASE-5 medium is difficult to work with and expensive. As a result, it is no longer used extensively. However, a large installed base makes a working knowledge of this medium essential.

10BASE-T Media

Because of its ease of use, 10BASE-T is the fastest growing Ethernet market segment. 10BASE-T uses Category 4 or 5 UTP medium. Unlike

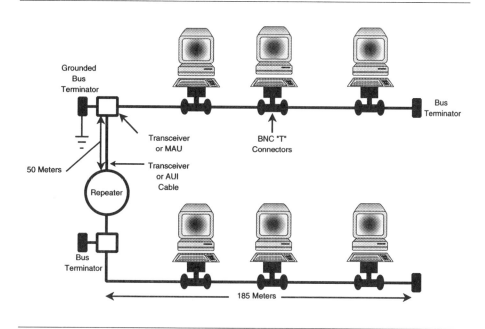

Figure 19-10. *A typical 10BASE-2 network with allowable distances.*

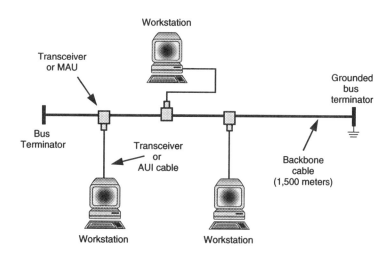

Figure 19-11. *A typical 10BASE-5 cable connection.*

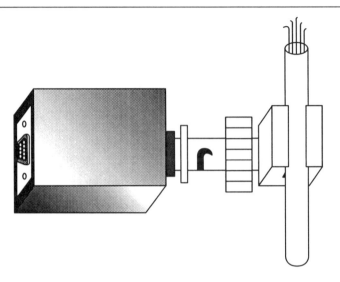

Figure 19-12. *A vampire tap cable connection to a transceiver.*

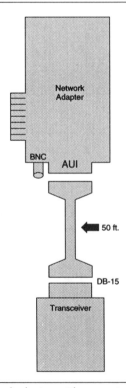

Figure 19-13. *A transceiver and adapter with connectors.*

10BASE-5 and 10BASE-2, 10BASE-T is star-wired, which makes connections easier to install and troubleshoot. Users upgrading from ARC-NET or UTP-based token-ring networks find that few or no changes are required to the medium.

In 10BASE-T, each connection between the adapter and concentrator is considered a populated segment. The maximum distance between the concentrator and adapter is 100 meters (328 feet). Interconnections between daisy-chained concentrators also can be up to 100 meters. (See Figure 19-14 on page 212.)

As a result of the limitations of the 5, 4, 3 rule, daisy-chaining is not the best way to connect large groups of concentrators. For large groups, it is best to use mixed 10BASE-2 and 10BASE-T. (See Figure 19-15 on page 212.) Concentrators count as one device on a 10BASE-2 segment, and most have an AUI port available. To link concentrators to a bus segment use 10BASE-2 transceivers on the concentrator's AUI port and use T-connectors to join concentrators into a bus. This configuration allows you 30 concentrators per segment.

Tip:
Do not try to use the flat silver satin cable from your telephone network to wire your Ethernet network. It is not twisted and causes problems in any size of network.

Tip:
Be sure to check both ends of the cable (adapter and concentrator) for link integrity. Because devices only monitor their receive pair, you must verify both cable ends for good cable connections.

UTP uses an RJ-45 connector at each end. Four wires make the Ethernet UTP connection—pins 1 and 2 and 3 and 6—as specified in the EIA/EIA 568B wiring standard. The pin configurations are given in Figure 19-16 on page 213.

UTP medium has a straight-through wiring scheme in which pin 1 connects to pin 1 and so on. UTP cables also may be wired in a reverse polarity connection. The requirement for a reverse polarity cable depends on the type of equipment you have. To make a reverse polarity cable, you would reverse the transmit and receive pairs so transmit positive on one end goes to receive positive on the other, and the transmit negative goes to receive negative. Thus, pin 1 goes to pin 3, and pin 2 goes to pin 6.

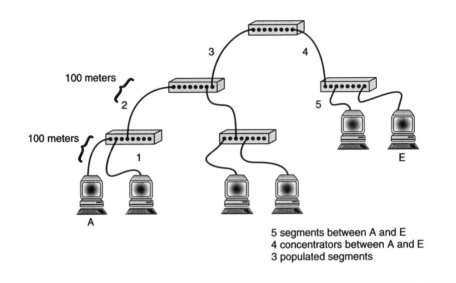

100 meters

2

100 meters

1

A

5 segments between A and E
4 concentrators between A and E
3 populated segments

Figure 19-14. *Daisy-chaining concentrators and the 5,4,3 rule.*

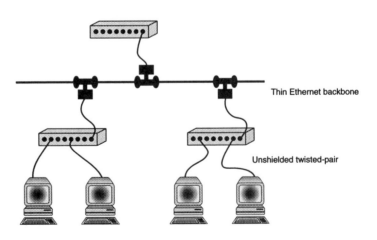

Thin Ethernet backbone

Unshielded twisted-pair

Figure 19-15. *Using mixed-media Ethernet.*

Pin	Color	Signal
1	**White/Orange**	**Transmit Positive**
2	**Orange/White**	**Transmit Negative**
3	**White/Green**	**Receive Positive**
4	Blue/White	Not Used
5	White/Blue	Not Used
6	**Green/White**	**Receive Negative**
7	White/Brown	Not Used
8	Brown/White	Not Used

Figure 19-16. *RJ-45 wired for 10BASE-T.*

Concentrators that follow the 10BASE-T specification have a series of ports labeled MDIX that have an internal crossover and use straight-through connections. Other ports are labeled MDI and do not have internal crossovers—these ports are designed to connect concentrators, but can be used for connecting adapters as well. Connections to MDI ports require reverse-polarity medium. (See Figure 19-17.)

If you are using twisted-pair medium, it is a good idea to invest in a cable scanner. The connections on twisted-pair medium are troublesome and require good termination and crimping. Using a pair scanner on new and suspected cables can save trouble later on. It spots problems with cable and warns of bad crimps or reversed cables.

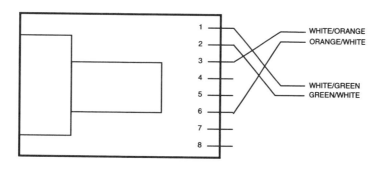

Figure 19-17. *A reverse-polarity wiring scheme.*

On large Ethernet networks, particularly in a mixed-media environment, you should use intelligent wiring devices or managed hubs. With these, you centralize wiring into fewer devices and make troubleshooting and management easier.

100VG-AnyLAN Media

100VG-AnyLAN operates on the same medium used for 10BASE-T networks. In addition it operates on shielded twisted-pair (STP) and 62.5/125-micron fiber-optic media.

100VG-AnyLAN over UTP

100VG-AnyLAN over UTP uses standard four-pair 100-ohm Category 3, 4, or 5 UTP media. Figure 19-18 shows the specifications for the different categories.

100VG-AnyLAN is still a proposed standard and may change before being officially adopted. As it currently exists, the 100VG-AnyLAN proposal calls for UTP medium run as point-to-point cable segments in which one end connects to a network adapter and the other to a hub, or run as an interconnection between hubs. In each case, the cable run is considered a populated segment.

The difference in medium quality between Category 3 and 4 media restricts the distance allowable for each segment. In most cases, Category 3 medium supports segment lengths of up to 100 meters. Category 5 medium supports segment lengths of up to 150 meters. In addition, you also may use punch-down blocks, patch panels, and wall plates that are consistent with the category of medium you are installing.

Category	Bandwidth	Grade	Pairs Required
Category 3	15MHz	Voice	4 pairs
Category 4	20MHz	Data grade	4 pairs
Category 5	100 MHz	Data grade	2 or 4 pairs

Figure 19-18. *The specifications for 100VG-AnyLAN on UTP.*

Tip:
If you are using Category 5 medium, but the accessories such as punch-down blocks, patch panels, connectors, or wall plates are not Category 5, your installation is not a Category 5 installation regardless of the medium quality. This implementation limits maximum cable segment distance to 100 meters. The best advice is to have the installation certified for Category 5.

Like 10BASE-T networks, 100VG-AnyLAN media is terminated with RJ-45 connectors. The cables are wired straight through, according to the EIA/TIA 568B standard, shown in Figure 19-19.

To transmit information, all four pairs are used at the same time in a single direction. 100VG-AnyLAN's demand access protocol requires that control signals from the node to the hub be transmitted on pairs 1 and 4, while control signals from the hub to the node are transmitted on pairs 2 and 3.

If you are using twisted-pair medium, it is a good idea to invest in a cable scanner. The connections on twisted-pair medium are troublesome and require a proper connection. Using a pair scanner on all new or suspected cables can save trouble. Cable scanners spot problems with media and warn of bad crimps or reversed wires. The scanner should be capable of scanning the category of medium you are using. Not all scanners work with Category 4 or 5 media. Verify with the manufacturer that the scanner certifies higher-grade media.

Pin	Color	Pair
1	White/Orange	2
2	Orange/White	2
3	White/Green	3
4	Blue/White	1
5	White/Blue	1
6	Green/White	3
7	White/Brown	4
8	Brown/White	4

Figure 19-19. *Pinouts for 100VG-AnyLAN over UTP.*

100VG-AnyLAN over STP media

Because 100VG-AnyLAN operates in token-ring environments, it also operates over standard two-pair 150-ohm shielded pair medium used in Type 1 token-ring networks. This medium should be wired according to the EIA/TIA 568B standard, TSB-36 and 40. STP also interoperates with existing token-ring patch panels, end connectors, and wall plates.

100VG-AnyLAN uses the same medium configuration as standard token-ring. The medium from node to hub uses a DB-9 connector to attach to the adapter and a Type I data connector to attach to the hub. (See Figure 19-20.)

100VG-AnyLAN uses both pairs for transmission and reception when using STP media. The pin assignments for STP follow token-ring assignments as follows:

EIA/TIA Conductor	Color Code	Pin	Transmission from Node	Transmission from Hub
Pair 1	Red	1	RX+	TX+
	Green	6	RX–	TX–
Pair 2	Orange	9	TX–	RX–
	Black	5	TX+	TX+

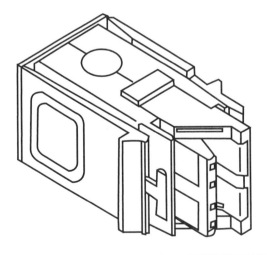

Figure 19-20. *A Type I data connector.*

100VG-AnyLAN using Fiber-Optic Media

The proposed standard for 100VG-AnyLAN over fiber-optic media follows the EIA/TIA 568 standard for SC connectors. The fiber-optic link as proposed uses single pair, dual-mode glass fiber-optic medium. The standard requires 62.5/125 micron cable and SC connectors. The SC connector is a bayonet-type connector similar to a BNC connector. The wavelength of the fiber-optic medium transmission is analogous to the frequency of transmission on copper media. It is measured in nanometers (nm). 62.5/125 micron medium operates at 850nm or 1330nm.

100BASE-T Medium

100BASE-T over UTP media uses Category 3, 4, or 5 two or four-pair 100-ohm UTP wiring, or fiber-optic media. The two-pair media implementation is called *100BASE-TX*; the four-pair implementation is called *100BASE-T4*, and, the fiber-optic version is called *100BASE-FX*.

Category	Bandwidth	Grade	Pairs Required
Category 3	10MHz	Voice	4 pairs
Category 4	20MHz	Data grade	4 pairs
Category 5	100MHz	Data grade	2 or 4 pairs

The wiring standard for 100BASE-T is the same as that for 10BASE-T and is specified by the same IEEE 802.3 committee. The specification calls for UTP cable as a point-to-point connection in which the adapter is at one end of the cable and the concentrator at the other. You also may have repeater connections or hub-to-hub connections. Each cable run is a populated segment.

The difference between Category 3 and 5 media restricts the allowable distance for each segment. In most cases, Category 3 medium supports segment lengths up to 100 meters. Category 5 medium supports segment lengths up to 150 meters. In addition, you can use standard cabling devices such as punch-down blocks, patch panels, and wall plates that are consistent with the category of medium you are installing.

Tip:
If you are using Category 5 medium, but the accessories such as punch-down blocks, patch panels, connectors, or wall plates are Category 5, you have a Category 5 installation regardless of medi-

um quality, which is limited to a maximum cable segment distance of 100 meters. Have a certified cable installer certify the medium installation for Category 5.

As with 10BASE-T networks, the cable terminates with RJ-45 connectors. The cables are wired straight through according to the EIA/TIA 568B standard as shown in Figure 19-21.

If you are using twisted-pair medium, it is a good idea to invest in a cable scanner. The connections on twisted-pair medium are troublesome and require good connections. Using a pair scanner on new and suspected cables can save trouble. Cable scanners spot problems with cables and warn of bad crimps or reversed cables. The scanner should be capable of scanning the category of medium you are using. Not all scanners work with Category 4 or 5 media. Verify with the manufacturer that the scanner certifies higher-grade media.

INTERNETWORKING

In Ethernet, bridges and routers connect multiple networks together. A bridge operates at the Data Link Layer of the OSI Model and can connect any access methods that conform to the Media Access Control (MAC) layer specifications of the IEEE 802.2 standard. Currently these access methods include Ethernet, token-ring, and the Fiber Distributed Data Interface (FDDI).

Routers operate at the Network Layer of the OSI Model and route Network Layer protocols such as IPX and IP, as well as different protocols and access methods. A router could connect an Ethernet network to an ARCNET network. A bridge could not.

Pin	Color	Pair
1	White/Orange	2
2	Orange/White	2
3	White/Green	3
4	Blue/White	1
5	White/Blue	1
6	Green/White	3
7	White/Brown	4
8	Brown/White	4

Figure 19-21. *The RJ-45 connection.*

Bridges

Bridges act as mail sorters. They maintain lists of network and source addresses and transfer packets across the bridge according to these lists. (See Figure 19-22.) As part of the switching process, a bridge has the following functions:

- Frame forwarding
- Loop resolution
- Network learning

In frame forwarding, the bridge must filter packets. When packets are sent to the bridge, it looks at the network address of each packet and sends it across the bridge if the packet's address indicates it is destined for another network. The bridge knows node addresses on its side, and assumes that an unrecognized address is on the other side. This prevents local packets from being sent across the bridge incorrectly and reduces unnecessary traffic off the network. Networks segmented by bridges can greatly reduce network traffic. However, filtering requires time and introduces latency to the network. As a result, most bridges are rated by the number of packets they can forward per second.

Network	Source Address
CDE	001686CE451C
123	001686AD3A17
456	001686FFD167
456	00168734CF26
123	0016867364F6

Figure 19-22. *A table of network and source addresses.*

Large networks using spanning tree can contain multiple bridges to the same network segment and cannot resolve differing routes to the same network, packets can continuously loop around particular segments. Many bridges eliminate packets existing on wrong segments.

Bridges used to be programmed manually with network addresses; when a node moved, the bridge had to be reprogrammed. Luckily, bridge manufacturers developed learning bridges to overcome this problem. There are two types of learning bridges, called *transparent* and *source routing bridging*. Transparent bridging on Ethernet networks uses the spanning tree algorithm to discover the route to a particular network segment. Token-ring networks also can use transparent bridging. However, they use source routing bridges more often. In source routing, the node rather than the router determines the path to a destination. A bridge that combines both Ethernet and token-ring uses a combination of the two methods called a *source-transparent bridge*.

In transparent bridging, the bridge handles the network address resolution for source addresses that are not known to it. When the bridge receives a frame, it initiates a search of the list it maintains for the frame's source address. The list is maintained on a constant basis. If the bridge can't determine a source address, it sends a discovery packet to every network connected to it. This method works well on smaller networks, but on large networks with multiple paths and bridges between networks, it can be inefficient.

The problems associated with transparent bridging led to the development of the Spanning Tree Algorithm. The spanning tree protocol, which is maintained by the IEEE 801.2-D committee, detects circular paths between networks. It stops looping in redundant bridges by shutting down the secondary bridge until needed.

The spanning tree protocol assigns a unique identifier to each bridge based on the MAC-layer address of the device. Each bridge receives a priority value, each port on the bridge is assigned an identifier, and each bridge port is then assigned a path cost value, which indicates the number of ports that must be crossed to move from one network to another. The path cost may be determined by the protocol or assigned by the network manager.

The bridge with the lowest identifier becomes the root bridge. The other bridges determine which of their ports provide access to the root bridge at the least cost. These ports become the root port to the bridge. Bridges and ports with the least cost provide the path across the network for frames. The other ports and bridges shut down and operate as secondary paths.

Routers

Routers are network switches that operate locally or over wide-area networks to interconnect different access methods and protocols. They operate at the Network Layer of the OSI Model, examine frames, and look at their routing information. Routers maintain a list of adjacent routers and LANs on the internetwork. Routers look at the destination information in the frame and check it against the router's internal list. If the router cannot ship the packet locally, it verifies the next router to send the packet to and sends the packet on its way.

Forwarding requires that the frame be fully received and opened to determine its routing information. Because packets may be broken into frames of different sizes depending on the access method to forward, the router must perform extra work processing each frame. For example, the router receives a 4,096-byte token-ring frame that it needs to pass to an ARCNET network. ARCNET has a maximum packet size of 512 bytes. The router needs to divide the token-ring frame into the appropriate number of ARCNET frames before transmitting it to the ARCNET network.

Routers may handle only single access methods or network protocols. In addition, they can be programmed to route only specific protocols to other networks. If, for example, a network in Dallas has both IPX and IP traffic and wants only the IP traffic routed to a network in Austin, Texas, the router can be programmed to reject any IPX traffic designated for Austin.

Routers use various protocols to perform their forwarding functions, depending on the network protocol or access method being routed. The following are some of the routing protocols used today:

- Address Resolution Protocol (ARP) is a protocol is used in TCP/IP networks.

- Routing Information Protocol (RIP) is a distance-vector protocol NetWare uses. It differs from the Router Information Protocol used by TCP/IP.

- Open Shortest Path First (OSPF) is an Open Systems Interconnect (OSI) link-state routing protocol.

- End System to Intermediate System (ES-IS) is an OSI discovery protocol that allows nodes to discover routers.

- Intermediate System to Intermediate System (IS-IS) is an OSI discovery protocol Intermediate routers use to discover each other.

As a result of the overhead in receiving and analyzing packets, routers are considerably slower than bridges. However, they provide additional services that bridges do not provide. In addition, many network services provide routing functions such as a Novell's internal router or its Multiprotocol Router. However, this ability depends on what protocol is being used. IPX and IP are routable protocols, while NetBIOS is not. Therefore, an NT server would be able to route IP traffic, but not NetBIOS traffic.

MANAGEMENT

Ethernet management operates at two different levels. The first is analysis that uses protocol analyzers to provide MAC-layer packet analysis. This form of management provides information to the network manager that allows him or her to make reliable decisions about changes made to the network. The second form of management is by the Simple Network Management Protocol (SNMP), which gathers information about network devices via management agents and reports them to a management console. SNMP also allows users to alter specific network objects by setting packet filters, disabling ports, or creating traps and alarms.

An Ethernet network is congested when network performance begins to degrade. A variety of occurrences cause network congestion. The foremost is collisions. Collisions increase latency on the network, thus increasing congestion and leading to degraded network performance. A large number of collisions generally occur when too many devices exist on the network segment. Another problem is high bandwidth utilization, caused by network applications that require a large amount of network traffic. Applications such as CAD programs, multimedia, and databases require a large amount of bandwidth to operate properly. A user who requires a particular application that uses a large amount of network traffic causes delays for other users on the network. Finally, congestion can be caused by incoming network traffic from bridges or routers.

Tip:
A special type of collision is a late collision, which occurs when a station attempts to transmit outside the standard waiting time

period. Late collisions only occur when stations exceed the maximum cable distance. Managed hubs or protocol analyzers are required to find late collisions. The alternative is to verify cable lengths individually. Cable distances may be increased by using the Signal Quality Error indicator, but all devices attached to the segment must have it enabled.

Protocol Analysis

Protocol analysis is performed with software- or hardware-based protocol analyzers that use the Ethernet chipset's promiscuous mode to capture packets traveling along the media. Protocol analyzers have drivers designed to capture all frames on the network and save them for analysis. Captured frames can be used to calculate network functions, including bandwidth utilization and number of frames, and to make some general network decisions. You should use this protocol analysis feature to baseline your network's performance, and then set the analyzer to look for items that exceed the baseline performance you determined.

 Tip:
One of the features you should look for in a protocol analyzer is the ability to generate network traffic. By generating network traffic in a controlled experiment, you can determine the resulting changes in your network before you actually make them. For example, if you have 30 nodes on your network and performance is acceptable, you can use the analyzer to increase your traffic by 50 percent to see the effect of adding 15 new workstations.

The other essential feature of protocol analyzers is the ability to capture all packets, so you can perform packet-level analysis. This unique level of analysis is best used to solve specific problems, such as protocols that are not routing properly or nodes that cannot find the network. You cannot use this form of analysis for extended periods of time, as it requires a large amount of disk space to store packets. Most packages let you set aside an amount of memory. When that memory is full, the capture buffer wraps, and the oldest packets are overwritten. The most popular software-based protocol analyzers include Triticom's LAN Decoder/E and LAN Decoder/TR; FTP's LANwatch; and Novell's LANAlyzer for DOS, Windows, or OS/2.

SNMP Management

The Simple Network Management Protocol (SNMP) is a communications protocol that collects information from devices and allows them to be managed. The information is collected by agents on each device that report to a designated management console. Devices may be workstations, printers, hubs, or any other network device that contains a management agent. The agent consists of built-in software or a software program that runs on the device. The agent collects information and responds to queries from a management console to provide its information.

SNMP allows the console to access agents to obtain information and to change the status of a device. As originally written, SNMP used TCP/IP as its network protocol. However, in 1992 SNMP was expanded to include support for NetWare's IPX, the OSI network protocols, and AppleTalk.

The information the console collects is stored in a management information base, also called an *MIB*. The MIB is written to the SNMP specification by the manufacturer of the device it manages. While MIBs must work within all SNMP-managed networks, they can contain information that is specific to a device, allowing the user to control almost every aspect of that device.

SNMP provides the following information functions:

- Network mapping
- Event trapping with alarms
- Traffic monitoring
- Diagnostic functions
- Report generation
- Historical management of information

It also provides these management functions:

- Automatic disconnection of nodes
- Network segmentation
- Connection or disconnection of workstations based on factors such as time of day
- Device management
- Protocol analysis
- Offsite management

Tip:
A feature of SNMP management is that you can gather information on almost any device. One university attached all the soda machines on campus to the Ethernet and placed an SNMP agent in each machine. These agents constantly query the number of drinks of each variety remaining in the machine. When a particular variety is sold out, the agents alert the management console to order more soda.

Management consoles are generic, allowing them to work with almost any vendor's MIB. The console uses SNMP to query the agent based upon the MIB loaded on the console. It then displays the information in an understandable manner. Devices are displayed as icons to represent network devices. The network also can be displayed graphically to illustrate the relationship between devices. Using the management console, you can monitor agents and set traps to alert you of events on the network such as increased utilization or excessive collisions. In addition, you can set traps to issue warnings or shut down offending nodes entirely.

The information that agents supply can be collected over an extended period of time, allowing you to perform trend analysis.

SNMP is best used with managed hubs in a structured wiring system. With all stations connected through an SNMP-managed hub, you can gather information on the network and use the information to control it. In addition, you can set traps to warn you of problems, and in extreme cases, control individual ports to stop problems.

Almost every device today is supplied with an SNMP agent. The leading vendors of SNMP management consoles are Hewlett-Packard, SunConnect, IBM, and Novell. As configurable and extensible as SNMP is, there are improvements on the horizon. The most important improvement is the Common Management Information Protocol, an OSI protocol that is more extensive and configurable than SNMP. Presently, more vendors have adopted SNMP than CMIP. As a result, SNMP has retained and expanded its popularity.

TOKEN-RING

20

In the early 1980s, International Business Machines Corp. (IBM) developed token-ring, a deterministic token-passing protocol that operates at four megabits per second (Mbps) on shielded or unshielded twisted-pair (STP or UTP) media. Since that time other vendors including IBM have designed a 16Mbps version of token-ring that operates on both STP and UTP, as well as fiber-optic, media.

After its original development, token-ring became the Institute of Electrical and Electronic Engineers (IEEE) standard called *IEEE 802.5*. The token-ring access method and protocol, which resides at the Open Systems Interconnection (OSI) Data Link layer, consists of two sublayers: the Logical Link Control (LLC) sublayer and the Data Link sublayer. The LLC became the IEEE 802.2 standard and serves as the interface between the Data Link sublayer and the OSI Network Layer. The Data Link layer provides an interface between the LLC and the medium.

Token-ring, a physical star topology, operates as an electrical ring. Each adapter in a token-ring network connects to a central hub called a *multistation access unit (MAU)*. In networks with standalone MAUs, the wiring within the MAU wraps back onto itself to form a closed communication loop and creates a ring in which stations attached to the MAU can logically pass data from one to the other. Relays in a token-ring MAU automatically close in the event of a faulty node, allowing ring operations to continue unabated. This mechanism represents one of the many secure, reliable features of token-ring.

In token-ring, adapters connect to the MAU by a cable called the *lobe*, which consists of STP, UTP, or fiber-optic media. The lobe wire can receive as well as transmit network data. Multiple MAUs connect to each other via separate ports called the *Ring In* and *Ring Out* ports to form larger rings.

MAUs may be passive unpowered or active powered or passive powered devices. By maintaining open relays at each port connection, MAUs allow communication to flow unimpeded to connected network adapters. The relay opens when the adapter driver sends voltage across the lobe wire to the relay. Once the relay opens and the adapter is electrically connected to the ring, the workstation sends a series of requests to the other stations on the ring to announce its presence.

In token-ring, one station (a workstation or file server) becomes the *active monitor* for all ring activity. This workstation is normally the first workstation to initialize the ring. All other stations on the ring are *standby monitors*; they listen for the presence of an active monitor. If they don't hear one after a predetermined amount of time, they will appoint one through a ring contention process. When the contention process is complete, the active monitor purges the ring, the ring is rebuilt, and each station collects the node IDs of both its neighbors.

Before a station attempts to transmit data on the ring, it sends a frame requesting insertion, checks that its adapter is operating at the proper transmission speed, and verifies that the adapter's node ID is not duplicated by another active network node. After the node performs these checks, the active monitor sends a packet that purges the ring of data. This packet forces nodes to temporarily leave the ring, before re-entering and reestablishing the nodes that are closest to them on the MAU. The two closest nodes, called *upstream* and *downstream* neighbors, are used to establish *fault domains* when troubleshooting problems occur on the network. The *nearest active upstream neighbor (NAUN)* reports errors from its *downstream* neighbor.

Token-ring is a deterministic, token-passing protocol, whose throughput degradation is known as nodes are added to the network. Because token-ring uses large packet sizes (up to 24 kilobytes [KB]), large amounts of data can be moved across the network quickly.

OPERATIONS

Token-ring is a physical star-wired topology that operates as an electrical ring. It uses baseband signaling with Differential Manchester encoding. In token-ring, adapters are wired to the MAU. Each MAU is equipped with one relay per port that automatically opens when the token-ring adapter sends voltage (called *phantom voltage*) to the MAU.

Otherwise, the ports on the MAU are closed, allowing the signal to pass by the port.

Originally MAUs were passive devices such as the IBM 8228 eight-port MAU, but in recent years powered, active MAUs have been introduced that amplify and retime the data signal, allowing greater cabling distances. In addition, copper and fiber-optic devices called *repeaters* are available to allow extended distances.

A typical token-ring network appears in Figure 20-1. Token-ring transmission is handled by the Logical Link Control and Data Link Control sublayers of the Open Systems Interconnect (OSI) Model.

The MAC Layer

The Media Access Control (MAC) layer is responsible for controlling access to the transmission media and for the following functions:

> **Frame formats**—The MAC sublayer defines three token-ring frame formats: the token; the MAC frame responsible for management, error recovery, and reporting; and the Logical Link Control (LLC) frame for data transmission.

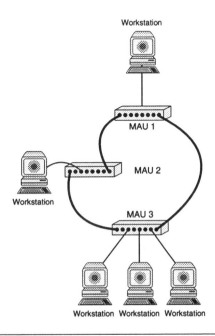

Figure 20-1. *A typical token-ring network.*

Error control—The MAC sublayer implements the Frame Check Sequence (FCS) with a Cyclic Redundancy Check (CRC).

Ring maintenance—The MAC sublayer is responsible for active and standby ring monitors, error recovery, and ring management.

MAC-layer error monitoring and recovery is a token-ring strength. Because token-ring originally was designed to provide IBM mainframe users with means to connect to PCs, diagnostics were built into the token-ring MAC layer that allows it to provide information about the adapters and the ring itself. Ring management programs such as IBM's NetView for Windows or OS/2 use this information.

The LLC Layer

The LLC sublayer defines the virtual data paths between nodes, including multiple links to logical entities called *Service Access Points* or SAPs. SAPs allow an adapter to provide communications services to NetBIOS and Systems Network Architecture (SNA) protocols. In token-ring, the connection-oriented SAPs result in sequential frame transmission with acknowledgment between frames. This service also is known as *Type 2 LLC*.

Monitor Stations

In token-ring networks, four types of monitors exist:

- The active and standby monitors supervise network operation.
- The Ring Error Monitor (REM) collects error reports from adapters and active and standby monitors. Management applications use the REM to monitor and control network functions.
- Configuration Report Servers (CRS) collect current network configurations and control adapter parameters such as ring access priority.
- The Ring Parameter Server (RPS) assigns operational parameters to the adapter upon ring insertion.

Monitor Frames
The token-ring monitors use a series of frames to provide information:

- The claim token frame starts the monitor contention process if the active monitor is no longer present.

- The ring purge frame establishes the ring after the monitor contention process is completed or after the active monitor detects a token error condition. All nodes repeat the ring purge frame until the active monitor receives it again without error. The active monitor then generates a new token.
- The neighbor notification frame allows all stations to determine the MAC-layer address of their nearest active upstream neighbor (NAUN) and generate a list of node IDs for the Configuration Report Server.
- The beacon frame alerts a downstream neighbor of the type of hard network errors present. When beacon frames are received, the upstream neighbor automatically enters self-test mode and may remove itself from the ring.
- The transmit forward frame relays information around the ring to test combinations.
- The hard error frame is generated whenever a node detects a wire fault, frequency error, or signal loss.
- The soft error frame lists network errors that degrade performance but don't cause the ring to fail.
- The active monitor present (AMP) frame is transmitted by the active monitor every seven seconds or after a ring purge to indicate its presence on the ring. The active monitor also provides buffer space to emulate a minimum ring length (the ring must contain the entire token).
- The standby monitor present (SMP) frame is transmitted in response to an AMP or another standby monitor present frame.
- The lobe media test frame is transmitted during the first phase of ring insertion to test the lobe wire between the MAU and the node.
- The duplicate address test frame verifies that nodes entering the ring have unique node IDs.
- The request initialization frame is transmitted from nodes to the Ring Parameter Server to request initialization parameters.
- The initialize ring station frame is transmitted by the RPS in response to request initialization frames.
- The report neighbor notification incomplete frame indicates that the station has not received a transmission from its upstream neighbor during the neighbor notification process.
- The report new monitor frame is transmitted by the winning station at the end of the claim token process.

- The report SUA (Stored Upstream Address) change frame reports changes in stations' stored upstream addresses from information gathered during the neighbor notification process.
- The remove ring station frame is sent by the CRS to force a station to remove itself from the ring.
- The change parameters frame allows the CRS to adjust ring parameters.

The extensive monitoring features of token-ring networks make the access method the obvious choice for networks where network management is important. Several products take advantage of token-ring's management features, including IBM's LAN Network Manager, Cabletron's Spectrum, Proteon's NetView, Madge's Ring Manager, and Thomas-Conrad's Spectra Token-Ring Server for DOS.

COMPONENTS

A token-ring network can be divided into three functional components: adapters, MAUs, and media. (See Figure 20-2 on page 233.) A token-ring adapter must reside in all devices attached to the network. These devices may include PCs, front-end mainframe processors, midrange computers such as the IBM AS/400, or network-attached printers. All devices on the network attach to the MAU, the device that gives the network its ring properties. The MAU may be a passive powered, passive unpowered, or active powered device. Active powered MAUs retime and retransmit signals and provide greater overall ring distance than passive powered or unpowered MAUs.

Adapters

IBM introduced the first token-ring adapter using a chipset of its own manufacture. Original token-ring adapters operated at 4Mbps only and used Type I STP media as their connection to the MAU. IBM's adapters did not include onboard media filters that allowed the use of Type III UTP media. They required external media filters.

For several years, IBM dominated the token-ring market. When other manufacturers introduced token-ring adapters, IBM upgraded

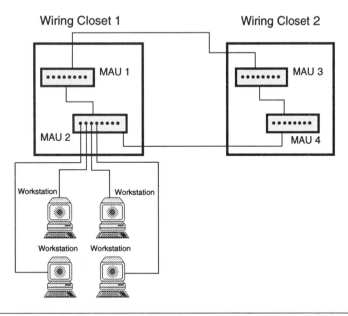

Figure 20-2. *Typical token-ring architecture.*

token-ring to 16Mbps transmission on Type I media. The company then introduced the IBM 16/4 token-ring adapter, which was switch-selectable to 4 or 16Mbps transmission. These adapters and earlier IBM adapters used a shared memory address, an interrupt, and a port address.

Texas Instruments (TI) announced an agreement with IBM to develop a token-ring chipset called the *TMS380* based on the IBM token-ring specification. This chipset had technological and performance advantages over the IBM chipset that allowed increased data buffers for data transfer and also allowed direct memory access (DMA) transfers, in which an onboard controller managed access to memory. Later, TI enhanced the TMS380 chipset to accommodate 16Mbps token-ring networks, resulting in the TMS380C16. Recently, TI announced an advanced token-ring chipset using the TMS380C26 chipset, which integrates more functionality than the previous two.

While the TI chipset is 100-percent compatible with the IEEE 802.5 and 802.2 token-ring specifications, it is not 100-percent compatible with IBM's LLC protocol implementation. As a result, IBM developed the Token-Ring Protocol Interface Controller (TROPIC) chipset for third-party vendor use, ensuring register-level compatibility for all IBM applications. Marketed by National Semiconductor under license from IBM, TROPIC manufacturers include vendors such as Madge Networks, Proteon, Thomas-Conrad Corp., Cabletron Systems, and 3Com. The TROPIC chipset allows use in applications and environments where IBM adapters were previously required. Recently Standard Microsystems Corp. introduced a token-ring chipset for its token-ring adapters, which it claims is 100-percent register-level compatible.

Tip:
Adapters based on TI chipsets allow more flexible adapter configuration and enhanced driver capabilities than TROPIC-based adapters. The TI chipset also supports bus-mastering, giving it a throughput advantage over the original IBM 16/4 shared-memory and TROPIC-based adapters. To counter the speed differences of the TI chipset, IBM introduced bus-mastering Micro Channel adapters in 1993.

For the majority of applications, 4Mbps token-ring transmission is sufficient. However, as network applications become larger and more complicated, 4Mbps token-ring is too slow. 16Mbps token-ring and the increasing number of adapter manufacturers has led to an increased use of the token-ring access method.

Tip:
Although the TROPIC and TI chipsets are IEEE 802.5- and 802.2-compliant and operate on the same network without error, in some IBM-specific environments, only the TROPIC chip or an original IBM Token-Ring adapter operates properly. These environments include some Systems Network Architecture (SNA) and Systems Application Architecture (SAA) environments.

Versions of Novell's NetWare for SAA prior to v1.3 require IBM- or TROPIC-based adapters in the server. Subsequent versions of NetWare for SAA allow use of any Open Data-Link Interface (ODI) revision 3 driver. These ODI drivers can be used with Novell's Virtual Loadable Modules (VLMs) in NetWare v3.11, v3.12, and 4.x.

Recent developments in bus design have led to the development of credit-card size PCMCIA token-ring adapters, which most often are used to connect laptops to the company's token-ring network. PCM-

CIA adapters, which are easy to store and install, have a hot-swap capability that allows them to be removed from the laptop and replaced with another adapter (such as a modem) while the computer is powered on. Early PCMCIA adapters used low-level drivers called *enablers* as conduits between the machine's BIOS and the adapter's reserved socket. Adapter services have been introduced that allow the adapter to be configured and work without enabling the PCMCIA socket.

Other high-performance bus environments such as VESA local bus and the PCI bus have led to increased token-ring adapter development. This increased capability allows increased throughput by eliminating bus bottlenecks.

The local bus architecture in particular provides a direct input to system memory via a 32-bit data path.

The PCI chipset autoconfigures the adapter each time the system is powered up. PCI allows only four PCI adapters in a station, three of which may be bus-mastering. Because most PCI-based token-ring adapters are bus-mastering, the number of installed token-ring adapters in the workstation is limited to three. As the PCI standard evolves, you should be able to increase the number of adapters in a station. Trend analysis indicates that the majority of machines sold over the next few years will contain PCI device slots.

 Tip:
PCI slot numbers are dynamically allocated each time the computer is powered up. The slot numbers are numbered 16–29. Drivers typically identify the adapter by slot number. However, if you add or remove an adapter, the slot numbers the adapter uses can change. If you use a configuration file that identifies the adapter by slot number, you may need to change the slot number in your configuration file.

CAUs, LAMs, and Other Devices

Each adapter in a token-ring network must be connected to the network via a Multistation Access Unit (MAU), which provides the "ring" portion of the network. MAUs may be passive powered, passive unpowered, or active powered. Active powered MAUs increase the overall network distance.

The MAU provides a dual-path device for the electrical signal that provides protection against cable breaks in the network. When the

MAU's relays detect a break, the relays on both sides of the break close. Type I medium contains self-sealing connections that complete the ring and keep the network up. If a cable break occurs in the medium between two MAUs, the relays also close, forming two separate rings. (See Figure 20-3.)

When a station wants to open onto the ring, its adapter sends a signal called *phantom voltage* to the MAU. This signal opens the relays on the MAU and electrically connects the adapter to the network. This action begins the ring insertion process. MAUs contain 8 or 16 ports and are patterned after IBM's 8228, a passive, unpowered MAU. Other manufacturers have developed powered, passive MAUs that provide diagnostics through LEDs on the front panel indicating ring activity and insertion. Still other manufacturers have introduced active powered MAUs that retime and resend the signal, extending overall network distance.

MAUs also contain two additional ports, Ring In and Ring Out, for daisy-chaining MAUs to each other. The Ring Out port on one MAU connects to the Ring In port on the other MAU.

🕦 Tip:
You do not need to connect the last MAU to the first MAU to complete the ring, as the relay on the Ring Out port wraps the signal back to the MAU automatically. However, this configuration

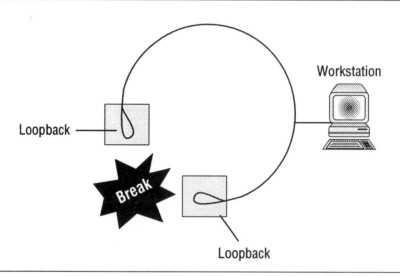

Figure 20-3. *When a break in the medium occurs, the relays close on either side of the break, causing the ring to reform around the broken area.*

allows no fault tolerance, which would be needed if a cable broke. Creating a bus of MAUs does not affect the Main Ring Length (MRL).

Originally IBM did not support 16Mbps on Type III media without external media filters. To support Type III media, IBM developed a two-tier approach using Cable Access Units (CAUs) and Lobe Access Modules (LAMs). CAUs connect Type III media to the network without using media filters. Up to four CAUs can be connected to a Lobe Access Module (LAM). This LAM connects the MAU to the ring.

Media and Connectors

Wiring on token-ring networks may be Type I, II, or VI STP, Type III UTP, or fiber-optic media. Token-ring has specific and inflexible cabling requirements. (See Figure 20-4.)

Type I connections, also called *hermaphroditic* connectors, are used for STP media while RJ-45 connectors are used for UTP media.

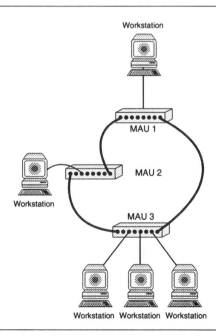

Figure 20-4. *Three daisy-chained MAUs.*

For transmission of data, token-ring uses four wires in each cable: transmit (+), transmit (–), receive (+), and receive (–). In Figure 20-5, these wires are designated 1, 6, 5, and 9.

Transmission flows in and out each adapter as active nodes repeat the signal. If a malfunctioning adapter or a cable fault causes a break in the ring, the resulting open ring causes errors.

Repeaters

To overcome distance limitations in token-ring networks, you can use *repeaters*. These devices, used in pairs, regenerate and retime the signal to allow it to travel longer distances. Repeaters are used between two MAUs or to extend the lobe wire length of a station. Used in this manner, a repeater exists at each end of the cable run.

Because the repeater transparently passes data, the distance covered by the repeater pair is not counted in distance calculations such as Main Ring Length. The cabling used between the repeater pairs can be fiber-optic or STP. The repeater's distance limitations depend on the medium used, its characteristics, and the network speed. For example, the maximum for Type I media on a 4Mbps token-ring network is 2,400 feet. The distance for 4Mbps rings on Type III cable can be between 800- and 1,100 feet, depending on the type of Type III cable used. Fiber-optic repeaters have similar limitations, but can be extended for much longer distances. In addition, fiber repeaters are immune to electromagnetic and radio-frequency interference.

Signal Lead	Pinout Type I connector	Pinout DB-9 connector
Receive +	Red (R)	Pin 1
Receive –	Green (G)	Pin 6
Transmit +	Orange (O)	Pin 9
Transmit –	Black (B)	Pin 5

Figure 20-5. *Cable pinouts for DPB-9 showing pins 1,6,5, and 9.*

Tip:
Repeaters are not the same as routers or bridges. Because they transparently handle data, they cannot be used to increase the number of nodes or to connect separate networks together.

TOKEN-RING DATA PACKET

The token-ring data packet is complicated because of the information required to complete data transfers around the ring. Its content is as follows:

> **Starting Delimiter**—One octet indicates the start of the frame.
>
> **Access Control Field**—One octet contains the frame priority bit, frame indicator bit, monitor counts, and the priority reservation bit.
>
> **Frame Control Field**—One octet contains frame format information, an address recognized bit, a frame copied bit, and reserved bits.
>
> **Destination Address**—2–6 octets that designate the frame's destination.
>
> **Source Address**—2–6 octets that designate the frame's source.
>
> **Routing Information**—0–30 octets that contain routing information for source routing.
>
> **Information Fields**—This field is of variable length and contains LLC information as well as data.
>
> **Frame Check Sequence (FCS)**—The FCS consists of four octets for error checking.
>
> **Ending Delimiter**—The last field contains the end-of-frame (EOF) sequence and a bit indicating the frame is part of a multiframe transmission.

LLC information is contained in the information field. Following is a list of that information:

> **Destination Service Access Point (DSAP)**—This eight-bit field identifies one or more Service Access Points that can receive infor-

mation. The IEEE assigns this number to vendors such as Standard Microsystems Corp for its adapters.

Source Services Access Point (SSAP)—This eight-bit field identifies the Service Access Point that transmitted the frame. The IEEE assigns this number.

Control Field—This field identifies unacknowledged connectionless frames, acknowledged connectionless frames, and acknowledged connection-oriented services.

Only seven bits of the address fields are used for addressing, thus maintaining a maximum of 128 distinct addresses for each Service Access Point. The eighth bit of the DSAP indicates whether the address is an individual or group address. The eighth bit of the SSAP indicates whether the frame contains a request or a response.

Type 1, 2, and 3 Services

Connectionless services are know as Type 1 services. In these services no Data Link connection exists between SAPs (Service Access Points). Because there is no connection overhead, data transfer is more rapid, but because no error recovery exists, higher-layer protocols must provide error control and recovery mechanisms.

Connection-oriented services are classified as Type 2 services. A direct data or logical link between the transmitting and receiving stations exists prior to data transfers. Once the connection is made, each frame is acknowledged at its destination. The acknowledgment provides error control at the Data Link layer and does not require intervention by higher-layer protocols. The overhead of acknowledgments sacrifices performance.

The IEEE has proposed a Type 3 connectionless service with acknowledgment that provides error control without the overhead of Type 2 services.

MEDIA

Token-ring cabling is straightforward in concept and difficult in practice. It uses six types of cables and two types of connectors. The cable limits are determined by the following formulas:

For Type I media:

- 16Mbps using nonpowered MAUs

The node distance equals 600 feet minus (two feet times the number of ports on the MAU) minus (the sum of all Ring In and Ring Out cables minus the length of the shortest Ring In/Ring Out cable).

- 4Mbps using nonpowered MAUs
  The node distance equals 1,200 feet minus (two feet times the number of ports on the MAU) minus (the sum of all Ring In and Ring Out cables minus the shortest Ring In/Ring Out cable).

For Type III media:

- 16Mbps with nonpowered MAUs
  The node distance equals 250 feet minus (two feet times the number of ports on the MAU) minus (the sum of all Ring In/Ring Out cables minus the shortest Ring In, Ring/Out cable)
- 4Mbps with nonpowered MAUs
  The node distance equals 500 feet less (two feet times the number of ports on the MAU) less (the sum of all Ring In, Ring Out cables less the shortest Ring In/Ring Out cable)

 Tip:
If you are using powered MAUs, check with the manufacturer to determine the correct distance calculations. Fiber-optic and copper repeaters are excluded from this calculation.

While there are six variants of token-ring cable, there are only two specific types: STP and UTP. IBM specifies these in the IBM Cabling Plan:

- Type I cable consists of two 22AWG shielded, solid twisted-pair wires. Type I media allows 16Mbps transmission with up to 260 workstations per network.
- Type II cable consists of two 22AWG shielded, solid twisted-pair wires and four 26AWG solid twisted-pair wires. The token-ring connection uses only the 22AWG gauge pairs.
- Type III cable is 22–24AWG UTP medium. It supports transmission at 4 or 16Mbps with 72 workstations and a maximum distance limitation of ⅓ that of Type I cable.
- Type V cable is 100/140 micron fiber-optic cable and is used for fiber repeaters.
- Type VI is 26AWG stranded STP wire. Its distance is ⅔ that of Type I cable. Type VI cable is used for patch cables between MAUs or to connect MAUs or adapters to a wall plate.

- Type IX is 26AWG solid STP media used for plenum installation. It has a distance limitation of ⅔ that of Type I cable.

⚡ Tip:
A series of wiring charts and documents are included here for your convenience.

Cabling with Type I Cable

Type I cable uses two types of cable connectors. Connections between MAUs and on wall plates use hermaphroditic Type I connectors; the connection to the adapter uses a DB-9 connector. (See Figure 20-6.) The pinouts for Type I connections are given in Figure 20-7 on page 243.

⚡ Tip:
The Type I connector is called *hermaphroditic* because it is not gender-specific: it has neither male pins nor female receptacles. The connector is self-shorting when not in place, which allows limited card diagnostics prior to adapter insertion in the ring. The hermaphroditic connector also allows you to check the cable between the adapter and the wall plate. Placing the pins of a volt-ohm meter (VOM) across the transmit + (pin 9) and transmit – (pin 5) or the receive + (pin 1) and receive – (pin 6) should yield zero ohms or a short condition. If the VOM does not register zero, the cable is probably bad.

Type VI patch cables use hermaphroditic connectors on each end of the cable. In these cables, the wiring is straight through—each end is wired the same. Patch cables connect MAUs to each other from the Ring Out port of one MAU to the Ring In of another. Patch cables also should be used between Type I patch panels and MAUs.

DB-9 Pin Assignment	Cable Color Code	Hermaphroditic Connector	Transmission From Node	Transmission From Hub
1	Red	Pair 1	RX +	TX +
6	Green		RX –	TX –
9	Orange	Pair 2	TX –	RX –
5	Black		TX +	RX +

Figure 20-6. *A Type I hermaphroditic connector and a DB-9 connector.*

Signal Lead	Pinout Type I connector	Pinout DB-9 connector
Receive +	Red (R)	Pin 1
Receive –	Green (G)	Pin 6
Transmit +	Orange (O)	Pin 9
Transmit –	Black (B)	Pin 5

Figure 20-7. *A DB-9 connector.*

Cabling with Type III Cable

While Type I cable offers greater distance and a larger number of nodes than Type III, it is difficult and bulky to work with. Most installers prefer working with Type III UTP cable. Type III uses an eight-position RJ-45 jack at both ends of the cable. Type III cable is divided into several grades or categories. Types III, IV, and V are the most commonly used:

- Category 3 also is known as *Level III* cable. Category 3 cable is 22–24AWG UTP cable that complies with standards set by the Electronic Industries Association/Telecommunications Industry Association (EIA/TIA) 568 Commercial Building Standards Guide. Category 3 cable is designed to carry 4Mbps token-ring with up to 72 stations.

- Category 4 also is known as *Level IV* cable. It is a 22–24AWG UTP cable that complies with the EIA/TIA standards in Bulletin PN-2841. Category 4 is designed to handle 10Mbps Ethernet and 16Mbps token-ring for short distances and in non-noisy environments.

- Category 5 also is known as *Level V*. It is 22-24AWG cable that complies with the Category 5 standards set in EIA/TIA Bulletin PN-2841. Category 5 is designed to handle 100Mbps transmission over UTP media. It easily handles 16Mbps token-ring.

Tip:
A Category 5 cable plant requires properly installed Category 5 cable components. Expensive improperly installed Category 5 components will not yield proper results.

The Type III RJ-45 connector uses the inner two connectors for one pair and the next inner two for the other. These pins are 3, 4, 5, and 6.

Pins 1, 2, 7, and 8 are not used. A 6-pin RJ-11 connector also can be used with pins 2, 3, 4, and 5. The connections are given in Figures 20-8 and 20-9 on page 245.

In Type III RJ-45 connections, the inner two wires are the receive pair and the two adjacent wires are the transmit pair. Original and second-generation TI-based adapters have both six- and eight-position connectors. By setting switches on the adapter, you can control the connector type. Newer TI-based adapters contain circuitry to automatically select the media connection. Most IBM- and TROPIC-based adapters come with only DB-9 connectors, although some newer IBM- and TROPIC-based adapters have automatic medium selection. Adapters that only have a DB-9 connector can be used with Type III media and a media filter.

 Tip:
The adage that you get what you pay for is particularly true when it comes to token-ring media filters. If you are trying to use media filters with 16Mbps token-ring, purchase the best ones you can find. A poor or unstable media filter causes unending problems that are almost impossible to find. The same is true for the quality of the cable you use. While Category 3 medium works for 4 and

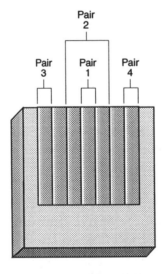

Pair 1- Blue/Blue White
Pair 2- Orange/Orange White
Pair 3- Green/Green White
Pair 4- Brown/Brown White

Figure 20-8. *The pin-outs for a six-position connector.*

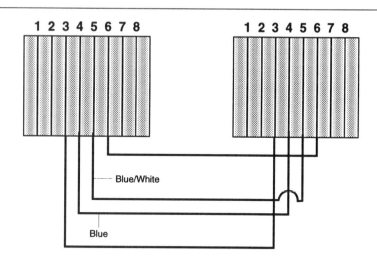

Figure 20-9. *The pin-outs for an eight-position connector.*

16Mbps token-ring in non-noisy environments and at short distances, most 16-bit applications require Category 4 or 5 media.

MONITORING AND MANAGING TOKEN-RING NETWORKS

Token-ring's strength is its extensive hardware and software monitoring and management capabilities. Token-ring LANs can be managed by hardware-based or software-only packages.

Hardware-Based Monitoring

Hardware-based monitoring requires attaching an additional hardware device to the network to test a variety of functions ranging from cable quality, packet and frame composition, and fault isolation. For transmission analysis, a cable testing device such as those from Fluke or Microtest can isolate network transmission problems and malformed frames that result from faulty media.

To diagnose and view protocol errors, a variety of hardware-protocol analysis tools are available from Network General, Network Communications Corp., and Hewlett-Packard. Network General's Sniffer provides one of the most effective hardware-based tools available. Like the LANalyzer from Network Communications Corp., the Sniffer provides analysis of frames on the wire. It attaches a special token-ring adapter to the network to capture network traffic, which it then decodes as necessary. Hardware-based analyzers provide enough buffer space and adapter speed to capture all frames completely. The protocol analyzers support a wide number of network protocols such as NetWare's Internetwork Packet Exchange and the Internet Protocol.

Software Monitoring and Management

Software monitoring and management can run the gamut of sophistication: from simple-to-use tools such as Cheyenne's Monitrix for NetWare to complex protocol analysis tools such as Novell's LANalyzer for Windows, which requires some knowledge of Novell's network protocol stacks. They monitor error frames generated by the token-ring protocol and often require a dedicated PC that has an adapter with a promiscuous mode driver. LANalyzer for Windows operates with all token-ring adapters using Open Data-Link Interface (ODI) drivers.

Software-based monitoring is less expensive but less comprehensive than hardware-based monitoring or managed hub products. One of the problems with software-based monitoring is that it doesn't capture as much data as hardware-based solutions or allow as extensive an analysis. However, for the vast majority of small and medium-sized networks, software-based monitoring provides essential information at a reasonable cost.

Many software-based monitoring packages also can use out-of-band monitoring to capture frames if the network becomes unusable.

 Tip:
It is a good idea to store the monitoring software on a local hard drive. If the network slows or goes down, you still can get to the software and analyze hardware problems.

Programs such as Triticom's Token Vision, Thomas-Conrad's Sectra, Madge's Ring Manager, and Cheyenne's Monitrix for NetWare read specific operating system shell, redirectory, and protocol information. They also provide relevant adapter and driver information and can generate network traffic for analysis. These programs require the station monitor to load and attach as a network node and provide analysis based upon the MAC layer diagnostic frames inherent in token-ring. By analyzing the number of error frames reported by the network, you can determine the health of the network and isolate errant nodes. Many of these packages also let you send a remove request, one of the MAC layer diagnostic packets, to force a node that has too many errors to remove itself from the ring. User-definable thresholds can be set that trigger an alarm when the threshold is exceeded.

Analysis programs that report errors in token-ring use promiscuous-mode drivers to capture MAC layer frames and report them to the monitoring application. This information can alert you to network problems and allow you to maintain information on the individual network nodes. They also allow nodes to be automatically removed. Performance monitors can provide either in-band or out-of-band diagnostics and can range from extremely sophisticated packages to mere error counters.

Network Management Protocols

Network information gathering and management is based upon rules and guidelines that have been refined into two standards: the Simple Network Management Protocol (SNMP) and the Common Management Information Protocol (CMIP).

Each of these management protocols establishes information-gathering and storage characteristics. SNMP is the oldest management protocol—it has undergone numerous updates by way of Requests for Comments (RFCs). SNMP defines the type of information collected and how it is stored, and provides a hierarchical control function that provides network security. SNMP-managed networks consist of a manager and a number of managed agents for the devices on the network. The manager collects information from the agents and stores it in a database called the *management information base (MIB)*. Users can access information contained in the MIB to make decisions about network activity. Most vendors' management packages support SNMP, including Novell's NetWare Management System (NMS) and Microsoft's System Management Server (SMS). Banyan VINES also has a SNMP management component.

CMIP is the OSI-compliant network management model that defines how CMIP-compliant devices interrelate on the network. The heart of CMIP is the Common Management Information System (CMIS), which defines the OSI standard for gathering and storing information on the network. Collected information is used by the CMIP management station to compile information from multiple vendors and display the information. CMIP functionality includes the following:

- Accounting Management, which tracks the use of network resources
- Configuration Management, which allows the manager to reconfigure network devices
- Fault Management, which detects and corrects faults in network equipment
- Performance Management, which monitors network traffic
- Security Management, which allows system managers to control access to the information databases

IBM currently supports CMIP through NetView and AT&T Sentry. If the OSI model gains acceptance, CMIP and its protocols will gain wider use in the marketplace.

Managed Workgroup, Departmental, and Enterprise Hubs

By and large, most token-ring networks are not managed. The most rudimentary token-ring MAUs offer LED diagnostics on the front panel for local, visual management, which indicate ring insertion and traffic, but little more. Adapters offer LEDs on the end bracket for management as well.

As networks become larger, the need to gather statistics on overall network traffic, monitor individual port activity, and control these ports has led companies such as Bay Networks, Standard Microsystems, and Cabletron to introduce single- or multiprotocol workgroup, departmental, or chassis-mounted enterprise managed hubs. (See Figure 20-10.) These hubs provide centralized devices for node management. Many vendors' hubs manage Ethernet, token-ring, and Fiber Distributed Data Interface networks. Other vendors such as Proteon have token-ring-only managed hubs. Although these hubs do not extend or change the wiring rules of the access method, they work within the access method to bring centralized control to the user. Combined with management software, managed hubs allow extensive local or remote fault isolation and network node management.

The network management component of these hubs commonly uses the Simple Network Management Protocol (SNMP) to poll individual devices and gather information for inclusion in a database. Contents of this database corresponds to criteria decided by the Internet groups responsible for database aspects of SNMP.

The Network Layer transport protocol for SNMP is the Transmission Control Protocol/Internet Protocol (TCP/IP), which is used to gather statistics and present them to the user at the designated management station. The management station also uses TCP/IP to transmit management control information to hubs.

In 1990, Novell introduced the NetWare Management System (NMS) to manage network devices, including hubs, adapters, and other network devices. NMS is based on SNMP and allows network managers to control NMS-compliant devices from a single management console. NMS incorporates the functions of a number of third-party management packages. Each vendor has a common set of instructions for managing its devices.

Workgroup Hubs

Workgroup hubs, which may be managed by remote software, consist of 8–16 Type I or Type III connections for a single access method and media.

Departmental Hubs

Departmental hubs, which provide 24–36 ports and include the popular stackable hubs, often have only single-protocol support. They most often are managed.

Enterprise Hubs

By definition, all enterprise hubs are managed. These hubs, which are designed for desktop or chassis-mounted enclosures, contain individual modules that contain token-ring, Ethernet, or Fiber Distributed Data Interface (FDDI) ports. The backplane of these hubs interconnects modules where necessary, allowing resegmentation and rerouting of traffic from disabled nodes if desired. Individual modules can be interconnected to other modules in the main chassis or to standalone hubs via a single port connection. Up to 144 nodes can be supported by most enterprise hubs. Multiprotocol and multiple access method support is common in enterprise hubs, and some hubs even incorporate bridging or routing hardware and software.

Additional management potential is introduced to enterprise hubs with dedicated management modules that fit in the chassis and provide users with more sophisticated analysis and control than simply observing LED activity on the front panels of MAUs. Management modules gather information about devices attached to the hub and store the information in a Management Information Base for use by a management console or workstation attached to the network. The management capability allows manual or automatic resegmentation, port disabling, or resetting of individual ports from the management station. You can also configure traps and alerts to identify potential problems.

The management console connects to the network as a network connection or to the hub via an RS-232C connection. It interprets data sent from the hub's management module, allowing the software to map the network. The information the management software gathers is based upon the addresses of individual nodes. Ports can be turned off and on. Entire modules can be turned off, attached to different networks, or made to stand alone.

The functionality of managed hubs depends on the hub and modules you purchase.

INTERNETWORKING

Internetworking token-ring networks can be performed via a variety of devices: bridges, routers, repeaters, and gateways.

Bridges

A bridge, which operates at the Data-Link Layer of the Open Systems Interconnect (OSI) Model, connects two or more networks using the same network access method such as Ethernet or token-ring and the same or different media. The bridge, which is transparent to the network protocol in use (IPX or IP), takes frames from one network and retransmits them to the other network by reading the destination address of the frame and transmitting the frame to its destination. If the address exists on the local network, the bridge retransmits the frame on the network. If the frame contains the address of an adapter on another network, the bridge transmits the frame on the other network. The bridge performs no other frame filtering. (See Figure 20-10.)

Bridges may be software- or hardware-based. A software-based bridge consists of a PC with two token-ring adapters installed that run

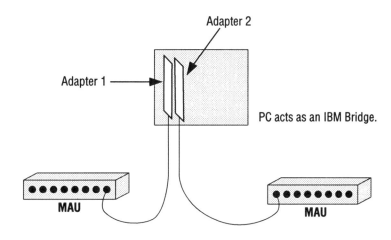

Figure 20-10. *The IBM 8228 MAU, a passive unpowered MAU.*

bridge software. The most widely used token-ring software bridge is the IBM Bridge Program.

A hardware bridge is a separate proprietary vendor device that connects two networks. The device contains software and must be programmed separately. Several types of token-ring bridges exist: transparent, source routing, and source-route transparent—a combination of the two.

Transparent Routing Bridges

In transparent routing, the bridge maintains a routing table of the node address of each device on the network. The bridge reads the network source and destination IDs of frames and compares them with the addresses contained in its routing tables. If the node address is on a network other than the source network, the bridge forwards the frame to that node.

Originally, bridges had to be programmed with the address of each device on the network. The need to program bridges led to the development of bridges called *learning bridges* that could learn the address of each device and build routing tables automatically. These bridges make up the majority of network bridges.

Source-Routing Bridges

Bridges may also be used to connect multiple networks with multiple paths to each network. In token-ring, the IBM Software Bridge runs on each network device and sends exploratory frames called *discovery frames* to determine the best route for packets between its source and destination. The discovery frame determines the least costly route in network hops and time to the destination address (ticks). The discovery frame is then returned to the source address, and the routing information gathered is placed in the information field of the token-ring data packet. Bridges read this field to be able to transfer the frame across the network to the destination address. If the route is not available, the node resends a discovery packet to discover a new network route. The advantage of source routing is that bridges are not responsible for routing information; its disadvantage is that source routing can increase network traffic.

Routers

A router is a software or hardware device that operates at the Network Layer of the OSI model to connect networks using the same network protocol (IPX or IP). Because it operates at a higher layer than a router, it may connect networks that use different access methods such as Ethernet or token-ring. Routers examine each frame and filter specific user-definable frames—they are more important to large internetworks than are bridges. Routers use algorithms to determine the best route for each frame.

As with bridges, there are several types of routers: transparent, source, protocol-dependant, and protocol-independent.

Transparent and Source Routers

Transparent routers open the frame and determine if it is intended for the local network or a remote network. If it is destined for a remote network, the router places the frame on the network for the destination address or for the address of another router.

Originally, routers could not discover the address of devices on the network and had to be programmed individually. Now, most routers discover the devices on the networks automatically.

Transparent routers do not support multiple network paths to nodes. To overcome the problems associated with handling multiple routes in transparent routing networks, the IEEE developed the Spanning Tree Protocol (IEEE 802.1). This protocol uses a tree structure in which each router is designated as a root of the tree. The Spanning Tree Algorithm determines the overall number of hops between the source and destination node and takes into account different routes between the two nodes. It counts one hop for each router the frame crosses and uses the path with the least number of hops. If the shortest path is unavailable, the route is recalculated for the next frame. This calculation is made by having each router respond to a MAC-layer frame called a *Bridge Protocol Data Unit*. Source routing also can be used in conjunction with transparent routers that use the spanning tree algorithm.

Since routers operate at the Network Layer of the OSI Model, they can filter frames transferred from one network to another. Network traffic routing depends on the access method the network uses and the routing protocol in use.

Protocol-Dependent Routers

A router that uses the Network Layer protocol to perform its routing function is called a *protocol-dependent router*. Each protocol uses network-specific addressing. For example, IPX uses the network address to set its routing tables for each network. IP uses a portion of the IP address as its network address. The router must maintain separate routing tables for each protocol it routes.

Protocol-Independent Routers

Another router is the protocol-independent router, which uses the physical address of adapters on the network and maintains a table of these addresses. It then assigns a network identifier to each network and maintains its routing table according to the network identifier and physical address of network devices. Protocol-independent routers automatically update their routing tables to build maps of the network. They can be used with nonroutable protocols.

Multiprotocol Routers

Routers that can route more than one protocol at a time are called *multiprotocol routers*. They must read each frame and look up the protocol used to find the address in its routing table for that protocol. This limits the packets that can be transferred over the router.

A multiprotocol router routes traffic of various types from network to network, but cannot route traffic between Network Layer protocols. Translation of a frame from one protocol requires encapsulating the frame into another type of frame. For instance, you have IPX traffic on network 1, and want to route frames to a remote IPX network on network 2. An IP network connects the two. To route data from one network to another, the IPX frame is encapsulated in the IP frame to route it over the IP network to the remote IPX network, where the IP information is stripped and the packet is routed as an IPX frame.

Routing Protocols

Each networking environment has its own routing protocol:

NetWare RIP	(Routing Information Protocol)
TCP/IP RIP	(Router Information Protocol)
ISO OSPF	(Open-Shortest-Path-First)
Digital's DRP	DECnet Routing Protocol
Banyan's VINES VRTP	(Sequenced/Nonsequenced Routing Update Protocol)

Network Layer protocols such as IPX and IP govern information transfer from one node to another and can typically be filtered or rejected by routers.

Nonroutable Protocols

Not all protocols are routable. The most notable is NetBIOS, the default protocol for IBM's LAN Server, and Microsoft's LAN Manager and Windows NT Advanced Server. NetBIOS uses device names on a network and cannot differentiate between networks. To route NetBIOS, you must use the physical address of the individual adapters.

BROUTERS

Because many routers and bridges do not provide adequate support, combination bridges and routers have been introduced. Called *brouters*, these devices combine the Data-Link Layer frame-passing properties of bridges with the frame-filtering capability of routers. As products mature, the line between bridges and routers will continue to blur.

GATEWAYS

The need to link IBM and compatible host mainframe computers with LANs has led to the need for gateway products that allow communication between diverse devices and operate at all layers of the OSI Model. All terminals and devices that connect to IBM mainframes or minicomputers must be defined and configured on the mainframe. If a station moves or an adapter is replaced, the gateway must be reconfigured. Network gateways, which provide access to all network nodes, simplify the configuration process; only the gateway device needs to be configured on the mainframe.

The number of logical unit or physical unit connections to the mainframe easily can be managed through gateway software. Active sessions on the gateway can be routed as Physical or Logical Units (PU/LU). Many gateway products are limited to a single PUs and 32 LUs. However, some vendors such as Eicon have introduced SNA gateways that support up to 32 PUs and 254 LUs. Each session uses a logical unit. Pooling the resources allows gateways to be managed more productively.

DIRECTIONS

Token-ring, like Ethernet, is moving toward a 100Mbps transmission solution that is compatible with existing 4 and 16Mbps token-ring networks. The 100VG-AnyLAN chip set is compatible with UTP token-ring as well as with Ethernet. 100VG-AnyLAN uses a demand priority-based system that provides greater access to workstations that require it. Research is also continuing into a switched token-ring implementation that is similar to switched Ethernet. In switched token-ring, two connections between two nodes exist for short time periods, allowing station greater access to the network. These additions to token-ring will allow the access method to grow toward applications that require more bandwidth.

ARCNET

ARCNET was developed by San Antonio, Texas–based Datapoint in 1977. One of the first network access methods, ARCNET provided a connection for the company's mini- and microcomputer-based devices. By 1990, when its decline in use started, ARCNET boasted six million installed nodes. Although this de facto access method's use has been declining in the past five years, it is still one of the most reliable and trouble-free technologies of its ilk. While the user community initially received ARCNET enthusiastically, neither the IEEE nor ANSI adopted it as a standard. Lack of standardization led to ARCNET's decrease in use for many networks. ARCNET continued to be used widely in networks where it filled a need by virtue of its simplicity, its relatively flexible cable requirements, or its deterministic token-passing nature. ARCNET supported fiber-optic media before other access methods did, which allowed its use in many environments such as factory floors that contained large amounts of electromagnetic or radio-frequency interference. In 1992, through the efforts of the ARCNET Trade Association, the ANSI standards committee adopted ARCNET as an ANSI standard (ANSI/ATIA 878.1).

OPERATIONS

ARCNET is a baseband, modified token-passing protocol that works as a logical ring supporting up to 255 nodes per network. In ARCNET, nodes circulate a packet—called a *token*—from node to node in sequential order from lowest to highest node ID. ARCNET does not send the token physically from node to node as token-ring networks do, unless the next highest node ID also happens to be adjacent to the sending node. Only a single media path may connect any two nodes on the network.

In ARCNET, only the workstation that possesses the token may transmit data. When a node transmits, all the active workstations on the network hear the transmission. Transmissions of data can be sent all nodes or to a single node on the network. The workstation accepting the token acknowledges token receipt. The overall network cabling distance for an ARCNET network is 20,000 feet for coaxial cable–based networks. The time a packet requires to traverse the entire network determines the overall network distance.

If workstations do not detect a token for 78.2 microseconds, they assume the token is lost and force the network to reconfigure itself. The reconfiguration process requires each network adapter to identify itself and its two closest sequential neighbors to the network, indicating the workstation that will transmit the token and the one that will receive it.

Because only one node transmits data at a time, collisions do not occur. Each node has equal access to the network, and the response time is deterministic, even as the number of network nodes increases.

Tip:

If you change the time-out period the adapter uses to extend the overall network distance, you must make the same change on all ARCNET adapters on the network. We don't recommend that you do this unless you need to have a single large network. If you need additional distance, split the network into two or more networks and internally route the segments to each other in the NetWare server.

ARCNET's transmission speed is 2.5 megabits per second (Mbps). Although this speed seems slow compared to 10Mbps Ethernet, 16Mbps token-ring, and especially 100Mbps access methods, the speed of ARCNET is relatively constant across the network regardless of the number of nodes. Unlike collision-based networks, the throughput of ARCNET decreases at a known rate as the number of nodes increases.

ARCNET owes its popularity to its simple-to-use-and-administer protocol characteristics, its media independence, and the deterministic nature of the token-passing protocol it uses. In ARCNET, the existence of only five packet types allows little management complexity but provides low overhead.

PACKET STRUCTURE

One of the assets of ARCNET is its low overhead packet structure. The ARCNET data packet has a length of 512 bytes; 508 of these bytes are data. In addition to the ARCNET data packet, ARCNET uses four other packets for communications. Although the simple packet structure of ARCNET does not leave room for extensive protocol management, the access method is very efficient.

These are the five ARCNET packet types:

- The Invitation-to-Transmit (ITT) (token)
- The Free Buffer Inquiry (FBE)
- The data packet
- The positive acknowledgment
- The negative acknowledgment

The Invitation-to-Transmit (ITT) consists of four fields: an alert burst followed by an end-of-transmission, two node IDs, and an ending delimiter. (See Figure 21-1.) The ITT is the packet that gives the node permission to transmit.

A Free Buffer Inquiry (FBE) consists of an alert burst, an ENQ statement, two destination IDs, and an ending delimiter. (See Figure 21-2 on page 260.) A node uses this packet to ask the destination node if it has a buffer in its adapter's onboard memory available to accept the data packet. When the adapter receives this packet, it checks this buffer and

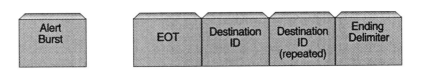

Figure 21-1. *An ARCNET Invitation-to-Transmit (ITT).*

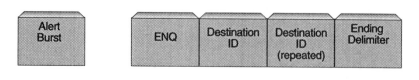

Figure 21-2. *A Free Buffer Inquiry (FBE).*

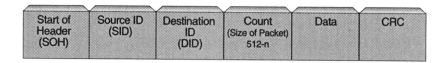

Figure 21-3. *An ARCNET packet.*

issues a negative or positive acknowledgment. If the node issues a positive acknowledgment, the source node will send the data packet; if the node issues a negative acknowledgment, the source node will relinquish the data packet to the workstation with the next sequential node ID.

The data packet consists of a starting delimiter, a header that identifies the frame type, the node address of the packet's source (SID), two destination IDs (DIDs), a count that identifies the packet as a short 256-byte or a long 512-byte packet, the data, a Cyclic Redundancy Check (CRC), and an ending delimiter. (See Figure 21-3.) ARCNET uses the Cyclic Redundancy Check to detect errors in packet transmission. A count is made of the number of ones and zeroes in the packet. The same count also is made upon receipt of the packet. If the counts do not match, the packet is rejected. Sent data packets must be positively or negatively acknowledged upon receipt. The 20 megabit per second (Mbps) ARCNETPlus, implemented by Datapoint, uses a different packet structure that remains compatible with 2.5Mbps ARCNET.

Positive and negative acknowledgments contain a starting delimiter, an ACK or NAK, and an ending delimiter. (See Figures 21-4 and 21-5.) The normal sequence of data transmission is as follows:

- When a workstation finishes transmitting a data packet, it issues the token to the node with the next highest node ID.
- The workstation receiving the token issues a positive or negative acknowledgment.
- The source workstation issues the data packet.
- The destination workstation checks the integrity of the packet it receives and issues a positive or negative acknowledgment.
- The source workstation receiving the acknowledgment issues the token to the workstation with the next highest node ID. If during the reconfiguration process, the workstation knows it has the highest node ID, it issues the token to the workstation with the lowest node ID.

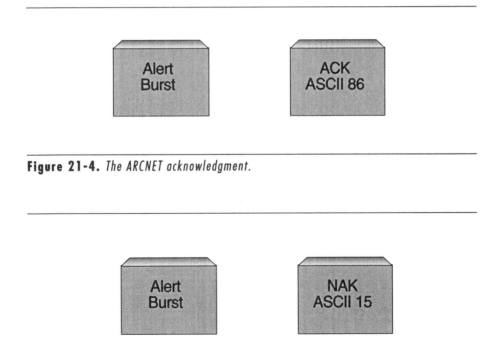

Figure 21-4. *The ARCNET acknowledgment.*

Figure 21-5. *A negative acknowledgment.*

TOPOLOGY

ARCNET networks can be implemented as star or bus topologies. You may also use a combination of the two topologies to create a distributed-star that uses the same or different media types.

A bus topology is created by cabling a series of network adapters from one to the other with T-connectors and terminating each end of the bus with a terminator. Up to eight adapters can exist on the bus, and the total cable distance is limited to 1,000 feet. Figure 21-6 shows a bus topology ARCNET network.

A star topology ARCNET network requires an additional piece of equipment called an *active hub*. An active hub is a device that concentrates the workstation connections and retimes and retransmits the signal to all nodes attached to it. Every signal passes through the hub before being relayed to the nodes. In a star topology, adapters radiate from the active hub. (See Figure 21-7 on page 263.) Active hubs can be daisy-chained to one another to create larger networks. Most active hubs consist of eight ports. On a coaxial-cabled star topology network, you can use a device called a *passive hub* that only splits the signal to the workstations attached to it.

The ARCNET access method also allows you to use both bus and star topologies in the same network. (See Figure 21-8 on page 263.) This configuration is called a *distributed-star topology* network. In a distributed-star network, successive active hubs are joined together using either one of the eight ports on the hub. Workstation buses can be extended from each active hub's port; the connector on the active hub acts as the terminator on one end of the bus. Like a simple bus topology ARCNET network, the cable distance of this configuration is limited to 1,000 feet. You can configure a passive hub off one of the active hub's

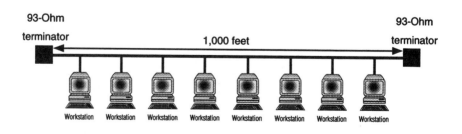

Figure 21-6. *A bus topology ARCNET network allows up to eight adapters and a total length of 1,000 feet.*

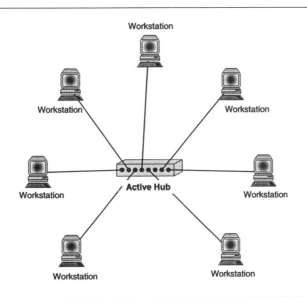

Figure 21-7. *A star topology ARCNET network.*

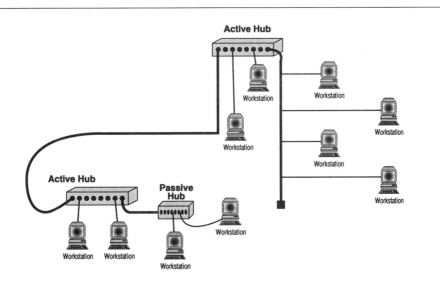

Figure 21-8. *A distributed-star topology ARCNET network.*

ports as long as you maintain a 100-foot distance between the active and passive hubs. The distributed-star topology is extremely flexible.

The cabling requirements of ARCNET are flexible. The cable can be either RG-62 A/U, unshielded twisted-pair (UTP) Category III, IV, or V, or fiber-optic media.

ADAPTERS

Each ARCNET adapter contains a controller chip such as the Standard Microsystems Corp. 90C26. This chip handles all protocol requirements for taking data from the computer's memory and passing it onto the wire.

ARCNET Adapter Configuration

Most ARCNET adapters used shared memory, in which the adapter shares a location in its memory with the CPU. Data received off the medium is stored in this shared area of memory where it can be processed by the CPU. In the same way, data from system memory stored in the shared memory area can be accessed and prepared for transmission by the adapter over the medium.

ARCNET typically uses a 16 kilobyte (KB) shared memory address in the memory range C000 to DFFF. However, only 8KB is used for data transfer. The boot ROM uses the remainder to store data. By default, most adapters use this memory address, which allows it to avoid conflicts with other devices, such as video adapters, in the workstation.

Tip:
If you are using a memory manager and memory is limited, you can exclude only the first 8KB of shared memory in the 16KB range. This exclusion will save memory. You will not be able to use a boot ROM in this configuration.

ARCNET adapters also use an interrupt request line (IRQ) and a port address for network communications. The port address is normally 2E0h. Some manufacturers take advantage of a seldom-used feature of the ARCNET chip set that allows the adapter to bypass the port address to create additional configuration options.

Diskless Workstations

Diskless workstations are configured for several reasons: to save the cost of a diskette drive, to protect the network against viruses, and to prevent corporate data loss. For each diskless workstation, the network manager must place a boot ROM on the adapter. As with other network access methods, NetWare supports ARCNET remote booting. LAN Server, Windows NT Advanced Server, Windows NT 3.5, Banyan VINES, and LAN Manager do not support remote ARCNET booting. The boot ROM consumes the last 8KB of the 16KB shared memory space.

 Tip:
No address needs to be added to the ARCNET adapter's configuration. In most cases, you should not use the address space reserved for boot ROMs.

HUBS

When ARCNET is wired in a star topology, adapters must be attached to a hub that congregates the nodes. Hubs may be either active, powered or passive, nonpowered. Passive hubs are normally four-port devices that split the signal among the four ports. Passive hubs are much less expensive than active hubs, but the nodes are restricted to 100 feet from the hub to the adapter. One of the four devices may be an active hub.

An active hub is a device that retimes and retransmits the signals to all ports. Each port connects to a workstation, another device, a series of network interface devices in a bus, another active hub, or a single passive hub.

 Tip:
Passive hubs may not be attached together. If you need more than four devices, you must use a bus configuration or an active hub.

 Tip:
Only coaxial-cabled ARCNET networks use passive hubs. Do not use passive hubs in networks that use UTP or fiber-optic cable.

CONNECTORS

In an ARCNET network that uses coaxial cable, the ends that attach to the adapters or to the active or passive hub use BNC connectors. (See Figure 21-9 on page 267.) Each BNC connector has a bayonet-style attachment that connects to the adapter with a twist.

Adapters in a bus topology attach to the media via a T-connector, in which the base of the T connects to the adapter and the cross members connect cables together. (See Figure 21-10 on page 267.) Terminators must end each end of the bus. (See Figure 21-11 on page 267.) ARCNET terminators place a 93-ohm load on the cable.

An ARCNET UTP network uses Category III, IV, or V media. The medium connection to the hub or adapter consists of an RJ-45 connector. In ARCNET, only pins 4 and 5 of the cable are used to make the network connection.

 Tip:
Even though many people consider the 2.5Mbps transmission speed of ARCNET to be slow, you can predict its throughput when you add the second-to-the-last node to the network. As you add 20 nodes to an ARCNET network, you will quickly realize that a well-tuned ARCNET network is nearly as fast as an Ethernet network with the same number of nodes.

MEDIA

Until several years ago, ARCNET was the only access method that was medium-independent. It presently offers coaxial, UTP, and fiber-optic media support.

The total cable distance for coaxial and UTP ARCNET networks is 20,000 feet using the default retiming and reconfiguration settings. Some manufacturers of ARCNET adapters allow you to change the retiming and reconfiguration time-out functions of the access method to increase the overall network distance. The distances will vary depending upon the time-outs you set. Fiber-optic ARCNET networks are limited to 17,600 feet.

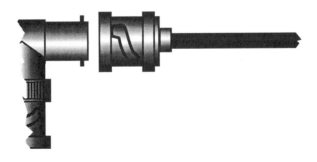

Figure 21-9. *A BNC connector.*

T Connector

Figure 21-10. *A T-connector.*

Terminator 93-Ohm

Figure 21-11. *A terminator.*

Cabling with RG-62 A/U

RG-62 A/U cable is coaxial cable similar to RG-59 cable television cable. The ends of RG-62 A/U use BNC connectors. The cabling distances for RG-62 A/U are shown in Figure 21-12 on page 269.

Most ARCNET adapter manufacturers require you to use different adapters for bus and star topologies. Star-topology adapters are self-terminating at 93 ohms, and bus-topology adapters require separate 93-ohm terminators. Some manufacturers sell adapters that perform in both bus and star topology networks.

 Tip:
In a pinch, you can use a bus-topology ARCNET adapter on an active hub by attaching a T-connector and terminator to the end of the adapter and by connecting the cable to that. As long as the adapter is on the end of the bus, you can use a star-topology adapter in a bus topology as the final adapter. If you do this, do not use a separate terminator and T connector for the star-topology adapter.

Star Topology
In star-topology ARCNET networks using active hubs, the following distances apply:

- 2,000 feet between two adapters is allowed in a two-node network
- 2,000 feet is allowed to separate the adapter from the active hub
- 2,000 feet between active hubs is allowed
- A bus of cards can extend from the port of an active hub

Using passive hubs, a different set of distance rules applies:

- 100 feet can exist between the adapter and the passive hub
- 100 feet can exist between an active and passive hub
- Unused ports on the passive hub must be terminated with 93-ohm terminators
- You cannot connect two passive hubs together.

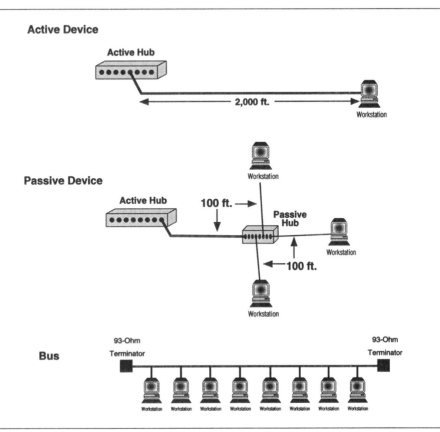

Figure 21-12. *ARCNET cabling distances using RG-62 A/U coaxial cable.*

Bus Topology

In bus-topology ARCNET networks using RG-62 A/U coaxial cable, the following distances and rules apply:

- Up to 1,000 feet can exist between the first and last adapter in the bus
- Bus segments are connected using T-connectors
- The first and last T-connectors require 93-ohm terminators
- A maximum of eight nodes can exist on a single bus
- You can bus adapters from an active hub port up to a distance of 1,000 feet from the hub

Cabling with UTP

Most adapter manufacturers recommend Category III UTP cable on ARCNET networks. UTP cable consists of two or more pairs of single strand 22–26 AWG wire in which each pair twists around the other. Category III UTP requires a minimum of 2–3 twists per foot. This cable is typically 100–110-ohm cable.

ARCNET only uses one pair of wires. One of the wires in the pair must have a solid color, and the other must have the same solid color broken with a white stripe. Individual wires are designated as blue, blue/white, orange, orange/white, and so on. In UTP ARCNET, you can use either an RJ-11 four-conductor connector or an RJ-45 eight-conductor connector. In both cases, you use the two center conductors and wire the cable straight through to the other end. Do not cross the wires.

 Tip:
To verify your connections, place the two connectors side by side. Verify that the color coding of the wire across the two connectors is the same. Also, check the ends of the connectors. If you cannot see the copper ends of all the wires, you should consider recabling the end. UTP ARCNET adapters have two end bracket RJ-45 connectors, for use in a star or bus configuration. The adapter also ships with a terminator. The UTP terminator consists of an RJ-45 connector with a 110-ohm resistor between the two center conductors. In a star topology, the connector remains in the unused port. In a bus topology, the terminator needs to be placed on the first and last card in the bus. Use cable connections on the other adapters as in and out connectors for the bus cabling.

Star Topology
Star-wired ARCNET networks observe the following distances and rules:

- 400 feet between two adapters on a two-node network
- 400 feet between the adapter and the active hub
- 400 feet between active hubs
- Buses of adapters can extend from the ports of an active hub
- Each adapter requires a 110-ohm terminator in its second port on the end bracket

Bus Topology
Bus topology UTP networks observe different distances and rules:

- 400 feet is the maximum distance of the bus
- A maximum of eight nodes can be placed on the bus
- The first and last adapters on the bus require 110-ohm terminators

Tip:
Thomas-Conrad produces extended distance ARCNET UTP adapters based on the RS-442 standard. These adapters can increase overall network distance by 800 feet and allow a maximum of 23 nodes on a bus. However, this enhanced implementation of ARCNET will not interconnect with existing ARCNET networks except through internal routing in the file server.

Tip:
Do not use UTP or coaxial cable outside or between buildings. Copper cabling uses the building's earth ground. Because different buildings have different ground potentials, signal scrambling can occur or generate additional network line voltages that can stop all network traffic or damage network equipment. Ground potential is the amount of voltage on the ground line.

Fiber-Optic Cabling

ARCNET also can use fiber-optic cable as its transmission medium. Fiber-optic ARCNET must be dual-stranded multimode filler. The fiber-optic adapter has two ports: one for transmission, the other for receipt of data. Fiber can be wired only in a star topology. However, two adapters can exist without an active or passive hub. If you choose to use fiber-optic cable, the cable from the transmitter of one adapter must connect to the receiver on the active hub and vice versa.

Fiber-optic cables use two different connectors. The first is a screw-on connector called an *SMA* connector. The second, a bayonet type connector, is called an *ST* connector. Because the cost of changing connectors can be enormous, be sure to check the connector type before you buy.

Tip:
To properly connect the transmit and receive cables between the adapters and the hub, connect the cables to the adapter and turn on the computer. This action will power up the transmitter on the adapter. The transmit cable will shine a light out of the other end of the cable. Place that end on the receive port of the active hub.

ARCNET cable distances vary depending on the type of cable you use. Fiber cable is designated by the size of the cable in microns. It is represented as two numbers such as 62.5/125. The first number represents the size of the fiber cable's inner core. The second number represents the size of the outer cladding surrounding the inner core fiber. ARCNET uses 62.5/125-, 50/125-, and 100/140-micron cable.

Most ARCNET manufacturers use 62.5/125-micron cable. This cable yields a distance of approximately 8,000 feet between active devices. Other cable types can yield longer distances.

Fiber-optic cable is more expensive than coaxial or UTP cable. Terminating fiber-optic cable costs approximately $1.00 per foot. However, fiber-optic's immunity to electromagnetic interference (EMI) makes it the only choice in some circumstances. Fiber-optic should be used between buildings or where a potential for interference exists.

ARCNET NETWORK MANAGEMENT

When an ARCNET node enters or leaves the network, it issues a reconfiguration burst that disrupts network traffic. This reconfiguration burst, the longest signal on the network, is virtually the only mechanism you have for managing the network. The only times reconfiguration bursts should occur are when workstations are powered on, causing the ARCNET adapter to reinitialize, or when workstations sense no activity on the network, indicating a possible hardware failure. When a node is powered down, the adapter leaving the ring causes the network to reinitialize itself.

Tip:
Do not confuse reconfiguration bursts with logging on or off the network. Logging on and off the network creates logical attachments to the network server. Reconfigurations should occur only when a physical attachment to the network changes.

A reconfiguration occurs each time nodes presume the token is destroyed. This occurs when the adapter hears an idle line for 78.2 microseconds. Reconfigurations, also called *recons,* should occur only when a node enters or leaves the physical network. Thus, recons are a normal occurrence on ARCNET networks. Managing an ARCNET network relies on determining when recons are excessive. Excessive recons can be caused by a bad cable, a duplicate node ID, poor cable runs, or cable runs that are too long or short.

To manage excessive recons, most ARCNET hubs have LEDs that record the number of recons occurring on a port and allow the network manager to disable ports that are generating an excessive amount.

A few vendors have introduced network management tools for ARCNET. Among them is Triticom's ARCvision, which allows a network manager to analyze ARCNET traffic. Another package, Thomas-Conrad's HubTalk, allows the network manager to view the number of recons per active hub port, and disable or re-enable ports remotely via serial connections.

INTERNETWORKING

Because of vendors' decreasing emphasis on ARCNET development, no ARCNET-specific bridges and routers exist. The majority of ARCNET routing is performed from within the NetWare server using NetWare's internal routing mechanisms, and most gateways support ARCNET. Devices such as Novell's Multiprotocol Router (MPR) have proved invaluable for ARCNET users. Most gateways will support ARCNET.

DIRECTION

ARCNET is declining in popularity. Few new ARCNET installations are being installed. Currently the most common reasons for adding ARCNET adapters and hubs are to expand present ARCNET installations and to replace ARCNET adapters and hubs that have failed.

THE FIBER
DISTRIBUTED DATA
INTERFACE (FDDI)

c h a p t e r

22

The Fiber Distributed Data Interface (FDDI) is the first access method designed for large enterprise networks. With a progeny of Copper Distributed Data Interface (CDDI) products, FDDI brings 100 megabit per second (Mbps) token-passing capability to the desktop for applications that require high speed, and to the enterprise network for joining servers along a high-speed backbone. The American National Standards Institute's (ANSI) Accredited Standards Committee Task Group X3T9.5, which introduced FDDI in 1986, also governs FDDI. As a result of the token-passing protocol it uses, FDDI is deterministic and offers many management functions similar to those of token-ring networks.

FEATURES

FDDI and its copper-based CDDI network derivatives operate in a dual counter-rotating ring topology for stations that have attachments to both rings, and in a tree topology for stations with an attachment to only one ring. The first ring is called the *main ring*; the second ring is called the *secondary ring*. Workstations with attachments to both rings are called *dual-attach stations (DAS)*; those with only one ring connection are called *single-attach stations (SAS)*. Single-attach stations connect to the secondary ring through a *single-* or *dual-attach concentrator*.

275

Dual counter-rotating rings offer redundant connections in the event of a medium malfunction. If a malfunction occurs, FDDI automatically reconfigures itself.

An FDDI network can have a maximum of 500 active stations.

Media

FDDI operates with single- or multimode fiber-optic cable. The maximum cable length for multimode fiber-optic media between two workstations is two kilometers (Km). Single-mode fiber-optic cable allows lengths of up to 60Km between stations. The maximum overall network length of an FDDI network is 200Km, making FDDI the most wide-flung access method, capable of spanning large distances. CDDI stations using shielded or unshielded twisted-pair (STP or UTP) media are limited to 100 meters from the adapter to concentrator.

Topology

FDDI uses a two-ring topology in which each ring operates in an opposite direction from the other. (See Figure 22-1.) If a break in the medium occurs along either ring, the network uses a mechanism within each station or concentrator called the *Configuration Control Element* (CCE) to reroute the intact ring. (See Figure 22-2 on page 277.) An FDDI network

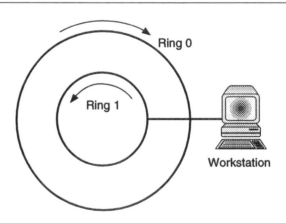

Figure 22-1. *An FDDI dual counter-rotating ring network.*

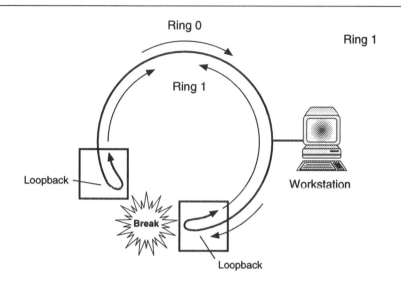

Figure 22-2. *The ring is rerouted when a break in the cable occurs.*

may also run in a single-ring configuration, but loses its redundancy and recovery qualities.

Signaling and Encoding

FDDI networks operate at 125 megahertz (MHz) or 100Mbps. To obtain these speeds and achieve 80 percent efficiency, the network uses a highly efficient signal encoding mechanism called 4B/5B encoding to create symbols, in which five bits convey four bits of data. Symbol transmission is accomplished with *Non-Return-to-Zero, Invert-on-Ones (NRZI)*. This two-step process takes the signal and converts it to a five-bit Non-Return-to-Zero (NRZ) symbol. In NRZ, a high-polarity signal represents a binary 0 and a low-priority signal represents a binary 1. The second conversion step converts the signal to an NRZI signal. In this signal, a transition represents a binary 1 and the absence of a transition represents a binary 0. This method guarantees that each transmitted signal contains at least one polarity transition every five bits. The transition maintains the network's clock synchronization. With clocking at 125MHz, the effective transmission rate with 4B/5B encoding is 100MHz.

Transmission

FDDI transmits in synchronous and asynchronous modes. In synchronous mode, FDDI's management mechanism, *Station Management (SMT)*, preallocates the bandwidth necessary for the communication. In asynchronous transmission, communications contend with other stations on the network for bandwidth.

Synchronous traffic is limited to delay-sensitive data traffic such as voice or real-time video. Asynchronous traffic consists of data packets or Open Systems Interconnect (OSI) Model Media Access Control (MAC) Layer traffic.

In FDDI, the MAC Layer maintains timers for synchronous and asynchronous transmission. The Token Hold Timer (THT) controls the length of time a station may transmit asynchronous frames. The Token Rotation Timer (TRT) schedules transmissions on the ring.

Management

The Station Management (SMT) function is responsible for FDDI management and provides control at the station level. SMT collects current configuration, connection, and ring management information from the FDDI MAC frames.

Frame Types

FDDI allows several types of frames to exist on the ring. The Media Access Control (MAC) frames operate in a manner similar to token-ring MAC frames. They are responsible for ring initialization, timing, and error counters.

For communication, there are two FDDI frames: a token and a frame. Two types of tokens and eight types of frames exist. Stations use nonrestricted tokens to transmit using the asynchronous bandwidth. Pairs of stations use restricted tokens to reserve all the bandwidth temporarily in a synchronous communication. The FDDI frames are as follows:

1. Void frame
2. Station management frame
3. SMT next-station addressing frame
4. MAC frame
5. MAC beacon frame

6. LLC frame
7. LLC information frame—asynchronous
8. LLC information frame—synchronous

FDDI's maximum frame size is 4,500 bytes.

Components

FDDI network components consist of dual- and single-attach stations and concentrators. Single-attach stations (SAS) attach to only one ring. Dual-attach stations (DAS), which provide greater security and redundancy and are more expensive than single-attach stations, connect to both rings. Stations that use copper-based media attach to a single ring.

Tip:
Single-attach stations do not have the same redundancy and fault-tolerance as dual-attach stations. If a break occurs in the medium between the SAS and the ring, the connection is severed and the SAS loses its network connection.

SAS workstations connect to the primary ring or to single-attach concentrators (SAC) with a single cable attachment. Consequently, SAS only have one PMD and one PHY. [FDDI's Physical Layer Medium Dependent (PMD) and Physical Medium Independent (PHY) components operate at the OSI Model's Physical Layer. The PMD concerns the optical network components such as fiber, connectors, transmitters, and receivers. It specifies, for instance, the characteristics of the pulses that travel through the fiber.]

SAS workstations may have multiple MAC Layer components. Because the SAS only connects to the primary ring, if this ring is disabled, the SAS loses connection depending on its installation. If the SAS directly connects to the primary ring, it loses its network connection. If the SAS connects through a device such as a dual-attach concentrator (DAC), it retains its network connection.

DAS workstations connect to both counter-rotating rings directly or via a dual-attach concentrator (DAC). They have two cables of four fiber-optic pairs each, which requires two PMDs and PHYs, as each attachment requires a PMD/PHY pair. The DAS has one SMT and one or more MAC Layer components. DAS's also require two ports on dual-attach concentrators (DACs). A MAC Layer DAS can transmit and receive frames on both rings. Remember, the secondary ring only provides redundancy for the main ring.

Concentrators, which consist of single-attach (SAC) or dual-attach concentrators (DAC), connect to one ring or both rings. SAS workstations attach to SACs; DAS workstations attach to DACs.

 Tip:
Both the SAC and DAC are nodes on the network for many calculations. However, they are not stations on the network because they do not retransmit or transmit frames.

FDDI AND THE OSI MODEL

FDDI operates at the OSI Model Data Link and Physical Layers. It consists of four components and an additional management layer (see Figure 22-3).

The first two components, FDDI's Physical Layer Medium Dependent (PMD) and Physical Medium Independent (PHY) components, operate at the OSI Model's Physical Layer.

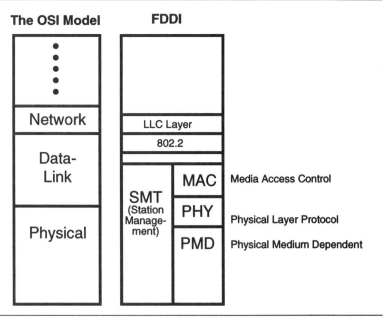

Figure 22-3. *The relation of FDDI to the OSI model.*

The PMD concerns the optical network components such as fiber, connectors, transmitters, and receivers. Among other functions, the PMD specifies the characteristics of the pulses that travel through the fiber medium. While several medium are available for FDDI, a different PMD must be used for each medium. If you switch to copper- from fiber-optic-based media, the PMD component must change.

The PHY designates the Physical Layer sections that are not media-dependent. It specifies algorithms to overcome clock rate differences, manages error detection, and encodes information into pulses that are transmitted on the physical medium.

The third and fourth components, the Logical Link Control (LLC) and Media Access Control (MAC), operate at the OSI Model Data Link Layer. The MAC Layer specifies the token and frame formats and the rules for initializing the token. The LLC Layer handles incoming packets from the various network protocols the LAN drivers are bound to. The LLC also specifies flow control and error recovery.

The Station Management (SMT) component spans the Physical Layer and the Data Link Layer portion responsible for MAC Layer protocols. SMT specifies protocol and frame formats to locate and isolate faults automatically and control network reconfigurations and initialization.

THE TOKEN-PASSING PROTOCOL

FDDI uses a token-passing protocol similar to token-ring. In token-ring, the time required for the token to traverse the ring (its token travel time, TTT) is determined by two time factors: the time the token is held by each station, and the time it takes the token to travel one ring rotation from node to node. These times are known as the Token Holding Time (THT) and the Token Rotation Time (TRT). The THT is constant.

The TRT is a function of the number of active stations times the THT, plus the token travel time (TTT). The TTT is a function of the ring's size. As the number of network stations grow, the TRT grows proportionally.

The time required for a single token round trip is called *latency*. As the number of stations grows, latency increases. The ability to calculate latency makes token-ring a deterministic protocol. A user knows exactly how long the station's wait is between tokens. Unfortunately, this wait may often be unacceptable.

FDDI seeks to overcome latency by having all stations agree on a Target Token Rotation Time (TTRT). Each station cooperates. If the time period is exceeded, no more stations may transmit during that rotation. This method is used for data- or asynchronous-class traffic. Synchronous-class traffic or interactive voice traffic may transmit on any token, but the duration of each synchronous transmission is limited.

FDDI also allows up to eight priority levels on transmitted data. The decision to implement priorities is left to the network administrator. If the TRT is below a set value, lower-priority stations can transmit.

THE FDDI FRAME FORMAT

The FDDI frame is similar to the token-ring frame. Its structure is as shown in Figure 22-4.

The frame consists of several fields:

The Preamble—The preamble consists of 216 octets.

The Starting Delimiter (SD)—The SD consists of two octets and indicates the start of the frame.

Frame Control—The frame control field consists of two octets and indicates whether the communication class is asynchronous or synchronous. It also contains the address length bit and the frame format bits that indicate the type of frame.

Destination Address (DA)—The DA consists of four or 12 octets, depending on the address type, that indicate the frame's destination.

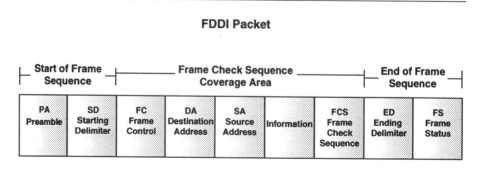

FDDI Packet

Figure 22-4. *The FDDI packet structure.*

Source Address (SA)—The SA consists of four or 12 octets, depending on the address type, that indicate the frame's source.

Information Field—This variable length field depends on the packet type and size and indicates data intended for upper proto-col layers.

Frame Check Sequence (FCS)—The FCS consists of eight octets and is responsible for error checking of frame control, destination and source address, and information fields.

Ending Delimiter (ED)—The ending delimiter indicates the end of the frame. It consists of one octet.

Frame Status—The frame status field is of a variable length that depends on the status of the frame and indicates whether the frame has been accepted and copied into memory or whether it is unacceptable, and thus rejected.

The frame control field indicates the class of frame (asynchronous or synchronous), the address field length, and the frame type. The first octet of this field signifies whether the service is asynchronous or synchronous. The second octet indicates the address length and the frame type.

Several frame types are possible:

Logical Link Control (LLC)—The LLC frame is the most common frame on the ring.

Tokens—Tokens can be restricted or nonrestricted. All stations use nonrestricted token to transmit using the asynchronous band-width. Pairs of stations use restricted tokens to reserve the band-width temporarily for synchronous communication.

Media Access Control (MAC)—There are a number of possible MAC frames, including those used for ring initialization and fault recovery. Among the most common MAC frames are claim frames and beacon frames.

Reserved—Reserved frames exist for future standardization of an Ethernet frame format.

The LLC frame contains the following information:

Destination Service Access Point (DSAP)—This eight-bit field identifies one or more Service Access Points (SAPs) for which information is to be delivered. The IEEE assigns DSAPs to vendors.

Source Service Access Point (SSAP)—This eight-bit field identifies the SAP that transmitted the frame. The IEEE assigns SSAPs to vendors.

Control Field—The control field indicates whether frames are connectionless (U-frames), unacknowledged frames, or acknowledged connection-oriented frames (I-frames).

Only several bits of the address fields are used for addressing, maintaining a maximum of 128 distinct addresses for each SAP. The eighth bit of the DSAP indicates whether the address is for an individual or group. The eighth bit of the SSAP indicates whether the frame contains a request or a response.

The frame's address portions follow the IEEE addressing conventions for use in IEEE 802.3, 802.4 and 802.5 LANs. The address length can be 16 or 48 bits, although 48-bit addressing is the only addressing method currently in use. The first bit specifies whether the address is an individual or group address. The second bit specifies whether the address is a universal or local address. Manufacturers assign universal addresses according to IEEE guidelines. Users define local addresses, which take effect when the adapter driver initializes. The next 24 bits of the address defines the manufacturer's unique identifier. The last 24 bits are assigned to the adapter according to an algorithm set at the time of manufacture.

 Tip:
If you use universal address IDs, the chances of having duplicate node addresses on the network are slim. If you assign local addresses to conform to application requirements, your chances of having a duplicate address increase. Because duplicate addresses can play havoc with the network, do not use them unless an application requires them.

FDDI uses a 32-bit Cycle Redundancy Check (CRC) character in the frame check sequence field that ensures the frame is transmitted in an error-free condition. The Cyclic Redundancy Check verifies that the ones and zeros sent in the transmitted frame are received correctly.

The frame status field can be of three types: error detected (E), address recognized (A), or frame copied (C). If E is set, no other station on the ring can change the frame's status. Although the FDDI specification allows status indicators in addition to these three, the total number of indicators must remain odd.

Service Classes

FDDI has three classes of service: connectionless Type 1, connection-oriented Type 2, and acknowledged connectionless Type 3. Connectionless services, also known as *Type 1 services*, require no data-link connection between Service Access Points (SAPs). Since no connection exists, data transfer is more rapid than in connection-oriented services.. Because no error recovery exists in connectionless Type 1 service, higher-layer protocols may need to provide it.

Connection-oriented services, classified as *Type 2 services*, establish a direct data or logical link between transmitting and receiving stations prior to data transfer. Once the connection is made, each frame transfer is acknowledged. Acknowledgment provides Data-Link Layer error control and does not require higher-layer protocol intervention. The overhead of acknowledgments sacrifices performance.

A Type 3 service has been proposed. In this service, no connection is established prior to data exchange. Once data exchange begins, all frames are acknowledged. This provides error control without Type 2 service overhead.

SMT Frame Format

Station management (SMT) operates as a subset of network management and allows initialization, control, and hardware and software component monitoring at the MAC, PHY, and PMD Layers. SMT is a frame-based management service that uses specific frames to initialize, monitor, and control normal ring operation. The SMT frame format is as follows:

Preamble

Starting Delimiter—This field designates the start of the frame.

Frame Control—This field indicates the SMT frame type.

Destination Address—This field indicates the station address the frame is sent to.

Source Address—This field is the station address sending the message

SMT Header—The SMT header contains a variety of information including the frame class and type, the SMT version used, and the information field length following.

SMT Information—This field contains an encoded parameter that indicates SMT information.

Frame Check Sequence (FCS)

Ending Delimiter

Frame Status

SMT Header

The SMT header contains the following information:

Frame class—This part of the field indicates the SMT frame function.

Frame type—Frame types can be request, response, or announcement.

Version ID—This part of the field indicates the version of SMT standard used.

Transaction ID—The transaction ID matches SMT requests with SMT response frames.

Station ID—The station ID is the unique identifier for the source station packet assembler/disassembler (PAD).

Information field length—This part of the SMT header indicates the information field length that follows.

SMT Frame Classes

SMT frames are divided into several classes according to function. The SMT frames are these:

Neighbor Information Frame—A MAC uses the neighbor information frame to determine or announce a neighboring MAC. Each MAC has one upstream and one downstream MAC. Frames flow from an upstream MAC to a downstream MAC.

Status Information Frame—This frame gathers detailed information about a station. It is divided into configuration and operational frames. Configuration frames gather information such as whether the station is a concentrator or a workstation, the number of MACs attached, and the addresses of the upstream and downstream neighbors. Operational frames gather information for performance monitoring and fault isolation.

Echo Frame—Loopback testing uses the echo frame.

Resource Allocation Frame—This frame grants resources. Currently the only defined network resource is synchronous bandwidth.

Request Denied Frame—The request denied frame indicates that a station is unable to respond to a request.

Status Report Frame—This frame announces specific events and abnormal station conditions.

Parameter Management Frame (PMF)—The SMT uses the PMF for remotely managing station parameters. PMF Get Request frames read station values, and PMF Set Request Frames modify station values.

Extended Service Frame—This frame is vendor-definable.

SMT Implementation

Implementation of FDDI SMT at the Physical Layer requires two components: Connection Management (CMT) and Ring Management (RMT). CMT has three pieces:

Configuration Management (CFM)—This component manages the configuration of MACs and ports within a node.

Entity Coordination Management (ECM)—This component manages the media interface, including the coordination of activities of all ports on the node.

Physical Connection Management (PCM)—This component covers physical connection management between a managed port and another port in the adjacent node.

CMT functions also include physical link testing and error monitoring, and ring purges.

RMT management (RMT) includes fault announcements such as beaconing, restricted token monitoring, and duplicate address detection. It also is responsible for fault detection and recovery such as those errors that occur when a cable breaks or develops a short.

FDDI SNMP Management

The SMT standard for FDDI defines a management standard for single FDDI LANs. Because most FDDI networks consist of more than a single LAN and may be part of larger MANs or WANs, additional management capability is required. As a result, FDDI is fully interoperable with the Simple Network Management Protocol (SNMP) and the Common Management Information Protocol/System (CMIP/CMIS) defined in the ISO's OSI model.

SNMP uses stations called *network management stations* to control and monitor the FDDI network. Monitored and controlled devices are called *network elements*. The management station uses a management entity that talks to *management agents* located on each network element. The information the agents gather, which the management station collects and maintains, is kept in a database the element's manufacturer defines. This database is called the *Management Information Base* (MIB). A generic MIB (MIB II) is supplied with each SNMP implementation. Manufacturers write management software to gather MIB II statistics and also often create separate MIBs for element statistics that are proprietary.

The MIB for FDDI is called the *FDDI MIB*. The FDDI MIB follows the OSI standard for MIB definition. The communication protocol the SNMP manager uses for information and control functions is defined by SNMP.

FDDI also interoperates with OSI-defined CMIP, an SNMP replacement that has not had wide acceptance in the marketplace. The information that management agents supply is often gathered over a long periods of time, allowing network managers to perform trend analysis on their networks. With SNMP, you can customize reports to provide the information you need most, and use SNMP with a managed hub in a structured wiring system to provide even more information. In addition, SNMP-managed hubs let you set traps to warn of network problems and, in extreme cases, control individual ports to stop problems.

Almost every network device contains an SNMP agent. The leading vendors of SNMP management consoles are Hewlett-Packard's Open View, SunConnect's Sun Net Manager, and IBM's NetView 6000. There are improvements such as CMIP that are even more extensive and configurable than SNMP, but their current interfaces are proprietary. As a result, SNMP retains and is expanding its popularity.

ADAPTERS

FDDI adapter chip sets are currently being manufactured by Advanced Micro Devices (AMD), Motorola, and National Semiconductor. Manufacturers currently producing FDDI adapters include Ascom Timeplex, Crescendo Communications, Digital, Hewlett-Packard, IBM Corp., Intel, Network Peripherals, and Optical Data Systems (ODS).

CABLING

FDDI fiber-optic media is available as either single-mode or multimode fiber-optic cable. Each type uses two cables, one for transmitting data, and one for receiving data. Single-mode fiber-optic cable passes one frequency of light at a time, while multimode passes several frequencies. Special receptacles or cable end-connectors are used depending on the type of connection being made.

Single-mode fiber is based on the X3.194 standard and is intended for campus- wide or metropolitan area networks (MAN). Single-mode fiber uses a laser light source and has a transmission distance of up to 60 kilometers between stations. If you intend to install a single-mode fiber network, it is best to consider using custom-made single-mode fiber that is installed by a qualified technician.

Multimode fiber is used for most FDDI installations. It allows distances of up to two kilometers between stations.

The following fiber-optic cable types are allowed in FDDI:

- 62.5/125 micron
- 50/125 micron
- 85/125 micron
- 100/140 micron

Multimode fiber-optic uses LED light sources with wavelengths between 1,270 and 1,380 nanometers. Multmode cable is readily available in precut lengths, but should still be left to a qualified technician.

Connectors

FDDI cable ends must be terminated with keyed connectors called *media interface connectors (MIC)*. Keyed connectors have special structures that can be inserted in only one way and only into receptacles that accept the keyed connector. Keyed connectors are used so users can't confuse receive and transmit cables, and also because only specific connections can be used on certain concentrators or adapters. As a result of these requirements, there are four types of connectors:

MIC A—Consists of a primary out/secondary out (used for DAS-to-FDDI main ring).

MIC B—Consists of a secondary in/primary out (used for DAS-to-FDDI main ring).

MIC M—A master connector fits into any connection receptacle.

MIC S—The connector for SAS station.

 Tip:
Terminating the ends of fiber cable and installing connectors is not for the uninitiated user. Attend a class on properly terminating fiber and purchase the proper materials, or leave installation to professional cable technicians. The money you spend terminating ends for yourself over and over is worth the price of a professional who does it right the first time.

CDDI cable uses either STP or UTP media. CDDI attachments must be single-attach stations (SAS) only. CDDI STP wiring is the same as token-ring uses. It uses four wires, as follows:

• Transmit +
• Transmit –
• Receive +
• Receive –

The specific pinouts are given in Figure 22-5 on page 291.

Signal Lead	Pinout Type I connector	Pinout DB-9
Receive +	Red (R)	Pin 1
Receive –	Green (G)	Pin 6
Transmit +	Orange (O)	Pin 9
Transmit –	Black (B)	Pin 5

Figure 22-5 on page 297. *Cable with DB-9 showing pins 1, 6, 5, and 9 labeled as 1, receive +; 6, receive –;5, transmit –; 9, transmit +.*

The distance limit for Type I connectors is 150 meters. The distance limit for Category V UTP is 100 meters.

While Type I cable offers greater distance than Category V, it is more difficult and bulky to work with. CDDI on UTP uses Category V cable exclusively: Category V cable, also known as Level V, is 22-24AWG UTP wire that complies with the Category V standards as set in EIA/TIA Technical Bulletin PN-2841. Category V is designed to handle 100Mbps transmission over UTP.

Tip:
A Category V cable plant requires properly installed Category V components. Expensive improperly installed Category V components won't yield proper results.

The Type III RJ-45 connector uses the inner two connectors for one pair and the next outer two connections for the other. These are pins 3, 4, 5, and 6. Pins 1, 2, 7, and 8 are not used.

BRIDGING AND ROUTING

Bridges and routers connect multiple networks together. A bridge operates at the OSI Model Data-Link Layer and connects networks using the same or different media or topologies, or the same or different access methods that conform to the IEEE 802.2 Media Access Control specifications. These access methods presently include Ethernet, token-ring, IEEE 802.5, and FDDI.

Routers, on the other hand, also connect networks of different access methods, media, or topology. They differ from bridges because they can route packets between networks that use different network transport protocols such as IP and IPX. Routers operate at the OSI Model Network Layer. Thus, any layers below that layer, such as the Physical or Data-Link Layers, are supported by routers.

Bridges

In a bridge, packets are forwarded across the bridge according to the list of network and source addresses the bridge maintains. As part of the forwarding process, a bridge has the following functions:

- Frame forwarding
- Loop resolution
- Network learning

In frame forwarding, the bridge filters frames. When the bridge receives a packet, it looks at the packet's network address and sends it if the packet is destined for the other network, thus preventing local packets from being sent across the bridge and reducing internetwork traffic. (See Figure 22-6.) Although a network segmented by a bridge can greatly reduce traffic, filtering requires time and introduces latency. As a result, most bridges are rated by the number of packets per second they can forward.

Network	Source Address
CDE	001686CE451C
123	001686AD3A17
456	001686FFD167
456	00168734CF26
123	0016867364F6

Figure 22-6. *A bridge's table of network and source addresses.*

Large networks may have multiple bridges that connect the same network segment. When bridges cannot resolve routes to the same network, packets can loop continuously around a segment, causing unwarranted traffic. Many bridges eliminate packets that are placed on the wrong segment.

Formerly, bridges had to be programmed with the individual address of each network node. When a node moved, the bridge had to be reprogrammed. Bridge manufacturers developed a method implemented in *learning bridges* that overcomes this problem. There are two types of learning bridges, called *transparent bridges* and *source routing bridges*. Ethernet and FDDI networks use transparent bridges to discover the route to a network segment by using the spanning tree algorithm. (See Figure 22-7.) Token-ring networks can also use learning

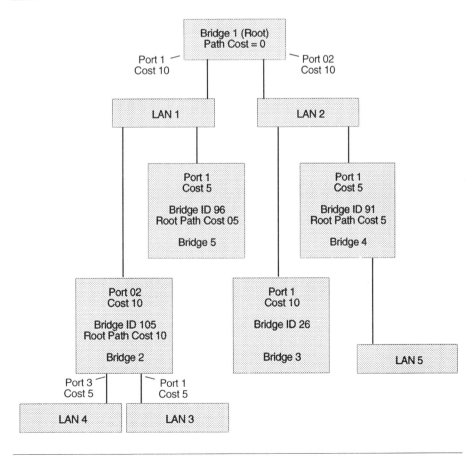

Figure 22-7. *A typical spanning-tree network.*

bridges; however, IBM developed the source routing bridge to handle traffic routing between IBM token ring networks. A bridge that combines FDDI, Ethernet, and token-ring uses a combination of the two learning bridges called *source-transparent bridging*.

In transparent bridging, the bridge controls the network address resolution for source addresses that are not known to the bridge. When the bridge receives a frame, it initiates a search of its source address table. If the bridge cannot find the source address, it sends a discovery packet to every interconnected network. The discovery packet collects network addresses so the bridge may forward the frame to the correct network. Each bridge constantly updates this list. Discovery works well, except in large networks that have multiple paths between network segments and a large number of bridges between any two networks.

The problems associated with transparent bridging led to spanning-tree algorithm development. The IEEE 801.2D committee maintains the spanning tree protocol, which detects circular paths between networks. It also stops redundant looping by creating an additional bridge, called a secondary bridge, and shutting down the secondary bridge until it is needed.

The spanning tree protocol assigns a unique identifier to each bridge, which normally is based on the MAC Layer device address. Each bridge then receives a priority value and each port receives an identifier. Each bridge port is then assigned a path cost value. The path cost, which is determined by the protocol or the network administrator, equals the number of ports that must be traversed to move from one network to another.

The bridge with the lowest number identifier becomes the root bridge. The other bridges determine which ports provide access to the root bridge at the least cost. This port becomes the root port to the bridge. Bridges and ports with the least cost provide the path across the network for frames. The other ports and bridges are shut down and maintained as secondary paths.

Routers

Routers, which operate at the OSI Model Network Layer, operate locally or over a wide-area network to interconnect differing network transport protocols. They maintain a list of adjacent routers and LANs on the internetwork. When a router receives a frame, it examines the frame for its destination information and checks the frame against its list of adjacent routers. If the router cannot ship the frame locally, it verifies the next router to send the packet to and transfers the frame.

The forwarding process requires that the router fully receive the frame and open it to determine the frame's routing information, creating a large amount of processing.

Routers may handle only single protocols, topologies, access methods, or media, or many of each. They are typically programmed to route only specific network transport protocols to other networks. For example, a network in Dallas with IPX and IP traffic wants only IP traffic to be routed to the network in Austin, Texas. The router could be programmed to reject IPX traffic bound for Austin.

Routing Protocols

Routers use various protocols to perform their forwarding functions depending upon the network transport protocol or access method routed. The following are some routing protocols used:

> **The Address Resolution Protocol (ARP)**—TCP/IP networks use ARP.
>
> **The Routing Information Protocol (RIP)**—RIP is a distance-vector protocol used in NetWare and other networks.
>
> **The Open Shortest Path First (OSPF) protocol**—OSPF is a link-state routing protocol that is commonly used as a gateway protocol.
>
> **The End System to Intermediate System (ES-IS) protocol**—ES-IS is an OSI discovery protocol end nodes use to discover routers.
>
> **The Intermediate System to Intermediate System (IS-IS) protocol**—IS-IS is an OSI discovery protocol intermediate routers use to discover each other.

As a result of the router overhead required to fully receive and analyze frames, routers are often slower than bridges. However, they provide additional services that bridges do not provide. In addition, many network operating systems provide routing functions such as NetWare's internal router. This ability depends on the protocol being used. IPX and IP are routable protocols, where NetBIOS is not. An NT server would be able to route IP, but not NetBIOS traffic. The decision to use a router or bridge must be made on the current and future network needs.

TROUBLESHOOTING FDDI

Troubleshooting FDDI networks takes two forms: network and adapter-level. Most problems occur at the network level.

Network-Level Diagnostics

Like many networks, most problems in FDDI occur with the cable plant. If you are working with FDDI or another fiber-based network, you'll want to buy a *time-domain reflectometer (TDR)*, which measures the power of the fiber light source. While TDRs are expensive, several on the market balance price and functionality. You'll also want to buy a link-confidence tester like that from Fotec that is designed for FDDI cabling.

To avoid problems when installing fiber-optic cable, make sure that the connectors terminating the cable ends are clean. You can clean them by blowing on the ends or by using special fiber-optic cleaning kits. The cable quality and the connection should be verified prior to installing the connector into equipment.

Other troubleshooting checkpoints include the following:

- Check that you have properly keyed connectors on the cable ends.
- Verify that all MICs go to the correct ports. Remember, MICs can use any connection.
- Verify that all ports on stations are operational.
- Check to see if the ring has been segmented. Rings automatically segment if problems exist.
- Verify that all single-attach stations (SAS) are functioning and that the ring they are attached to is still active.
- Use SMT to verify whether a station or node is beaconing. If one is, the problem is isolated to the beaconing station's upstream link. The correction process is similar the fault domain isolation and recovery process in token-ring networks.

Adapter-Level Diagnostics

The majority of problems with FDDI adapters are related to conflicts with other adapters or bus-timing issues. FDDI adapters use the following resources:

- I/O port

- DMA channel
- Interrupt Request Line (IRQ)

FDDI adapters that exhibit conflicts with other system resources often fail to load the LAN driver. If this occurs, look for a conflict with the Interrupt Request Line (IRQ). FDDI adapters default to IRQ 2.

Next in order of importance after interrupt conflicts, FDDI adapters have problems with shared RAM addresses. Address settings for FDDI adapters can range from C000h to DC000h. This range causes conflicts with other adapters such as video adapters, SCSI controllers, system shadowing, and memory managers. Programs such as CheckIT LAN or Microsoft's Diagnostic Utility (MSD) are useful for verifying shared RAM problems. Another source of adapter problems is conflicts with adapters that use DMA or bus-mastering. The adapters likely to cause DMA conflicts are these:

- SCSI controllers
- CD-ROM controllers
- Sound adapters
- Other network adapters

One of the hardest problems to diagnose is the use of bus-mastering devices on ISA machines. Adapters may be set at different DMA addresses, but still conflict with each other. These conflicts result from bus-mastering priority. In bus-mastering, the adapter's DMA controller takes over the bus until it is finished transferring data or until the CPU must complete a memory refresh cycle. The problem occurs when two controllers want to control the bus at the same time. The DMA channel number solves this problem. The adapter with the lowest number has priority. This is similar to interrupt priority with IRQs. To keep one adapter from keeping the bus when others need it, the IEEE developed a concept called *fairness*. Some vendor drivers implement fairness; others do not. If a driver doesn't implement fairness, the best idea is to place it at the highest DMA channel available. This usually solves the problem.

FUTURE DIRECTION

While 100Mbps access methods may be the fastest networks for the immediate future, the next generation of network applications will require additional speed. FDDI is compatible with circuit-switched traffic such as ISDN-B channel voice communications, which requires require additional speed. FDDI is compatible with circuit-switched traffic such as ISDN-B channel voice communications, which requires isochronous services and transmission at a constant interval. FDDI II provides support for time-specific isochronous services and is backward-compatible with 100Mbps FDDI nodes. The additional isochronous mode of operation is called *hybrid mode*. The requirements of FDDI II necessitate changes to the SMT.

The move to FDDI II led to changes in the MAC specifications. MAC II is the result. The changes relate to isochronous and hybrid operation. Additional bridge and support for source and transparent routing is also available.

appendix

GLOSSARY AND ACRONYM LIST

A

NUMBERS

1BASE-5   1BASE-5 is Ethernet over UTP media at 1Mbps for transmission distances of 500 meters per segment. Very few 1BASE-5 installations exist.

10BASE-2   10BASE-2 is known as *thin Ethernet* or *Thinnet* and supports up to 185 meters per segment. 10BASE-2 uses RG-58 A/U media.

10BASE-5   10BASE-5 also is known as *thick Ethernet* and supports a maximum segment length of 500 meters. 10BASE-5 uses double-shielded, .04-inch diameter coaxial media.

10BASE-F   10BASE-F is Ethernet over fiber-optic media. Fiber-optic Ethernet is commonly used as a backbone between repeaters at a transmission distance of up to 4 kilometers (Km).

10BASE-FL   10BASE-FL is 10Mbps Ethernet on fiber-optic media.

10BASE-T   10BASE-T is Ethernet over UTP Category III, IV, or V unshielded twisted-pair media.

100BASE-FX   The fiber-optic version of 100BASE-T.

100BASE-T   100BASE-T is 100Mbps Ethernet on shielded or unshielded twisted-pair.

100BASE-T4   The four-pair twisted-pair implementation of 100BASE-T is called *100BASE-T4*.

100BASE-TX   The two-pair twisted-pair media implementation of 100BASE-T is called *100BASE-TX*.

100VG-AnyLAN

100VG-AnyLAN is 100Mbps Ethernet over variable grade (VG) twisted-pair wiring. Also called *100VG-AnyLAN*, it refers to the access method's ability to use Ethernet or token-ring frame formats. This standard is controlled by the IEEE 802.12 committee, which normally handles token-passing protocols.

100BASE-X   100BASE-X is 100Mbps Ethernet over twisted-pair media. It is a hierarchical transmission protocol over Category V twisted-pair media with a maximum distance of 100 meters per segment.

10BROAD-36   10BROAD-36 is Ethernet over RG-59 broadband media with a maximum distance per segment of 3,600 meters.

4B/5B encoding

FDDI uses 4B/5B signal encoding in which four bits of data are represented by five bits.

802.3   802.3 is the IEEE standard for CSMA/CD-based Ethernet.

802.5   802.5 is the IEEE standard for token-passing token-ring.

A

access method

The access method controls data access to the media. Common access methods are Ethernet, token-ring, ARCNET, and FDDI. The network's access method designates how data is transmitted over the medium from client node to client node. Access methods are implemented as Carrier Sense Multiple Access with Collision Detection or token-passing protocols. Each access method uses different types of medium and operates at different transmission speeds.

Access Rights List (ARL)

The ARL designates the devices or users that have access to the networked resource.

acknowledgment

An acknowledgment consists of a packet sent from the recipient indicating it has received and processed data.

active hub   A central wiring device that actively repeats and retimes the signal is called an active hub. The active hub allows longer network distances.

active powered MAU

The active powered MAU is an AC-powered Multistation Access Unit (MAU) that actively retimes and retransmits the network data signals sends by attached network adapters. This 8- to 16-port device allows for greater communication distance than passive powered or unpowered MAUs. Most active powered MAUs do not require a separate reset tool to reset their relays. When power is applied to the device, the relays reset automatically.

adapter

In networking, the adapter represents the network adapter, which allows the workstation, server, or other network device to communicate with the network.

adapter address

The address is the hexadecimal number that identifies the adapter on the LAN.

address

A variety of addresses exist in networking that designate how a network device will receive data.

ADSP

The AppleTalk Data Stream Protocol manages data transmission across the network.

Advanced Server (AS)

Advanced Server designates Windows NT Advanced Server, a recent version of Microsoft's server-based network operating system.

AEP

The AppleTalk Echo Protocol determines if a session with another node can be established.

AFP

The AppleTalk Filing Protocol provides file-sharing services.

AHI

Adapter Handler Interface. The AHI is a Texas Instruments specification that substitutes for part of the IBM token-ring adapter implementation.

AMP

Active Monitor Present. This token-ring frame is released by the workstation that has temporary monitoring responsibilities for the ring.

amplitude

An electrical signal only travels so far without losing signal strength The strength of the signal is called its *amplitude*. A decrease in amplitude as the signal traverses the media is called *attenuation*.

ANSI

The American National Standards Institute is an organization in the United States charged with publishing standards.

API   Application Program Interface. An API is a specification that indicates how an application may use a defined set of services.

AppleShare   This term is applied to AppleTalk networks that use a centralized server.

AppleTalk   AppleTalk is Apple Computer's network architecture.

application   An application is a program or set of programs that supply a common function.

Application Layer
                   The Application is layer 7 of the OSI Model—it dictates how applications talk to the network.

ARCNET   ARCNET is an access method that is wired as a bus or a star and communicates at 2.5Mbps.

ARP   Address Resolution Protocol. ARP is a protocol that resides at the TCP/IP Internet layer that delivers data on the same network by translating an IP address to a physical address.

ARPANET   This network is also known as the Advanced Research Projects Agency Network.

ASP   The AppleTalk Session Protocol provides connection-oriented communication services.

ATM   Asynchronous Transfer Mode. ATM is a 25- or 125Mbps access protocol for local and wide-area networks.

ATP   The AppleTalk Transaction Protocol establishes and maintains communication sessions.

Attenuation   Attenuation is a characteristic of data as it traverses the network medium. The further data travels, the weaker its signal becomes.

AUI   Attachment Unit Interface. The DB-15 AUI connector allows the Ethernet adapter to attach to a variety of media. Attachment Unit Interfaces are used with 10BASE-5 networks.

AURP   The AppleTalk Update Routing Protocol updates the routing tables if changes are made to the network configuration.

AWG   American Wire Gauge. AWG specifies the thickness of the copper wire in coax and twisted-pair networks.

B

backup domain controller

In LAN Manager, a server may act as a domain controller or a backup domain controller. The backup domain controller stands ready to take over if the domain controller fails.

bandwidth   The bandwidth represents the frequency of the communication. In networks, bandwidth is measured in bits per second. For example, Ethernet has a theoretical bandwidth of 10 million bits per second.

baseband   Baseband is the most common type of transmission in LAN access methods. In a baseband network, one data signal can exist on the network medium at a time.

beacon   The beacon in a token-ring LAN consists of a special frame that indicates trouble has occurred.

bend ratio   Each cable has a ratio past which it should not be bent. In fiber-optic cable, the bend ratio is particularly important because the core of the cable is made of glass, and bends past a certain ratio can result in data loss or breakage of cable.

bindery   The bindery is a database maintained in NetWare v2.x and v3.x that lists the resources on the network and their characteristics.

binding   When a LAN driver and IPXODI (the protocol stack) are loaded, they are joined together in a process called binding.

B-ISDN   Broadband ISDN.

BNC   The bayonet connector is used in Ethernet networks to join adapters, hubs, and cables together. The BNC may be either male or female. Female connectors connect the network adapter to the medium. Male connectors attach the medium to the adapter. BNC T-connectors connect pieces of cable together and attach the cables to the network adapter or other device.

bottleneck   When the resource needs of the network are greater than the bandwidth that exists, a bottleneck exists.

bridge   A bridge exists at the Data-Link Layer of the OSI model and connects networks using the same or different access methods, the same or different media, and the same or different speeds.

broadcast   A broadcast is a special packet that all workstations receive. It also indicates a transmission form for Ethernet and ARCNET that all workstations hear, but only the workstation the frame is addressed to receives.

brouter   A brouter combines the technology of a router and a bridge. It can act as a router on some occasions and as a bridge on others.

bus   The bus refers to the topology 10BASE-5 and 10BASE-2 Ethernet use or to the length of medium workstations or repeaters attach to.

bus-mastering   Bus-mastering is a technique used by LAN adapters that increases data transfer between the computer's memory and the network. In bus-mastering, the adapter takes control of the computer bus to transfer data, leaving the CPU free to do work of its own.

bus topology   One of three network topologies, the bus arranges nodes along a single segment of cable. All nodes on the network hear messages at the same time. ARCNET and Ethernet both use bus topologies.

C

CAU   Controlled Access Unit. This device, part of an IBM active MAU, is used with a Lobe Access Module (LAM) to connect individual workstations to the MAU.

CCE   Configuration Control Element. The CCE is a protocol within SAS, DAS, and concentrators that controls the port and its configuration. When a failure occurs, the CCE determines the subsequent port configuration.

CCITT   Consultative Committee for International Telephone and Telegraph.

CDDI   Copper Distributed Data Interface is an implementation of FDDI over copper media.

CFM   Configuration Management. This component manages the configuration of MACs and ports within a node.

client   Networks consists of clients and servers. Clients request and receive services from servers. Traditional clients are DOS, Windows, OS/2, UNIX, or Macintosh workstations. Each has its own client operating system that works in concert with the network operating system to exchange service requests. A printer may work operating system to exchange service requests. A printer may also be a client of the file server, requesting services from it to perform the printing operations of the network.

client/server   Client/server is a form of networking in which client workstations request and receive services from servers. Banyan VINES, Windows NT 3.5, and NetWare are client/server network operating systems.

CMIP   Common Management Information Protocol. CMIP is an OSI network management specification originally intended to replace SNMP. It defines how CMIP-compliant devices interrelate on the network.

CMIS   Common Management Information System. The heart of CMIP is the Common Management Information System (CMIS), which defines the OSI standard for gathering and storing information on the network. Collected information is used by the CMIP management station to compile information from multiple vendors and display the information.

CMOT   Common Management Information Protocol over IP

CMT   Connection Management. Implementation of FDDI SMT at the Physical Layer requires two components: Connection Management and Ring Management (RMT). CMT has three pieces. They are Configuration Management, Entity Coordination Management, and Physical Connection Management.

coaxial cable   Coaxial cable consists of a solid or stranded copper core surrounded by a sheath and outer coating. ARCNET and Ethernet use coaxial cable.

collision   In a CSMA/CD network when two adapters attempt to transmit at the same time, the signals interfere with each other or collide. When collisions occur, each station stops transmitting and waits an amount of time calculated by a randomizing algorithm. This waiting period is different for each workstation. The stations then listen to the medium again and if it appears clear, transmit.

communication

Communication has four components: sender, receiver, message, and medium. In networks, devices and application tasks and processes communicate messages to each other over media. They represent the sender and receivers. The data they send is the message. The cabling or transmission method they use is the medium.

concentrator   A concentrator is a device that centralizes message transfer between clients and servers in an Ethernet network. Concentrators are intelligent and allow management of attached nodes. They are used in 10BASE-T and 100Mbps Ethernet networks and retime and retransmit the signal.

connection   In networking, two devices establish a connection to communicate with each other.

connectionless Communications can be either connection-oriented or connection-less. In a connectionless protocol, the protocol does not establish a connection before sending data. IPX and IP are examples of connectionless protocols.

connection-oriented

Connection-oriented communications requires a protocol to establish a connection before transmitting data. TCP and SPX are connection-oriented protocols.

console   The console refers to the station from which management operations are performed in a local area network.

Copper Distributed Data Interface (CDDI)

FDDI over shielded and unshielded twisted-pair cable is called CDDI.

core   The core represents the center of the medium. In coaxial and twisted-pair media, the core is copper. In fiber-optic media, the core is glass.

counter-rotating ring

FDDI uses a dual counter-rotating ring topology, in which two rings, operating in opposite directions, provide network fault-tolerance by allowing FDDI to respond to a break in a single ring.

CRC   Cyclic Redundancy Check is an error-checking mechanism used in local area networks.

CSMA/CA   Collision Sense Multiple Access with Collision Avoidance is used by the AppleTalk protocol suite.

CSMA/CD   Collision Sense Multiple Access with Collision Detection is a Data Link protocol in which each station has access to the network and may communicate anytime it does not hear other data traveling on the medium.

D

DAC	Dual-Attach Concentrator. This concentrator allows nodes to attach to both rings at the same time.
DARPA	This agency is also known as the Defense Advanced Research Projects Agency.
DAS	Dual Attach Station. The DAS is a node that attaches to both rings.
data	Information travels across the network in the form of data.
Datagram	The datagram represents the data packet passed between the upper protocol layers. Datagrams pass between routers.

Data-Link Layer

The Data-Link Layer consists of two types of protocols, token-passing and CSMA/CD, which validate the integrity of data flow between communication partners and provide reliable transmission.

Data-Link Protocol

Data-Link protocols are implemented by access methods such as Ethernet, token-ring, and the Fiber Distributed Data Interface (FDDI), which accomplish their actions through LAN adapter hardware, firmware, and LAN driver software.

DB-15	A DB-15 connector is used for shielded twisted-pair media.
DCA	This agency is also known as the Defense Communications Agency.
DCBD	Domain Control Database. In LAN Server, the domain controller maintains this database, which contains the list of users and group definitions. Security for the network is maintained in individual Access Control Profiles stored on the domain controller.
DDN	This network is also known as the Defense Data Network.
DDP	The Datagram Delivery Protocol provides connectionless data delivery of packets.
decapsulation	As data is handed from a lower protocol layer to a higher one, the higher protocol layer removes protocol-specific information before passing the data on.
de facto	A *de facto* standard is not associated with any specific standards group, but is simply a standard because of its wide use.

de jure A *de jure* standard is one that is defined and supported by a standards group such as the IEEE.

Demand Priority Protocol (DPP)
In 100VG-AnyLAN, a two-layer priority system for frames exists, in which high-priority frames are assigned to high-demand applications such as real-time video. Other applications use lower-priority frames. In mixed-priority environments, lower-priority frames are guaranteed access to the media.

DeMarc DeMarc is the distributed network management system in Banyan VINES V6.0.

destination address
The destination address represents the node on the network that will receive data.

destination node
The node that receives data is termed the destination node.

DET Directory Entry Table

device A device consists of a computer, printer, server, or other hardware entity that exists on the network.

DHCP Dynamic Host Configuration Protocol was developed by Microsoft to allow dynamic addressing in a TCP/IP network. Workstations use DHCP to get their IP addresses from the Windows NT server.

Differential Manchester
Differential Manchester is a form of signal encoding used by token-ring.

discovery packet
If the bridge can't determine a source address, it sends a discovery packet to every network connected to it.

dispersion Optical signals are subject to attenuation as well as light-source spreading, called dispersion, as they travel down the medium.

DIX Digital–Intel–Xerox. This informal consortium of companies adopted Ethernet and developed it further.

DMA Direct Memory Access. The TI token-ring chipset had technological and performance advantages over the IBM chipset that allowed increased data buffers for data transfer and also allowed direct memory access (DMA) transfers, in which an onboard controller managed access to memory.

DOD This agency of the federal government is also known as the Department of Defense.

domain In LAN Server, a domain is a group of servers and workstations that create an administrative unit.

domain controller
In LAN Server, *domain controller* is a server within a group that controls and manages the group (domain). Each domain has a domain controller.

downstream The node in a counterclockwise relation to another node is called that node's downstream neighbor in token-ring and FDDI networks.

DPP The Demand Priority Protocol is used by 100VG-AnyLAN networks to give priority to designated nodes.

driver Drivers may be implemented in hardware or software. Software drivers are used to provide the intelligence for network devices. The LAN driver is a common example.

DSAP Destination Service Access Point.

dumb terminal
See terminal.

E

ECM Entity Coordination Management. This FDDI component manages the media interface, including the coordination of activities of all ports on the node.

EIA Electronic Industries Association. The EIA/TIA develops wiring standards for all aspects of the communications and electronic industries, including the RS-232C specification.

EISA Extended Industry Standard Architecture. EISA is a 32-bit bus architecture.

ELAP The EtherTalk Link Access Protocol provides Ethernet connectivity for AppleTalk.

encapsulation

As data flows from a higher to a lower protocol layer, it is encapsulated in protocol information from that layer.

encoding   Data is encoded in digital forms for transfer over the medium.

ENS   The Enterprise Network System (ENS) is a StreetTalk derivative for NetWare networks.

enterprise network

An enterprise network consists of collections of networks connected to each other over a geographically dispersed area. The enterprise network serves the needs of a widely distributed company and operates the company's mission-critical applications.

entity   In a network, an entity may consist of software or a hardware device that communicates on the network.

Entity Coordination Management (ECM)

This FDDI component manages the media interface, including the coordination of activities of all ports on the node.

environment subsystems

NT's modular architecture consists of the Hardware Abstraction Layer (HAL), the kernel, the *NT Executive*, and the client environment subsystems. The client operating modules, called *environment subsystems,* handle file, memory, process, display, network and other subsystems and operate in user mode.

Ethernet   Ethernet is an implementation of CSMA/CD that operates in a bus or star topology at 10 or 100Mbps.

Ethernet I   Ethernet I was the first implementation of DIX Ethernet.

Ethernet II   Ethernet II replaced DIX Ethernet and is still used today.

EtherTalk   EtherTalk is an Ethernet implementation for the AppleTalk protocol suite.

ETR   Early Token Release is a feature of 16Mbps token-ring, which allows a workstation to append data to the token once the workstation determines that the original data has been received.

ES-IS   End System to Intermediate System (ES-IS) is an OSI discovery protocol that allows nodes to discover routers.

Executive Module

NT's modular architecture consists of the Hardware Abstraction Layer (HAL), the kernel, the NT Executive, and the client environment subsystems. The kernel and the NT Executive, which make up the basic system, operate with the HAL, which increases portability between hardware platforms and operates below the kernel in privileged mode to access system data and hardware to make their access transparent to the operating system. The kernel and NT Executive handle thread scheduling, message passing, device drivers, and virtual memory allocation. Collectively these modules are referred to as *kernel mode.* The NT Executive serves as the interface between the kernel and the client subsystems.

export server In LAN Manager, file replication synchronizes the files on one server to another server. The server originating the replication is called the *export server*; the destination server is called the *import server*.

F

fairness To keep one adapter from keeping the bus when others need it, the IEEE developed a concept called *fairness.* Some vendor drivers implement fairness; others do not. If a driver doesn't implement fairness, the best idea is to place it at the highest DMA channel available. This usually solves the problem.

Fast Ethernet Fast Ethernet, also called 100BASE-T, operates at 10 or 100Mbps per second over UTP, STP, or fiber-optic media.

FAT The File Allocation Table (FAT) is the file system DOS uses to store and recall files.

fault-tolerance Fault-tolerance is provided in many network operating systems to protect data and system resources. Among the fault-tolerance methods are Hot Fix, disk mirroring, and disk duplexing, which are used by Microsoft and Novell client/server implementations.

FCS The Frame Check Sequence (FCS) is used for error checking.

FDDI The Fiber Distributed Data Interface (FDDI) is a 100Mbps access method that has a dual-counter-rotating ring topology and uses the token-passing protocol.

fiber-optic Fiber-optic is a type of cable used for high-speed transmission.

file server A file server is a dedicated or nondedicated machine that provides file services to clients on a network.

frame   The frame indicates the datagram and the Data Link protocol headers and control information. Frames travel across the medium. They consist of data and information required to transmit the data to the proper node on the network. Data packets may be divided into several frames for transmission across the media. The maximum frame size conforms to the maximum packet size of the access method. For example, the maximum frame size for Ethernet is 1,518 bytes. In Ethernet, there are four frame types: 802.2, 802.3, Ethernet_II, and Ethernet_SNAP.

FTP   File Transfer Protocol. FTP is a connection-oriented protocol that is part of the TCP/IP suite.

full-duplex Ethernet

A new development, full-duplex Ethernet, allows adapters to transmit and receive data at the same time, thus increasing network bandwidth. Full-duplex Ethernet requires duplex-enabled adapters and devices.

G

gateway   A gateway links computers that use different data formats together.

GBps   Gigabytes per second. 1,0243 bytes per second.

Gbps   Gigabits per second. 1,0243 bits per second.

GOSIP   The Government Open System Interconnection Profile represents the U.S. government's plan to migrate its systems to OSI standards.

group   Groups consist of several user machines that have similar characteristics such as being in the same department.

H

HAL   The Hardware Abstraction Layer is a dynamic-link library (DLL) that protects the Windows NT kernel and NT Executive from variations in hardware. The HAL implements I/O interfaces, interrupt controllers, and communication mechanisms.

header
The header is attached to the front of a packet to identify it to successive protocol layers.

hermaphroditic
Type I token-ring uses hermaphroditic connectors to join the medium to the multistation access unit.

host
In networks, the host is loosely referred to as the system that provides services to all the other machines.

HPFS
The High Performance File System is a Microsoft OS/2-based file system that provides increased performance over DOS FAT file systems. LAN Manager requires an upgraded HPFS386 that operates only on 386- or 486-class machines to provide additional security.

HSM
Hardware Support Module. In NetWare's Open Data-Link Interface, the adapter vendor provides the HSM as its server driver for the adapter.

hub
A hub consists of a hardware device that attaches each node to the network.

hybrid
Hybrid refers to a mix of topologies.

I

IAB
Internet Activities Board.

ICA
The ICA is a communications adapter used for internetwork communications.

ICMP
The Internet Control Message Protocol provides diagnostic features.

IEEE
Institute of Electrical and Electronic Engineers.

IETF
Internet Engineering Task Force.

import server
In LAN Manager, file replication synchronizes the files on one server to another server. The server originating the replication is called the *export server*; the destination server is called the *import server*.

Intelligent Messaging
IM is Banyan VINES' messaging system.

Internet   The Internet is a worldwide network of dissimilar machines origi-
                        nated by the Department of Defense.

Internet address
                        To participate in Internet communications and on Internet
                        Protocol–based networks, a node must have an Internet address
                        that identifies it to the other nodes. All Internet addresses are IP
                        addresses.

internetwork   An internetwork consists of collections of networks connected to
                        each other over a local or geographically dispersed area.

Internetwork Packet Exchange/Sequenced Packet Exchange (IPX/SPX)
                        IPX/SPX are network transport protocols developed by Novell as
                        the primary transport protocol for its network operating systems.
                        They are derived from the Xerox Network Services protocols.
                        Microsoft has rewritten IPX/SPX as the default transport protocols
                        for Windows NT 3.5.

Inter-repeater Link (IRL)
                        The segment between two repeaters is called the *inter-repeater link*.
                        Sometimes the IRL is also called an *unpopulated segment*, as it does
                        not contain stations or other devices.

IOS   I/O Supervisor.

IP   The Internet Protocol provides connectionless transmission of data
                        on TCP/IP networks.

IP address   *See* Internet address. Not all IP addresses guarantee access to the
                        Internet.

IRQ   Interrupt Request Line. Nodes use interrupts to communicate data
                        over the system bus.

ISA   Industry Standard Architecture. ISA is a 16-bit bus architecture
                        commonly found in PCs.

ISDN   Integrated Services Digital Network. ISDN is a wide-area commu-
                        nication service.

IS-IS   Intermediate System to Intermediate System (IS-IS) is an OSI dis-
                        covery protocol Intermediate routers use to discover each other.

ISO   International Standards Organization. ISO developed the Open
                        Systems Interconnect (OSI) model for networking. This organiza-
                        tion is represented in the United States by ANSI.

ITT	Invitation-to-Transmit. In ARCNET, the ITT represents the token, the special packet that gives nodes permission to transmit data on the network.
ITU	International Telecommunications Union. The ITU-T is also called the Comite Consultatif Internationale de Telephonie and Telegraphie (CCITT). It is based in Geneva, Switzerland. Standards promulgated by the CCITT are also known as ITU standards.

J

jabber	Jabber is a signal on a 10BASE-T network that it is out of specification and disrupts network traffic.

K

KBps	Kilobytes per second. 1,024 bytes per second.
Kbps	Kilobits per second. 1,024 bits per second.
kernel	The kernel in Windows NT manages the processor, including thread scheduling, interrupt and exception handling, and multi-processor synchronization. NetWare also has a kernel that provides core network operating services.

L

LAM	Lobe Access Module. The part of an IBM active MAU that connects the MAU to the ring.
LAN	Local Area Network.
LAN adapter	The LAN adapter is hardware that connects the PC to the network and allows it to communicate.
LAN Manager	LAN Manager is a Microsoft server-based network operating system.

LAN Server

OS/2 LAN Server is an IBM server- and peer-to-peer-based network operating system.

LANtastic   LANtastic is a peer-to-peer network operating system from Artisoft.

LAP   The Link Access Protocol provides Data-Link Layer protocols for AppleTalk using ELAP, LLAP, or TLAP.

learning bridge

Bridges used to be programmed manually with network addresses; when a node moved, the bridge had to be reprogrammed. Luckily, bridge manufacturers developed learning bridges to overcome this problem. There are two types of learning bridges, called *transparent* and *source routing bridging*.

linear bus   *See* bus.

link training In 100VG-AnyLAN, link training is part of the OSI Data-Link Layer specification. Link training allows the Ethernet hub to verify the medium between the hub and the node, as well as determine information about the node including type, operational mode, and MAC-layer address.

LLAP   The LocalTalk Link Access protocol provides LocalTalk connectivity for AppleTalk.

LLC   *See* Logical Link Control.

lobe wire   The network cable that extends from the adapter to the token-ring MAU. The lobe wire receives and transmits information.

LocalTalk   The AppleTalk protocol operates on LocalTalk networks, which allow data to be transmitted at 230 characters per second.

Logical Link Control (LLC)

This component multiplexes and demultiplexes packets received from other Network Layer protocols. The LLC is specified in the IEEE 802.2 specification.

LSL   Link Support Layer. In ODI, the Link Support Layer routes packets between the MLID and the protocol stacks.

M

MAC frame   Media Access Control (MAC) frame. This is the upper-layer packet relayed to the adapter and broken into frames for transmission over the media.

main ring   FDDI networks consist of two rings: a main ring and a secondary ring. Data transfer takes place on the main ring. In the event of main ring failure, the secondary ring is used.

Main Ring Length (MRL)
              The aggregate amount of wire located in the MAUs, between MAUs, and between the farthest ports (MLL).

MAN   Metropolitan Area Network

Manchester encoding
              Manchester encoding is a form of signal encoding used in Ethernet networks.

MAU   Multistation Access Unit. The MAU is the central wiring device through which token-ring adapters communicate with the network. MAUs may be active powered, passive powered, or passive non-powered devices.

MAU   Medium or Media Attachment Unit

Maximum Lobe Length (MLL)
              The longest length of medium from the adapter to the MAU. This distance is a function of the Main Ring Length (MRL).

MBps   1,0242 bits per second.

Mbps   1,0242 bits per second.

MCA   Micro Channel Architecture. Micro Channel is a bus interface developed by IBM for its PS/2 model computers.

media   Media are the cables that join network devices together. Numerous types of media are available: shielded twisted-pair, unshielded twisted-pair, coaxial, and fiber-optic. Nontraditional wireless, infrared, and satellite media also exist.

Media Interface Connection (MIC)
              The MIC is the keyed connector used to attach the FDDI adapter to the cable.

MHz   Megahertz.

MIB   Management Information Base. In SNMP, gathered information is stored in the Management Information Base.

MIC   Media Interface Connector. In FDDI, the MIC represents the fiber-optic connector.

MLID   Multiple Link Interface Driver. The MLID represents the LAN driver in NetWare ODI networks.

MLL   *See* Maximum Lobe Length.

MNET   MNET is a performance management tool.

MPR   Multiprotocol Router (NetWare). MPR is a software-based router for NetWare LANs.

MRL   *See* Main Ring Length.

MSL   Mirrored Server Link. The MSL is used in NetWare SFT Level III to join mirrored file servers together. It consists of two LAN adapters and special LAN drivers.

MSM   Media Support Module. The MSM is the interface between the MLID and the HSM in ODI.

multimode   Multimode is a type of fiber-optic medium used by ARCNET, Ethernet, token-ring, and FDDI.

multitasking Multitasking is the operating system's method for sharing a single processor among multiple threads—the operating system can handle more than one process at a time.

MUSER   System administrators use MUSER to create users and assign or modify access rights.

N

NAUN   Next Active Upstream Neighbor. In a token-ring or FDDI network, the NAUN is the node in a clockwise relation to the present node. The NAUN passes frames to the downstream neighbor.

NBF   NetBIOS Frame. NBF provides Windows NT's Network and Transport Layer services by encapsulating SMB data for transport via the access method across the network. Like NetBIOS and NetBEUI, it is not routable.

NBP   The Name Binding Protocol translates node IDs into network names.

NBT   NetBIOS over TCP/IP.

NCP   NetWare Core Protocol. NCP is a service protocol used by NetWare or Windows NT 3.5, which consists of requests and responses between network partners.

NCP   This protocol is also known as the Network Control Protocol. Do not confuse it with the NetWare Core Protocol (NCP).

NDIS   Network Driver Interface Specification. NDIS is a protocol interface used in OS/2 LAN Server, LAN Manager, VINES, Windows NT Advanced Server, and Windows NT 3.5 networks to provide a standard method for LAN driver and protocol development. It lets DOS- and OS/2-based machines support multiple network adapters and protocol drivers.

NetBEUI NetBEUI is a protocol used in Windows NT Advanced Server and 3.5 and LAN Manager environments. It provides more features than NetBIOS and operates at the OSI Network and Transport layers. It was developed by IBM and Microsoft to integrate with NetBIOS to form an efficient communications system.

NetBIOS Network Basic Input/Output Specification. NetBIOS is an API and protocol developed by IBM and Sytek for data transport across a network. NetBIOS provides messaging, printing, and file server functions in Microsoft peer-to-peer implementations.

NetBIOS Frame
      See NBF.

NetWare NetWare is a server-based operating system developed by Novell, which has an 80 percent market share.

NetWare Lite Protocol
      In NetWare Lite, the first implementation of Novell's peer-to-peer network, the NetWare Lite Protocol replaces IPX as the transport protocol.

NetWare Loadable Module
      See NLM.

network   A network consists of a collection of two or more devices, people, or components that communicate with each other over physical or virtual media.

network-centric
In a network-centric network, the user logs into the network rather than into a file server.

network interface adapter
See LAN adapter.

Network Information File (NIF)
The NIF is a descriptor file for device drivers that defines configuration characteristics for the drivers during installation.

Network Layer
The Network Layer of the OSI Model is responsible for routing information between peer partners and between different networks. Its protocols provide a best-effort, nonguaranteed delivery system and seldom employ error control. Common Network Layer protocols are the Internetwork Packet Exchange (IPX) protocol and the Internet Protocol (IP), both of which are used by NetWare and Windows NT 3.5.

network operating system
The network operating system provides the intelligence for the collection of networked devices. It provides a means of sharing resources and information, access to the network, and other services.

NEXT   Near-End Crosstalk. NEXT occurs when wire pairs are adjacent to each other and the signals on the pairs cross over, creating crosstalk.

NFS   Network File System. NFS is an Application Layer file system and protocol used by UNIX-based Sun and other workstation-based network operating systems.

NIC   Network Interface Card. In a network workstation or server, the NIC is the intelligent hardware that allows the PC to communicate with the network.

NLM   NetWare Loadable Module. An NLM is a program loaded at the file server which becomes an integral part of the network operating system. NLMs may be network management programs, NetWare utilities such as MONITOR, backup software, LAN drivers, or other device drivers.

NLSP   NetWare Link Service Protocol. In NetWare, NLSP can be used to replace RIPs and SAPs, thus reducing unnecessary traffic in internetworks and wide-area networks.

node   Networks consist of nodes—computers or other devices—that request or provide network services. A node may be a server, printer, user workstation, or other specialized device such as a concentrator used in particular network access methods. The number of nodes allowed on a network depends on the access method the network uses.

NOS   Network Operating System. A network operating system is software that allows PCs to communicate with each other.

NRZI   Non-Return-to-Zero, Invert on Ones. NRZI is a form of signal encoding for FDDI signals.

N-series connector
                  This connector connects thick Ethernet cables to network devices. Male N-series connectors attach the medium to the network device. Female connectors are used on the network device.

NSFnet   This network is also known as the National Science Foundation network.

NT   New Technology. NT is Microsoft's peer-to-peer and server-based network operating system.

NTFS   NT File System. NTFS is the advanced file system Microsoft Windows NT uses.

NWLink   A protocol that allows NetWare workstations to access a Windows NT server.

0

ODI   Open Data-Link Interface. ODI is a specification for writing NetWare LAN adapters and protocols.

ODINSUP   This file is used to join NetWare clients to LAN Manager and Windows NT LANs.

operating system
> The operating system provides the intelligence for the client work-stations and other PC devices on the network that allow them to share data and resources.

OSI
> Open Systems Interconnection. OSI represents a reference model for network communication.

OSPF
> Open Shortest Path First is an Open Systems Interconnect (OSI) link-state routing protocol.

P

packet
> Packets consist of data and additional information required to transmit data to the proper network node. Packets are broken into frames for transmission across the medium. They contain identifying information, data, and control information that provides error checking. The size of a packet is dictated by the network's transport protocol and service protocols.

PAP
> The Printer Access Protocol provides network printer services.

passive hub
> A wiring device that splits the signal to the network nodes on a bus-topology network. A passive hub may connect a maximum of four devices. The passive hub does not regenerate or amplify the signal. Two passive hubs can not be contiguous in a bus.

passive powered MAU
> An AC-powered MAU that does not actively retime or retransmit signals. Applying power to the device resets the relays. Many passive, powered MAUs have diagnostic LEDs the network manager can monitor for indications of trouble.

PCI
> The Peripheral Components Interface is a bus architecture for PCs.

PCM
> Physical Connection Management. This component covers physical connection management between a managed port and another port in the adjacent node.

PCN
> IBM PC Network. The PCN was IBM's first attempt at local area networking.

peer-to-peer   Protocols dictate how communication takes place between equal entities on the network. It also represents a network in which all nodes are equals—each node may act as either a server or a client.

phantom voltage

In CSMA/CD networks, nodes listen for the presence of a phantom voltage before communicating.

PHY   *See* Physical Layer.

Physical Layer Medium Independent (PHY)

This component deals with the part of the Physical Layer that does not depend on the network medium. The PHY specifies the algorithms to overcome clock rate differences among stations.

Physical Layer Medium Dependent (PMD)

The PMD is the portion of the ANSI standard for the protocol that handles the physical connection to the medium. It includes the standards for Physical Layer Medium Dependent; single-mode fiber-optic Physical Layer Medium Dependent; and new standards for copper-based media access.

Physical Layer The Physical Layer is the lowest layer of the OSI Model. It defines the characteristics of the medium and the data flowing across it, including encoding, frequency, connector type, and medium type.

PMD   Physical Medium Dependent Layer.

preemptive multitasking

This mechanism allows a process with a greater priority to interrupt a currently running process rather than wait for the lower-level process to complete. If a process such as disk I/O becomes bogged down because of a slow hard drive, another process can take over the processor, reducing the number of wasted process cycles.

Presentation Layer

The Presentation Layer is the sixth layer in the OSI Model and is responsible for data representation, including format and encoding.

process   A process is a part of a program operating on the network.

propagation delay

CSMA/CD networks are characterized by propagation delay, which consists of the time lapse between nodes on the Ethernet segment.

protocol   Communication on the network is governed by sets of rules called *protocols*. Protocols provide the guidelines devices use to communicate with each other, and thus they have different functions. Some protocols are responsible for formatting and presenting data that will be transferred from file server memory to the file server's network adapter. Others are responsible for filtering information between networks and forwarding data to its destination. Still other protocols dictate how data is transferred across the medium, and how servers respond to workstation requests and vice versa. Common network protocols responsible for the presentation and formatting of data for a network operating system are the Internetwork Packet Exchange (IPX) protocol or the Internet Protocol (IP). Protocols that dictate the format of data for transfer across the medium include token-passing and Carrier Sense Multiple Access with Collision Detection (CSMA/CD), implemented as token-ring, ARCNET, FDDI, or Ethernet. The Router Information Protocol (RIP), a part of the Transmission Control Protocol/Internet Protocol (TCP/IP) suite, forwards packets from one network to another using the same network protocol.

protocol driver
                      The protocol driver provides higher-level communication services from the Data Link through Application layers such as NetBIOS.

PROTOCOL.INI
                      The PROTOCOL.INI file contains configuration and binding information for NDIS drivers and protocols.

R

RAID   Redundant Arrays of Independent (Inexpensive) Disks. What ever the I stands for, RAID consists of a group of disks with varying functions.

RARP   Reverse Address Resolution Protocol provides physical adapter-to-IP address resolution.

reassembly   In communication, data packets are divided into frames for transport across the medium. At the destination end, these frames must be reassembled to form the original packet.

recons	In ARCNET, when a node enters or leaves the network, it issues a reconfiguration blast, called a recon, that disrupts network traffic and notifies other nodes that it is present on the network or leaving the network. Excessive recons can reduce network performance and may indicate cabling or adapter problems.
redirector	The redirector consists of software that handles workstation requests for local or network service. For local requests to a hard or diskette drive, the redirector hands those requests to the client operating system; requests for network services are handed to the network operating system.
repeater	A repeater is used to join network segments of the same medium type together. Repeaters amplify the data signal across distance. It also regenerates and retimes signals to increase the cable segment's transmission distance. Repeaters can be managed and used to connect dissimilar segments.
requester	*See* redirector.
resource	Each network consists of numerous devices and entities called *resources*. A print server may provide printing resources to network users. A user's workstation hard disk may be a resource for shared data on the network. A file server provides file- and data-sharing resources.
RG-62 A/U	The type of coaxial medium used by ARCNET LANs.
ring	The path of the electrical signal in FDDI and token-ring. It travels from node to node until it reaches to the original sending station. In token-ring networks, the frame travels from the source adapter to stations intervening between it and the frame's destination. The destination adapter reads the frame, copies it to its buffers, updates a field in the frame indicating that the frame has been received, and strips the token from the frame before releasing it to the next physical workstation on the ring. If the destination workstation fails to strip the token from the frame, the source workstation strips, then releases the token to the next active physically attached node in a counterclockwise order.
RIP	Router Information Protocol (TCP/IP).
RIP	Routing Information Protocol (NetWare). In NetWare, routers exchange information about their networks by using RIP packets.

router   A router is the network software or hardware entity charged with routing packets between networks.

RIPL   Remote Initial Program Load (RIPL) allows booting a requester from the files contained on a server. It allows diskless workstations to participate in network resources.

RTMP   The Routing Table Maintenance Protocol maintains routing tables on the network.

S

SAA   Systems Application Architecture. SAA is IBM's umbrella architecture for network and data communications.

SAC   Single-Attach Concentrator. A SAC attaches to a single FDDI ring.

SAP   Service Advertising Protocol. NetWare and Windows NT 3.5 use SAPs to let other network devices know of their presence.

SAS   Single Attach Station. An SAS is a workstation that attaches to one ring in an FDDI network.

secondary ring FDDI networks consist of two rings: a primary ring and a secondary ring. The secondary ring provides redundancy in the event of primary ring failure.

segment   The segment is the length of medium between the network adapter and the concentrator on 10BASE-T networks. On 10BASE-2 and 10BASE-5 networks, a segment contains workstations or transceivers.

sequence   The sequence is the order frames are transmitted in TCP transmissions.

server   In a network, a machine that provides services to user workstations and other devices is called a *server*. Servers may share data or provide other services such as printing to the network. Several kinds of servers exist. There are print servers, database servers, application servers, communication servers, fax servers, and mail servers. Each server may be dedicated to a particular function (or functions). Print servers control and centralize the printing resources on the network. Communication servers provide remote communication services to network users or users calling in over modems to the network. Database servers congregate data- and disk-intensive database operations, relieving other servers of these tasks. Servers may be dedicated to server processes or nondedicated. Several servers may also exist on the same machine.

server-centric   In a server-centric network, users log into the server.

Session Layer   The Session Layer, the fifth layer in the OSI Model, is responsible for creating, maintaining and terminating connections or sessions between communication partners.

SFT   System Fault Tolerance. NetWare has implemented three forms of SFT: SFT Levels I, II, and III. SFT provides bad disk redirection, duplicate FAT tables, disk mirroring and duplexing, and server mirroring.

shared applications

These application programs are located on a server and used as network resources by client requesters.

Single-Attach Concentrator (SAC)

The SAC is a concentrator that allows nodes to attach to a single ring. This concentrator creates branches from the main ring.

Single-Attach Station (SAS)

The SAS is a station that attaches to a single ring of the dual rings.

SIP   The Simple Internet Protocol is designed to replace IP as the shortage of IP addresses grows.

SLIP   Serial Line IP is a transmission protocol for serial line communication.

SMP   Symmetric multiprocessing extends the multitasking model to more than one processor. A single processor can only execute one thread at a time. A multiprocessing model allows a single thread to execute on each processor in a system with multiple processors. Thus, multiple threads can execute at one time. Symmetric multiprocessing is simply a way of assigning the threads to the processors. In asymmetric multiprocessing, a processor is assigned a particular type of thread, such as system I/O. If there is no I/O to be performed, the processor is idle. In the symmetric multiprocessing model, tasks are assigned to the first processor available. If the processor finishes before another, it is assigned another task to perform. This method is harder to implement, but provides superior performance.

SMT
: Station Management. This is a management layer in the FDDI communications model responsible for preallocating the bandwidth necessary for the communication.

SMTP
: The Simple Mail Transfer Protocol is used for Internet mail.

SNA
: Systems Network Architecture.

SNAP
: The Subnetwork Access Protocol is part of the Logical Link Control (LLC) Layer required for TCP/IP transmission.

SNMP
: Simple Network Management Protocol. SNMP was designed to provide a common foundation for managing network devices.

socket
: The socket represents the address in an application for transmission of data.

source address
: The source address refers to the address of the node that sent the packet.

source routing
: There are two types of learning bridges, called *transparent* and *source routing bridging*. In source routing, the node rather than the router determines the path to a destination.

source/transparent bridge
: A bridge that combines both Ethernet and token-ring uses a combination of the two methods called a *source-transparent bridge*.

spanning tree
: The problems associated with transparent bridging led to the development of the Spanning Tree Algorithm. The spanning tree protocol, which is maintained by the IEEE 801.2-D committee, detects circular paths between networks. It stops looping in redundant bridges by shutting down the secondary bridge until needed.

SPX
: Sequenced Packet Exchange. SPX is a Transport Layer protocol NetWare uses for guarantee delivery of data. It is rarely used except in diagnostic applications.

star
: The star is a topology that ARCNET, Ethernet, and token-ring use. In a star topology, each device connects to the network via its own length of cable.

station
: In LANs, a station consists of a device that can communicate data on the network. In FDDI, a station includes both physical nodes and addressable logical devices. Workstations, single-attach stations, dual-attach stations, and concentrators are FDDI stations.

Station Management Algorithm (SMT)
> The SMT algorithm provides the station's management functions.

STP   Shielded twisted-pair.

StreetTalk StreetTalk is Banyan VINES' directory services organization.

subnet mask
> In TCP/IP, the bits used to create the subnet are called the subnet mask.

T

TCNS   Thomas-Conrad Networking System. TCNS is a 100Mbps proprietary access method that uses fiber-optic, RG-62 A/U, shielded twisted-pair and unshielded-twisted-pair media. TCNS is wired in a star or distributed-star topology.

TCP   The Transmission Control Protocol provides connection-oriented transmission on a TCP/IP network.

(TCP/IP)   Transmission Control Protocol/Internet Protocol is a widely used transport protocol that connects diverse computers of various transmission methods. It was developed by the Department of Defense to connect different computer types and led to the development of the Internet.

TELNET   TELNET is the TCP/IP remote login protocol.

terminal   Terminal refers to the user input device in mainframe or minicomputer host/terminal networks. A terminal is nonintelligent—it is not able to perform without the presence of the host computer. It simply presents screens of information to users and provides a mechanism for responding with input to host requests. Intelligent workstations, those with their own microprocessors, may act as terminals by using terminal emulation programs to access host-based applications over a network gateway. Terminals are called *dumb terminals*.

TFTP   Trivial File Transfer Protocol.

thick Ethernet
> Called 10BASE-5 Ethernet, this was the original implementation of bus-based Ethernet.

thin Ethernet

Called 10BASE-2 Ethernet, this implementation uses RG-58 coaxial cable on a bus topology.

thread

A thread is an executable entity that belongs to one process. It consists of a program counter, mode stack, and register values. Each thread has equal access to the processor's address space.

throughput

Throughput indicates the speed of the network. Network communication is measured in bits per second. For example although Ethernet is a 10Mbps access method, its realistic throughput is 600–1,200Kbps.

TLAP

The TokenTalk Link Access Protocol provides token-ring connectivity for AppleTalk.

token

The token is a special packet used by token-ring, ARCNET, and FDDI to designate the device that has permission to transmit data.

token bus

Token bus is represented by IEEE 802.4. It is a token-passing bus topology that has seen limited implementation in General Motors' MAP/TOP.

token-passing

Token-passing is one of the two forms of communication used in LANs. Token-passing protocols are token-ring, ARCNET, and FDDI. In these access methods, a token grants a network device permission to transmit data.

TokenTalk

TokenTalk is the token-ring implementation of the AppleTalk protocol suite.

token-passing

Token-passing is a deterministic protocol that requires a node to have permission to transmit by possessing a token. The token passes around the network, addressed to each adapter in turn.

token-ring

Token-ring is a network access method that is wired as a physical star and uses a token to regulate workstation ability to send data.

Token-Ring Interface Controller (TIC)

The TIC is the adapter in an AS/400 midrange computer, a frontend processor (FEP) for a mainframe computer, or in an IBM 327x-type controller that congregates signals sent from the LAN to the other device.

topology

The topology represents the shape of the network. Networks can be wired as bus, star, or ring topologies. Topology may be physical or logical and is dictated by the access method used. For example, Ethernet networks may be wired as buses, stars, or distributed stars. Token-ring networks are logical rings wired as physical rings.

transceiver   A transceiver joins two network segments together. Transceivers can also be used to join a segment that uses one medium to a segment that uses a different medium. On a 10BASE-5 network, the transceiver connects the network adapter or other network device to the medium. Transceivers also can be used on 10BASE-2 or 10BASE-T networks to attach devices with AUI ports.

transport protocol

The transport protocol is responsible for conveying data between the Data Link through Application Layers of the OSI Model. Common transport protocols are IPX and IP. The transport protocol is encapsulated in the data-link protocol for transmission across the medium.

TREL   Transaction Release closes transactions in ATP.

TRESP   Transaction Response responds to a transaction request in ATP.

TREQ   Transaction Request asks for a transaction session in ATP.

TROPIC   Token Ring Protocol Interface Controller. The TROPIC chip set is a 100 percent register-level IBM-compatible chip set used by a number of vendors in the manufacture of token-ring adapters.

terminator   A terminator is used on the end of a coaxial cable to terminate the medium. In Ethernet, the cable termination value is 50 ohms.

trunk   The trunk is the cable segment on a 10BASE-2 or 10BASE-5 network.

TSB   Technical Service Bulletin.

TSM   Topology Support Module. The TSM represents the ODI NLM in the NetWare file for access method type.

TSR   Terminate-and-Stay-Resident. A TSR is a program that is loaded into the workstation's RAM. SNMP agents and client requester software may run as TSRs.

TTS   Transaction Tracking System. In NetWare, TTS is responsible for maintaining the integrity of transaction-type data. In the event of a server failure, TTS rolls back a transaction to its beginning, thus disposing of bad data.

U

UDP   The User Datagram Protocol is a connectionless protocol that resides above IP in the TCP/IP suite.

ULP   The upper-layer protocol refers to Application Layer protocols such as FTP, SNMP, and SMTP.

upstream   In a token-ring or FDDI network, the upstream neighbor passes the token to the downstream neighbor in a counterclockwise fashion.

USERNAME   The USERNAME is the unique name assigned to each person who has access to the LAN.

UTP   Unshielded twisted-pair. UTP is a form of cable used by all access methods. It consists of several pairs of wires enclosed in an unshielded sheath.

V

vampire tap   The vampire tap cuts directly into and attaches to 10BASE-2 or 10BASE-5 media to allow stations to attach without the need to splice the media or use a T-connector. Many 10BASE-5 transceivers include a vampire tap to make connections to the medium easier.

Vanguard   Vanguard represents the security mechanism in Banyan VINES.

VAP   Value-Added Process. A Value-Added Process is a program or series of programs that operate on a NetWare v2.x file server.

VINES   Virtual Network System. VINES is a preemptive, multitasking, server-based network operating system developed by Banyan Systems.

VFS   VINES File System. VFS is the file system specification used by Banyan VINES.

VINES IP   VINES Internet Protocol. VINES IP is the proprietary network transport protocol Banyan VINES uses.

VLM   Virtual Loadable Modules consist of programs that are dynamically loaded and unloaded within NetWare v3.x and v4.x.

virtual memory

Virtual memory provides the means to allocate more memory to the operating system and applications than is physically available on the computer. As system memory runs low, part of the memory is swapped to disk to free up more memory for other processes.

W

WAN

Wide-Area Network. A wide-area network consists of groups of interconnected computers that are separated by a wide distance and communicate with each other via common carrier telecommunication techniques.

WFW

Windows for Workgroups. WFW is a peer-to-peer network operating system from Microsoft.

Windows

Windows is a graphical user interface for workstations that use DOS.

Windows for Workgroups

Windows for Workgroups is a peer-to-peer network operating system from Microsoft.

Windows NT 3.5

Windows NT 3.5 is a server-based and peer-to-peer network operating system from Microsoft.

Windows NT Advanced Server

Windows NTAS is the server-based network operating system from Microsoft that preceded Windows NT 3.5.

WINS

Windows Internet Naming Service is a protocol that locates network resources in an IP network by automatically configuring and maintaining the computer name and IP-address tables.

workgroup

A workgroup is a group of users who are physically located together and connected to the same LAN, or a group of users who are scattered throughout an organization but are logically connected by work and are connected to the same network group.

workstations

Workstation refers to the intelligent computer on the user's desktop. This computer may be an Intel-based PC, a Macintosh, or a UNIX-based workstation. The workstation is any intelligent device a user works from.

Windows Open Systems Architecture (WOSA)
> WOSA is Microsoft's strategy to assist developers in building work-group-enabling features for the Windows environment.

X

X.25   X.25 is a Physical Layer wide-area networking implementation that uses public data networks.

XNS   Xerox Network System. XNS is the a network transport protocol developed by Xerox. NetWare's IPX is derived from XNS.

Z

ZIP   The Zone Information Protocol maintains the network zone tables.

Zone   A zone consists of an logical configuration of network devices in an AppleTalk network.

appendix

VENDOR LIST

B

These are some of the vendors that make products for the technologies discussed in this book.

ADAPTERS (ARCNET)

3Com Corp. (Ethernet, FDDI, token-ring)
5400 Bayfront Plaza
Santa Clara, Calif. 95052-8145
(800) NET-3COM
(415) 764-5000
Fax (408) 764-5001

Accton Technology Corp. (Ethernet, token-ring)
1962 Zanker Road
San Jose, Calif. 95112
(800) 926-9288
(408) 452-8900
Fax (408) 452-8988

Addtron Technology Inc. (ARCnet, Ethernet, token-ring)
47968 Fremont Blvd.
Fremont, Calif. 94538
(800) 998-4638
Fax (510) 770-0120

Alfa Inc. (Ethernet, FDDI)
325 E. North Ave.
Westfield, N.J. 07090
(908) 789-2068
Fax (908) 789-2403

Allied Telesis Inc. (Ethernet)
575 E. Middlefield Road
Mountain View, Calif. 94043
(800) 424-4284
Fax (415) 964-8250

Alta Research Corp. (Ethernet, token-ring)
600 S. Federal Highway
Deerfield Beach, Fla. 33441
(800) 423-8535
(305) 428-8535
Fax (305) 428-8678

Andrew Corp. (token-ring)
10500 W. 153rd St.
Orland Park, Ill. 60462
(800) 328-2696

Artisoft Inc. (Ethernet)
2202 N. Forbes Blvd.
Tucson, Ariz. 85745
(800) 233-5564
Fax (602) 670-7359

Asante Technologies Inc. (Ethernet, token-ring)
821 Fox Lane
San Jose, Calif. 95131
(800) 662-9686
(408) 438-8388
Fax (408) 432-7511

Boca Research Inc. (Ethernet)
6413 Congress Avenue
Boca Raton, Fla. 33487
(407) 997-6227
Fax (407) 997-0918

Cabletron Systems (Ethernet, FDDI, token-ring)
35 Industrial Way
Rochester, N.H. 03867
(603) 332-9400
Fax (603) 337-2444

Cache Computers Inc. (Ethernet)
46600 Landings Parkway
Fremont, Calif. 94538
(510) 226-9922
Fax (510) 226-9911

Cactus Computer (LocalTalk)
1120 Metrocrest Drive, Suite 103
Carrollton, Tex. 75006
(214) 416-0525

Canary Communications Inc. (Ethernet)
1851 Zanker Road
San Jose, Calif. 95112-9201
(800) 883-9201
(408) 453-9201
Fax (408) 453-0940

Cisco Systems, Inc. (FDDI)
930 E. Arquez Avenue
Sunnyvale, Calif. 94086
(800) 238-2334
(408) 526-4000
Fax (408) 526-8401

CNet Technology Corp. (ARCnet, Ethernet,
    token-ring)
2199 Zanker Road
San Jose, Calif. 95131
(408) 954-8000
Fax (408) 954-8866

Codenoll Technology Corp. (Ethernet, FDDI)
1086 N. Broadway
Yonkers, N.Y. 10701
(914) 965-6300
Fax (914) 965-9811

Cogent Data Technologies Inc. (Ethernet)
175 West St., P.O. Box 926
Friday Harbor, Wash. 98250
(800) 426-4368
(206) 378-2929
Fax (206) 378-2882

Compex Inc. (ARCnet, Ethernet, token-ring)
4051 E. La Palma
Anaheim, Calif. 92807
(800) 279-8891, pin #1071
(714) 630-7302
Fax (714) 630-6521

CompuLAN Inc. (ARCnet, Ethernet, token-ring)
1630 Oakland Road, Suite A111
San Jose, Calif. 95131
(408) 432-8899
Fax (408) 432-8699

Contemporary Control Systems (ARCnet)
Rock Landing Corporate Center
11846 Rock Landing
Newport News, Va. 23606
(800) 873-9000

Cray Communications (Ethernet)
9020 Junction Drive
Annapolis Junction, Md. 20701
(800) FOR-CRAY
(301) 317-7710
Fax (408) 270-1170

D-Link Systems Inc. (ARCnet, Ethernet, token-
ring)
5 Musick
Irvine, Calif. 92718
(800) 326-1688
(714) 455-1688
Fax (714) 713-6331

Danpex Corp. (ARCnet, Ethernet, token-ring)
1342 Ridder Park Drive
San Jose, Calif. 85131
(800) 452-1551
(408) 437-7557
Fax (408) 437-7559

Dayna Communications (Ethernet, LocalTalk)
Sorenson Research Park
849 W. Levoy Drive
Salt Lake City, Utah 84123
(801) 269-7200

DCA (token-ring)
1000 Alderman Drive
Alpharetta, Ga. 30202
(800) 348-3221
Fax (404) 442-4366

DFI (Ethernet)
135 Main Avenue
Sacramento, Calif. 95838
(916) 568-1234
Fax (916) 568-1233

Digital Equipment Corp. (Ethernet, FDDI)
550 King St., LKG1-3/J17
Littleton, Mass. 01480
(800) DIGITAL
(508) 486-6963
Fax (508) 486-6311

Eagle Technology (Ethernet)
2202 N. Forbes Blvd.
Tucson, Ariz. 85745

EFA Corp. (Ethernet)
3040 Oakmead Village Drive
Santa Clara, Calif. 95051
(408) 987-5400
Fax (408) 987-5415

Elisa Technology Inc. (Ethernet)
4368 Enterprise St.
Fremont, Calif. 94538
(510) 651-5817
Fax 510) 651-4834

Farallon Computing Inc. (Ethernet)
2470 Mariner Square Loop
Alameda, Calif. 94501-1010
(510) 814-5000
Fax (510) 814-5023

Grand Junction Networks (Ethernet)
47281 Bayside Parkway
Fremont, Calif. 94538
(510) 252-0726
Fax (510) 252-0915

GVC Technologies Inc. (Ethernet)
376 Lafayette Road
Sparta, N.M. 07871
(201) 579-3630
Fax (201) 579-2702

HTI Networks (Ethernet)
532 Weddell Drive, Suite 1
Sunnyvale, Calif. 94089
(408) 745-0101
Fax (408) 745-7711

Hewlett-Packard Co. (Ethernet)
8000 Foothills Blvd.
Roseville, Calif. 95747
(800) 533-1333
Fax (800) 333-1917

IBM Corp. (Ethernet, token-ring)
P.O. Box 12195, Department C09/8060
Research Triangle Park, N.C. 27709
(800) IBM-CALL
Fax (800) 2-IBMFAX

IBM Personal Computer Co. (Ethernet, token-ring)
Route 100
Somers, N.Y. 10589
(914) 766-1900
Fax (914) 766-0116

IMC Networks (Ethernet)
16931 Millikan Ave.
Irvine, Calif. 92714
(714) 724-1070
Fax (714) 724-1020

Intech (Ethernet)
28346 Pueblo Drive
Trabuco Canyon, Calif. 92679
(800) 552-5267
(714) 589-0164
Fax (714) 589-0999

Intel Corp. (Ethernet, token-ring)
5200 N.E. Elam Parkway
Hillsboro, Oreg. 97124
(800) 538-3373
Fax (800) 525-3019

Interphase Corp. (FDDI)
13800 Senlac
Dallas, Tex. 75234-8823
(800) FASTNET
(214) 919-9111

IQ Technologies (token-ring)
13625 N.E. 126th Place, Suite 400
Kirkland, Wash. 98034
(800) 227-2817
Fax (206) 821-3961

Katron Technologies Inc. (ARCnet, Ethernet, token-ring)
7400 Harwin Drive, Suite 120
Houston, Tex. 77036
(713) 266-3891
Fax (713) 266-3893

Kingston Technology Corp. (Ethernet, token-ring)

17600 Newhope St.
Fountain Valley, Calif. 92708
(800) 435-2620
(714) 435-2600
Fax (714) 435-2699

Klever Computers Inc. (Ethernet, token-ring)
1028 W. Maude Ave.
Sunnyvale, Calif. 94086
(800) 745-4660
Fax (408) 735-7723

LAN Performance Labs (Ethernet)
4901 Morena Blvd., Suite 805
San Diego, Calif. 92117
(800) 726-8101
(619) 273-1442
Fax (619) 273-2706

Lancast (Ethernet)
10 Northern Blvd., Unit 5
Amherst, N.H. 03031
(800) 752-2768
Fax (603) 881-9888

Madge Networks (FDDI, token-ring)
2310 N. First St.
San Jose, Calif. 95131
(800) 876-2343
(408) 955-0700
Fax (408) 955-0970

MagicRAM Inc. (token-ring)
1850 Beverly Blvd.
Los Angeles, Calif. 90057
(213) 413-9999
Fax (213) 413-0828

Microdyne Corp. (Ethernet, token-ring)
3601 Eisenhower Ave.
Alexandria, Va. 22304
(800) 255-3967
Fax (703) 683-8924

National Semiconductor Inc. (Ethernet, FDDI)
2900 Semiconductor Drive
Santa Clara, Calif. 95052-8090
(800) 227-1817
Network Peripherals (FDDI)

1371 McCarthy Blvd
Milpitas, Calif. 95035
(800) NPI-8855
(818) 321-9218

NetWorth (Ethernet)
8040 Esters Blvd.
Irving, Tex. 75063
(800) 544-5255
(214) 929-1700
Fax (214) 929-1720

New Media Corp. (Ethernet)
One Technology, Building A
Irvine, Calif. 92718
(714) 453-0100
(800) CARDS-4-U
Fax (714) 453-0114

Northern Telecom (FDDI)
620 W. Oakton St.
Morton Grove, Ill. 60053-2756
(800) 262-9334
Fax (800) 262-9334

Olicom USA Inc. (Ethernet, token-ring)
900 West Park Blvd., Suite 180
Plano, Tex. 75054
(800) 2-OLICOM
Fax (214) 423-7261

Protec Microsystems Inc. (Ethernet)
297 Labrosse
Pointe-Claire, Que. H9R 1A3
Canada
(800) 363-8156
Fax (514) 694-0973

Proteon Inc. (token-ring)
9 Technology Drive
Westborough, Mass. 01581
(508) 898-2800
Fax (366) 8901

Racal InterLan Inc. (Ethernet)
155 Swanson Road
Boxborough, Mass. 01719
(800) LAN-TALK
Fax (508) 263-8655

Racore Computer Products (Ethernet, token-ring)
170 Knowles Drive, Suite 204
Los Gatos, Calif. 95030
(800) 635-1274
(408) 374-8290
Fax (408) 374-8290

Relia Technologies (Ethernet, token-ring)
761 University Ave., Suite B
Los Gatos, Calif. 95030
(408) 399-4350
Fax (408) 354-2545

Rockwell Network Systems (Ethernet, token-ring)
7402 Hollister Ave.
Santa Barbara, Calif. 93117
(800) 262-8023
Fax (805) 868-6478

Silicom Connectivity Solutions Inc. (ARCnet, Ethernet, token-ring)
14311 N.E. 90th St.
Redmond, Wash. 98052
(800) 474-5426
(206) 882-7995
Fax (206) 882-4775

SilCom Manufacturing Technology Inc. (token-ring)
4854 Odl National Highway, Suite 110
Atlanta, Ga. 30337
(800) 388-3807
(404) 767-0706
Fax (404) 767-0709

Standard Microsystems Corp. (ARCnet, Ethernet, token-ring)
80 Arkay Drive
Hauppauge, N.Y. 11788
(801) SMC-4-YOU
(516) 435-6900
Fax (516) 273-1803

SVEC Computer Corp. (Ethernet, token-ring)
2691 Richter Ave., Suite 130
Irvine, Calif. 92714
(714) 756-2233
Fax (714) 756-1340

SysKonnect Inc. (FDDI)
1922 Zanker Road
San Jose, Calif. 95112
(800) SK2-FDDI
(408) 725-4650
Fax (408) 725-4654

Thomas-Conrad Corp. (ARCnet, Ethernet,
token-ring)
1908-R Kramer Lane
Austin, Tex. 78758
(800) 332-8683
(512) 836-1935

Top Microsystems Corp. (ARCnet, Ethernet,
LocalTalk, token-ring)
3320 Victor Court
Santa Clara, Calif. 95054
(800) 827-8721
(408) 980-9813
Fax (408) 980-8626

Transition Engineering Inc. (Ethernet)
7090 Shady Oak Road
Eden Prairie, Minn. 55344
(800) 267-4908
Fax (714) 693-0225

TRENDware International Inc. (Ethernet)
2421 W. 205th St., D-102
Torrance, Calif. 90501
(310) 328-7795
Fax (310) 328-7798

Unicom Electric Inc. (Ethernet, token-ring)
11980 Telegraph Road, Suite 103
Santa Fe Springs, Calif. 90670
(800) 346-6668
(310) 946-9650
Fax (310) 946-9167

Xinetron Inc. (ARCnet, Ethernet)
2302 Walsh Ave.
Santa Clara, Calif. 95051
(800) 345-4415
(408) 727-5509
Fax (408) 727-6499

Xircom (ARCnet, Ethernet, LocalTalk, token-
ring)
26025 Mureau Road
Calabasas, Calif. 91302
(818) 878-7600
Fax (818) 878-7630
(818) 878-7175

BRIDGES, ROUTERS, AND REPEATERS

3Com Corp.
5400 Bayfront Plaza
Santa Clara, Calif. 95052-8145
(800) NET-3COM
(415) 764-5000
Fax (408) 764-5001

Addtron Technology Corp. Ltd
47968 Fremont Blvd.
Fremont, Calif. 94538
(800) 998-4638
Fax (510) 770-0120

Advanced Computer Communications
10261 Bubb Road
Cupertino, Calif. 95014
(800) 444-7854
(408) 366-9654

ALANTEC
70 Plumeria Drrive
San Jose, Calif. 95134
(408) 955-9000
Fax (408) 955-9500

Allied Telesis
575 E. Middlefield Road
Mountain View, Calif. 94043
(800) 424-4284
Fax (415) 964-8250

Andrew Corp.
10500 W. 153rd St.
Orland Park, Ill. 60462
(800) 328-2696

Cabletron Systems
35 Industrial Way
Rochester, N.H. 03867
(603) 332-9400
Fax (603) 337-2444

Cameo Communications
71 Spitbrook Road
Nashua, N.H. 03060
(800) 438-4827
(603) 888-8869
Fax (603) 888-8906

Canary Communications
1851 Zanker Road
San Jose, Calif. 95112-9201
(800) 883-9201
(408) 453-9201
Fax (408) 453-0940

Cayman Systems
400 Unicorn Park Drive
Woburn, Mass. 01801
(800) 473-4776
(617) 932-1100
Fax (617) 932-3861

Chipcom Corp.
118 Turnpike Road
Southborough, Mass. 01772
(800) 228-9930
(508) 460-8900
Fax (508) 460-8950

Cisco Systems Inc.
930 E. Arquez Ave.
Sunnyvale, Calif. 94086
(800) 238-2334
(408) 526-4000
Fax (408) 526-8401

Compatible Systems Corp.
4730 Walnut St., Suite 102
P.O. Box 17220
Boulder, Colo. 80801
(303) 444-9532
(800) 356-0283
Fax (714) 630-6521

CompuLAN Technology Inc.
1630 Oakland Road, Suite A111
San Jose, Calif. 95131
(408) 432-8899
(408) 432-8699

Cray Communications
9020 Junction Drive
Annapolis Junction, Md. 20701
(800) FOR-CRAY
(301) 317-7710
Fax (408) 270-1170

D-Link Systems
5 Musick
Irvine, Calif. 92718
(800) 326-1988
(714) 455-1688
Fax (714) 455-2521

David Systems Inc.
615 Tasman drive
Sunnyvale, Calif. 94088-3718
(800) 762-7848
(408) 541-6000
Fax (408) 541-6985

Dayna Communications Inc.
Sorenson Research Park
849 W. Levoy Drive
Salt Lake City, Utah 84123
(801) 269-7200

Develcon
856-51st St. East
Saskatoon, Sask. S7K 5C7
Canada
(800) 667-9333
(306) 933-3300
Fax (306) 931-1370

Digital Equipment Corp.
550 King St., LKG1-3/J17
Littleton, Mass. 01480
(800) DIGITAL
(508) 486-6963
Fax (508) 486-6311

Eicon Technology
2196-32nd Ave.
Montreal, Que. H8T 3H7
Canada
(800) 80-EICON
Fax (214) 239-3304

Farallon Computng Inc.
2470 Mariner Square Loop
Alameda, Calif. 94501-1010
(510) 814-5000
Fax (510) 814-5023

Fibronics International Inc.
33 Riverside Drive
Pembroke, Mass. 02359
(617) 826-0099
Fax (617) 826-7745

Galaxy Networks
9348 De Soto Avenue
Chatsworth, Calif. 91311
(818) 998-7851
Fax (818) 998-1758

Galcom Inc.
211 Perry Parkway, Suite 4
Gaithersburg, Md. 20877
(800) 966-4444
(301) 990-7100
Fax (301) 963-6383

Gandalf Technologies
Cherry Hill Industrial Center - 9
Cherry Hill, N.J. 08003-1688
(800) GANDALF
Fax (613) 226-1717

General DataCom Inc.
1579 Straits Turnpike
Middlebury, Conn. 06762-1299
(203) 574-1118
Fax (203) 758-9468

Hewlett-Packard
8000 Foothills Blvd.
Roseville, Calif. 95747
(800) 533-1333
Fax (800) 333-1917

IBM Corp.
P.O. Box 12195, Department C09/8060
Research Triangle Park, N.C. 27709
(800) IBM-CALL
Fax (800 2-IBMFAX

IDEA
29 Dunham Road
San Jose, Calif. 95134
(800) SNA-3270
(408) 663-6878
Fax (508) 663-8851

IMC Networks
16931 Millikan Ave.
Irvine, Calif. 92714
(714) 724-1070
Fax (714) 724-1020

LAN Performance Labs
4901 Morena Blvd., Suite 805
San Diego, Calif. 92117
(800) 726-8101
(619) 273-1442
Fax (619) 273-2706

Lancast
10 Northern Blvd., Unit 5
Amherst, N.H. 03031
(800) 752-2768
Fax (603) 881-9888

LANQuest
1225 Qume Drive
San Jose, Calif. 95131
(800) 487-7779
(408) 894-1000
Fax (408) 894-1001

Lantronix
15353 Barranca Parkway
Irvine, Calif. 92718
(800) 422-7055
(714) 453-3990
Fax (714) 453-3995

Madge Networks
2310 N. First St.
San Jose, Calif. 95131
(800) 876-2343
(408) 955-0700
Fax (408) 955-0970

Micom Communications Corp.
4100 Los Angeles Ave.
Simi Valley, Calif. 93063
(800) 642-6687
(805) 583-8600
Fax (805) 583-1997

Microdye Corp.
3601 Eisenhower Ave.
Alexandria, Va. 22304
(800) 255-3967
Fax (703) 683-8924

MiLAN Technology Corp.
894 Ross Drive, Suite 101
Sunnyvale, Calif. 94089-1443
(800) GO-MILAN
(408) 752-2770
Fax (408) 752-2790

Netrix Corp.
13595 Dulles Technology Drive
Herndon, Va. 22071
(703) 742-6000
Fax (703) 742-4048

Network Application Technology Inc.
1686 Dell Avenue
Campbell, Calif. 95008
(800) 474-7888
(408) 370-4300
Fax (408) 776-8448

Network Equipment Technologies bInc.
800 Saginaw Drive
Redwood City, Calif. 94063-4740
(415) 366-4400
Fax (415) 780-5160

Network Peripherals Inc.
1371 McCarthy Blvd
Milpitas, Calif. 95035
(800) NPI-8855
(818) 321-9218

Network Resources Corp.
61 E. Daggett Drive
San Jose, Calif. 95134
(408) 383-9300

Network Systems Corp.
7600 Boone Avenue North
Minneapolis, Minn. 55428
(612) 424-4888
Fax (612) 424-2853

Networks Northwest Inc.
3633 136th Place, SE, Suite 100
Bellevue, Wash. 98006
(800) 835-9462
(206) 641-8779
Fax (206) 641-8909

NetWorth
8040 Esters Blvd.
Irving, Tex. 75063
(800) 544-5255
(214) 929-1700
Fax (214) 929-1720

Newbridge Networks Inc.
594 Herndon Parkway
Herndon, Va. 22070
(800) DO VIVID
(703) 834-3600
Fax (703) 708-5959

Niwot Networks Inc.
2200 Central Avenue, Suite B
Boulder, Colo. 80301
(303) 444-7765
Fax (303) 444-7767

Olicom USA Inc.
900 West Park Blvd., Suite 180
Plano, Tex. 75054
(800) 2-OLICOM
Fax (214) 423-7261

OST Inc.
14225 Sullyfield Circle
Chantilly, VA 22021
(703) 817-0400
Fax (703) 817-0402

Penril Datability Networks
Corporate Headquarters
1300 Quince Orchard Blvd.
Gaitherburg, Md. 20878
(800) 4-PENRIL
(301) 921-8600
Fax (301) 921-8376

Plaintree Systems
70 Walnut St.
Wellesley, Mass. 02181
(800) 370-2724
Fax (617) 239-7570

Plexcom Inc.
2255 Agate Court
Simi Valley, Calif. 93065
(805) 522-3333
Fax (805) 583-4764

Proteon Inc.
9 Technology Drive
Westborough, Mass. 01581
(508) 898-2800
Fax (508) 366-8901

Rad Data Communications
900 Corporate Drive
Mahwah, N.J. 07430
(201) 529-1100
Fax (201) 529-5777

Rad Network Devices
3505 Cadillac Avenue, Suite G5
Costa Mesa, Calif. 92626
(714) 436-9700
Fax (714) 436-1941

Retix
2401 Colorado Avenue
Santa Monica, Calif. 90404-3563
(800) 255-2333
(310) 828-3400
Fax (310) 828-2255

Telco Systems
63 Nahatan St.
Norwood, Mass. 02062
(617) 255-9400
Fax (617) 255-5885

Telebit Corp.
1315 Chesapeake Terrace
Sunnyvale, Calif. 94089
(800) TELEBIT
Fax (408) 745-3310

Transition Engineering
7090 Shady Oak Road
Eden Prairie, Minn. 55344
(800) 267-4908
Fax (612) 941-2322

Wellfleet Communications Inc.
8 Federal St.
Billerica, Mass. 01821
(508) 670-8888
Fax (508) 436-3658

XNET Technology Inc.
426 S. Hillview Drive
Milpitas, Calif. 95035-5464
(800) 788-0148
(408) 263-6888
Fax (408) 263-8898

Xyplex Inc.
295 Foster St.
Littleton, Mass. 01460
(800) 338-5316
Fax (508) 952-4702

Cable Testing

AMP
P.O. Box 3608
Harrisburg, Penn. 17105-3608
(800) 522-6752
Fax (717) 986-7575

Cable Management Systems
3510 S. Susan St.
Santa Ana, Calif. 92704
(714) 662-0554
Fax (714) 662-1083

Fluke Corp.
P.O. Box 9090
Everett, Wash. 98206
(800) 44-FLUKE
Fax (206) 356-5116

FOTEC Inc.
529 Main St.
P.O. Box 246
Boston, Mass. 02129
(800) 537-8254
(617) 241-7810
Fax (617) 241-8616

Microtest
4747 N. 22nd St.
Phoenix, Ariz. 85016-4708
(800) 526-9675
Fax (602) 952-6401

Noyes Fiber Systems
P.O. Box 398
Laconia, N.H. 03247
(800) 321-5298
(603) 528-7780
Fax (603) 528-2025

Siecor Corp.
P.O. Box 489
Hickory, N.C. 28603-0489
(704) 327-5000
Fax (704) 327-5973

Unicom Electrix Inc.
11980 Telegraph Road, Suite 103
Santa Fe Spring, Calif. 90670
(800) 346-6668
(310) 946-9650
Fax (310) 946-9167

Wavetek Corp.
9145 Balboa Avenue
San Diego, Calif. 92123
(800) 854-2708
(619) 279-2200
Fax (619) 450-0325

Gateways

Adacom Network Routers Ltd.
P.O. Box 118
Industrial Park
Yokneam, Israel 20698
Andrew Corp.
10500 W. 153rd St.
Orland Park, Ill. 60462
(800) 328-2696

Apertus Technologies Inc.
7275 Flying Cloud Drive
Eden Prairie, Minn. 55344
(800) 876-7671
(612) 828-0300
Fax (612) 828-0454

Artisoft Inc.
2202 N. Forbes Blvd.
Tucson, Ariz. 85745
(800) 233-5564
Fax (602) 670-7359

Async Systems
203 Middlesex Turnpike
Burlington, Mass. 01803
(617) 270-3530
Fax (617) 270-3580

Attachmate Corp.
3617 131st Avenue SE
Bellevue, Wash. 98006
(800) 426-6283
(206) 644-4010
Fax (206) 747-9924

Banyan Systems Inc.
120 Banyan System Inc.
Westboro, Mass. 01581-5013
(800) 462-4565
(617) 783-0080
Fax (508) 898-1755

Brixton Systems Inc.
125 Cambridge Park Drive
Cambridge, Mass. 02140
(617) 661-6262
Fax (617) 547-9820

Bus-Tech Inc.
129 Middlesex Turnpike
Burlington, Mass. 01803
(800) 284-3172
(617) 272-8200
Fax (617) 272-0342

Cabletron Systems
35 Industrial Way
Rochester, N.H. 03867
(603) 332-9400
Fax (603) 337-2444

CGS Research Inc.
46560 Fremont Blvd. Suite 119
Fremont, Calif. 94538
(800) 875-3224
(510) 226-5776
Fax (510) 226-5775

CLEO Communications
3796 Plaza Drive
Ann Arbor, Mich. 48108
(800) 233-2536
Fax (313) 662-1965

Cray Communications
9020 Junction Drive
Annapolis Junction, Md. 20701
(800) FOR-CRAY
(301) 317-7710
Fax (408) 270-1170

Crystal Point Inc.
22232 17th Avenue, Suite 301
Santa Cruz, Calif. 98021
(800) 982-0628
(206) 487-3656
Fax (206) 487-3773

Data Interface Systems Corp.
11130 Jollyville Road, Suite 300
Austin, Tex. 78759
(800) 351-4244
(512) 346-5641
Fax (305) 238-0017

DCA
1000 Alderman Drive
Alpharetta, Ga. 30202
(800) 348-3221
Fax (404) 442-4366

Eicon Technology
2196-32nd Ave.
Montreal, QUE H8T 3H7
Canada
(800) 80-EICON
Fax (214) 239-3304

Firefox Inc.
2841 Junction Avenue, Suite 103
San Jose, Calif. 95134
(408) 321-8344
(800) 230-6090
Fax (408) 321-8311

Galaxy Networks Inc.
9348 De Soto Avenue
Chatsworth, Calif. 91311
(818) 998-7851
Fax (818) 998-1758

Hummingbird Communications Ltd.
2900 John Street
Markham, Ont. L3R 5G3
Canada
(905) 470-1203
Fax (905) 470-1207

ICOT Corp.
3801 Zanker Road
San Jose, Calif. 95134
(800) SNA-3270
(408) 432-3138
Fax (408) 433-9466

IDEA
29 Dunham Road
Billerica, Mass. 01821
(800) 257-5027
(408) 663-6878
Fax (508) 663-8851

InterCon Systems Inc.
950 Herndon Parkway
Herndon, VA. 22070
(703) 709-5555

Interconnections
14711 NE 29th Place
Bellevue, Wash. 98007
(800) 950-5773
(206) 881-4023
Fax (206) 867-5022

Interlink Computer Sciences Inc.
47370 Fremont Blvd.
Fremont, Calif. 94538
(800) 422-3711
Fax (510) 659-6381

Ipswitch Inc.
669 Main Street
Wakefield, Mass. 01880
(617) 246-1150
Fax (617) 245-2975

James River Group
125 N. First St.
Minneapolis, Minn. 55401
(612) 339-2521

Memorex Telex
Tex. Commerce Tower
545 E. John Carpenter Freeway
Irving, Tex. 75062
(214) 444-3500
Fax (214) 444-3501

Meridian Technology Corp.
11 McBride Corporate Center Drive
Suite 250
Chesterfield, Mo. 63005-1406
(314) 532-7708
Fax (314) 532-3242

Micro-Integration Corp.
One Science Park
Frostburg, Md. 21532
(800) 832-4526
Fax (301) 689-0808

Microdyne Corp.
3601 Eisenhower Ave.
Alexandria, VA. 22304
(800) 255-3967
Fax (703) 683-8924

Multi-Tech Systems Inc.
2205 Woodale Drive
Mounds View, Minn. 55112
(612) 785-3500
(800) 328-9717
Fax (612) 785-9874

Netlink Inc.
3214 Sprint Forest Road
Raleigh, N.C. 27604
(919) 878-8612
Fax (919) 872-2132

NetManage Inc.
10725 N. De Anza Blvd.
Cupertino, Calif. 95014
(408) 973-7171
Fax (408) 257-6405

NetSoft
39 Argonaut
Laguna Hills, Calif. 92656
(800) 352-3270
(714) 768-4013
Fax (714) 768-5049

Network Products Group
1400 W. Colorado Blvd.
Pasadena, Calif. 91105
(800) 638-7765
(818) 441-6504
Fax (818) 441-6894

Olicom Communications
900 West Park Blvd., Suite 180
Plano, Tex. 75054
(800) 2-OLICOM
Fax (214) 423-7261

OpenConnect Systems Inc.
2711 LBJ Freeway
Suite 800
Dallas, Tex. 75234
(214) 484-5200
Fax (214) 888-0688

Passport Communications Inc.
1101 S. Capital of Tex. Hwy
Suite 250-F
Austin, Tex. 78746
(512) 328-9830
Fax (512) 328-3847

Radlinx Ltd.
900 Corporate Drive
Mahwah, N.J. 07430
(201) 529-1100
Fax (201) 529-5777

Renex Corp.
Lakepoint 1
2750 Killarney Drive
Woodbridge, VA. 22192
(703) 878-2400
Fax (703) 878-4625

Sealevel Systems Inc.
P.O. Box 830
102 W. Main Street
Liberty, S.C. 29657
(803) 843-4343
Fax (803) 843-3067

Software AG of North America
11190 Sunrise VAlley Drive
Reston, VA. 22091
(800) 423-2227
(703) 860-5050
Fax (703) 391-8200

TGV Inc.
101 Cooper Street
Santa Cruz, Calif. 95060
(408) 457-5200
Fax (408) 457-5205

Top Microsystems Corp.
3320 Victor Court
Santa Clara, Calif. 95054
(800) 827-8721
(408) 980-9813
Fax (408) 980-8626

Wollongong Group Inc.
1129 San Antonio Road
Palo Alto, Calif. 94086
(415) 962-7202
Fax (415) 962-0286

Xyplex
295 Foster St.
Littleton, Mass. 01460
(800) 338-5316
Fax (508) 952-4702

Zephyr Development Corp.
Summit Tower, 11 Greenway Plaza
Suite 1610
Houston, Tex. 77046-1104
(800) 966-3270
(713) 623-0089
Fax (713) 623-0091

HUBS, CONCENTRATORS, AND MAUS

Accton Technology Corp.
1962 Zanker Road
San Jose, Calif. 95112
(800) 926-9288
(408) 452-8900
Fax (408) 452-8988

Ace/North Hills
7934 Nieman Road
Lenexa, Kans. 66214
(800) 998-4223
(913) 888-4999
Fax (913) 888-4103

Addtron Technology Co. Ltd.
47968 Fremont Blvd.
Fremont, Calif. 94538
(800) 998-4638
Fax (510) 770-0120

Allied Telesis
575 E. Middlefield Road
Mountain View, Calif. 94043
(800) 424-4284
Fax (415) 964-8250

Alta Research Corp.
600 S. Federal Highway
Deerfield Beach, Fla. 33441
(800) 423-8535
(305) 428-8535
Fax (305) 428-8678

Apertus Technologies
7275 Flying Cloud Drive
Eden Prairie, Minn. 55344
(800) 876-7671
(612) 828-0300
Fax (612) 828-0454

Asante Technologies
821 Fox Lane
San Jose, Calif. 95131
(800) 662-9686
(408) 438-8388
Fax (408) 432-7511

ASP Computer Products
160 San Gabriel Drive
Sunnyvale, Calif. 94086
(800) 445-6190
(408) 746-2965
Fax (408) 746-2803

Boca Research Inc.
6413 Congress Avenue
Boca Raton, Fla. 33487
(407) 997-6227
Fax (407) 997-0918

Bytex Corp.
4 Technology Drive
Westborough, Mass. 01581-1760
(800) 227-1145
(508) 366-8000
Fax (508) 366-7970

Cabletron Systems
35 Industrial Way
Rochester, N.H. 03867
(603) 332-9400
Fax (603) 337-2444

Cameo Communications Inc.
71 Spitbrook Road
Nashua, N.H. 03060
(800) 438-4827
(603) 888-8869
Fax (603) 888-8906

Canary Communications Inc.
1851 Zanker Road
San Jose, Calif. 95112-9201
(800) 883-9201
(408) 453-9201
Fax (408) 453-0940

Chipcom Corp.
118 Turnpike Road
Southborough, Mass. 01772
(800) 228-9930
(508) 460-8900
Fax (508) 460-8950

Cisco Systems
930 E. Arquez Avenue
Sunnyvale, Calif. 94086
(800) 238-2334
(408) 526-4000
Fax (408) 526-8401

CNET Technology Corp.
2199 Zanker Road
San Jose, Calif. 95131
(408) 954-8000
Fax (408) 954-8866

Compex Inc.
4051 E. La Palma
Anaheim, Calif. 92807
(800) 279-8891, pin #1071
(714) 630-7302
Fax (714) 630-6521

CompuLAN Technology Inc.
1630 Oakland Road, Suite A111
San Jose, Calif. 95131
(408) 432-8899
Fax (408) 432-8699

Cray Communications
9020 Junction Drive
Annapolis Junction, Md. 20701
(800) FOR-CRAY
(301) 317-7710
Fax (408) 270-1170

D-Link Systems Inc.
5 Musick
Irvine, Calif. 92718
(800) 326-1688
(714) 455-1688
Fax (714) 713-6331

Danpex Corp.
1342 Ridder Park Drive
San Jose, Calif. 85131
(800) 452-1551
(408) 437-7557
Fax (408) 437-7559

David Systems
615 Tasman Drive
Sunnyvale, Calif. 94088-3718
(800) 762-7848
(408) 541-6000
Fax (408) 541-6985

Dayna Communications Inc.
Sorenson Research Park
849 W. Levoy Drive
Salt Lake City, Utah 84123
(801) 269-7200

Develcon
856-51st St. East
Saskatoon, Sask. S7K 5C7
Canada
(800) 667-9333
(306) 933-3300
Fax (306) 931-1370

Digital Equipment Corp
550 King St., LKG1-3/J17
Littleton, Mass. 01480
(800) DIGITAL
(508) 486-6963
Fax (508) 486-6311

Farallon Computing Inc.
2470 Mariner Square Loop
Alameda, Calif. 94501-1010
(510) 814-5000
Fax (510) 814-5023

Fibercom Inc.
3353 Orange Avenue, NE
Roanoke, VA. 24012
(800) 537-6801
Fax (703) 342-5961

Fibermux Corp.
21415 Plummer Street
Chatsworth, Calif. 91311
(800) 088-4624
Fax (703) 342-5961

Fibronics International Inc.
33 Riverside Drive
Pembroke, Mass. 02359
(617) 826-0099
Fax (617) 826-7745

General Datacomm Inc.
1579 Straits Turnpike
Middlebury, Conn. 06762-1299
(203) 574-1118
Fax (203) 758-9468

Grand Junction Networks
47281 Bayside Parkway
Fremont, Calif. 94538
(510) 252-0726
Fax (510) 252-0915

General Technology Inc.
415 Pineda Court
Melbourne, Fla. 32940
(800) 274-2733
(407) 242-2733
Fax (407) 254-1407

GVC Technologies
376 Lafayette Road
Sparta,. N.M. 07871
(201) 579-3630
Fax (201) 579-2702

HTI Networks
532 Weddell Drive, Suite 1
Sunnyvale, Calif. 94089
(408) 745-0101
Fax (408 745-7711

Hewlett-Packard Co.
8000 Foothills Blvd.
Roseville, Calif. 95747
(800) 533-1333
Fax (800) 333-1917

IBM Corp.
P.O. Box 12195, Department C09/8060
Research Triangle Park, N.C. 27709
(800) IBM-CALL
Fax (800 2-IBMFAX

IBM Personal Computer Co.
Route 100
Somers, N.Y. 10589
(914) 766-1900
Fax (914) 766-0116

IDEA
29 Dunham Road
San Jose, Calif. 95134
(800) SNA-3270
(408) 663-6878
Fax (508) 663-8851

IMC Networks
16931 Millikan Ave.
Irvine, Calif. 92714
(714) 724-1070
Fax (714) 724-1020

Intellicom Inc.
20415 Nordhoff Street
Chatsworth, Calif. 91311
(818) 407-3900
Fax (818) 882-2404

Interphase Corp.
13800 Senlac
Dallas, Tex. 75234-8823
(800) FASTNET
(214) 919-9111

Kalpana Inc.
1154 E. Arques Avenue
Sunnyvale, Calif. 94086-4602
(800) 488-0775
(408) 749-1600
Fax (408) 749-1690

Katron Technologies Inc.
7400 Harwin Drive, Suite 120
Houston, Tex. 77036
(713) 266-3891
Fax (713) 266-3893

Klever Computers Inc.
1028 W. Maude Ave.
Sunnyvale, Calif. 94086
(800) 745-4660
Fax (408) 735-7723

LAN Performance Labs
4901 Morena Blvd., Suite 805
San Diego, Calif. 92117
(800) 726-8101
(619) 273-1442
Fax (619) 273-2706

LANart Corp.
145 Rosemary Street
Needham, Mass. 02194
(800) 292-1994
(617) 444-1994
Fax (617) 444-3692

LANcast
10 Northern Blvd., Unit 5
Amherst, N.H. 03031
(800) 752-2768
Fax (603) 881-9888

LANNET Inc.
17942 Cowan Avenue
Irvine, Calif. 92714
(800) 522-6638
Fax (714) 752-6641

Lantronix
15353 Barranca Parkway
Irvine, Calif. 92718
(800) 422-7055
(714) 453-3990
Fax (714) 453-3995

Microdyne Corp
3601 Eisenhower Ave.
Alexandria, VA. 22304
(800) 255-3967
Fax (703) 683-8924

MiLAN Technology
894 Ross Drive, Suite 101
Sunnyvale, Calif. 94089-1443
(800) GO-MILAN
(408) 752-2770
Fax (408) 752-2790

Network Peripherals Inc.
1371 McCarthy Blvd.
Milpitas, Calif. 95035
(800) NPI-8855
(818) 321-9218

NetWorth
8040 Esters Blvd.
Irving, Tex. 75063
(800) 544-5255
(214) 929-1700
Fax (214) 929-1720

Newbridge Networks Inc.
594 Herndon Parkway
Herndon, VA. 22070
(800) DO VIVID
(703) 834-3600
Fax (703) 708-5959

Northern Telecom Inc.
620 W. Oakton St.
Morton Grove, Ill. 60053-2756
(800) 262-9334
Fax (800) 262-9334

Olicom USA Inc.
900 West Park Blvd., Suite 180
Plano, Tex. 75054
(800) 2-OLICOM
Fax (214) 423-7261

Penril Datability Networks
Corporate Headquarters
1300 Quince Orchard Blvd.
Gaitherburg, Md. 20878
(800) 4-PENRIL
(301) 921-8600
Fax (301) 921-8376

Plexcom Inc.
2255 Agate Court
Simi VAlley, Calif. 93065
(805) 522-3333
Fax (805) 583-4764

Protec Microsystems Inc.
297 Labrosse
Pointe-Claire, QC H9R 1A3
Canada
(800) 363-8156
Fax (514) 694-0973

Racal InterLan Inc.
155 Swanson Road
Boxborough, Mass. 01719
(800) LAN-TALK
Fax (508) 263-8655

Relia Technogies Inc.
761 University Ave., Suite B
Los Gatos, Calif. 95030
(408) 399-4350
Fax (408) 354-2545

Retix
2401 Colorado Avenue
Santa Monica, Calif. 90404-3563
(800) 255-2333
(310) 828-3400
Fax (310) 828-2255

Rockwell Network Systems
7402 Hollister Ave.
Santa Barbara, Calif. 93117
(800) 262-8023
Fax (805) 868-6478

SilCom Manufacturing
4854 Old National Highway, Suite 110
Atlanta, Ga. 30337
(800) 388-3807
(404) 767-0706
Fax (404) 767-07090

Standard Microsystems Corp.
80 Arkay Drive
Hauppauge, N.Y. 11788
(801) SMC-4-YOU
(516) 435-6900
Fax (516) 273-1803

SVEC Computer Corp.
2691 Richter Ave., Suite 130
Irvine, Calif. 92714
(714) 756-2233
Fax (714) 756-1340

SynOptics Communications Corp. (now Bay
Networks)
4401 Great America Parkway
P.O. Box 58185
Santa Clara, Calif. 95052-8185
(800) PRO-NTWK
Fax (408) 988-5525

SysKonnect Inc.
1922 Zanker Road
San Jose, Calif. 95112
(800) SK2-FDDI
(408) 725-4650
Fax (408) 725-4654

Thomas-Conrad Corp.
1908-R Kramer Lane
Austin, Tex. 78758
(800) 332-8683
(512) 836-1935

Top Microsystems Corp.
3320 Victor Court
Santa Clara, Calif. 95054
(800) 827-8721
(408) 980-9813
Fax (408) 980-8626

Transition Engineering Inc.
7090 Shady Oak Road
Eden Prairie, Minn. 55344
(800) 267-4908
Fax (714) 693-0225

TRENDware International
2421 W. 205th St., D-102
Torrance, Calif. 90501
(310) 328-7795
(Fax) 328-7798

Xinetron Inc.
2302 Walsh Ave.
Santa Clara, Calif. 95051
(800) 345-4415
(408) 727-5509
Fax (408) 727-6499

Xyplex Inc.
295 Foster St.
Littleton, Mass. 01460
(800) 338-5316
Fax (508) 952-4702

Zero One/Networking
4920 E. La Palma Avenue
Anaheim, Calif. 92807
(714) 693-0804
Fax (714) 693-0705

Hayes Microcompuer Products Inc.
5835 Peachtree Corners East
Norcross, Ga. 30092
(404) 441-1617
Fax (404) 449-0087

Microsoft
One Microsoft Way
Redmond, Wash. 98052-6399
(800) 227-4679

Moses Computers Inc.
15466 Los Gatos Blvd., Suite 201
Los Gatos, Calif. 95032
(408) 358-1550
Fax (408) 356-9049

Novell Inc.
122 E. 1700 South
Provo, Utah 84606
(800) NETWARE
(801) 429-5588

Saber Software Inc.
5944 Luther Lane
Suite 1007
Dallas, Tex. 75225
(800) 338-8754
(214) 361-8086
Fax (214) 361-1882

OPERATING SYSTEMS

Artisoft Inc.
2202 N. Forbes Blvd.
Tucson, Ariz. 85745
(800) 233-5564
Fax (602) 670-7359

Banyan Systems Inc.
120 Banyan System Inc.
Westboro, Mass. 01581-5013
(800) 462-4565
(617) 783-0080
Fax (508) 898-1755

PROTOCOL ANALYZERS DIGILOG (ETHERNET, TOKEN-RING)

Digital Equipment Corporation
900 Business Center Drive
Horsham, Penn. 19044
(800) DIGILOG
Fax (215) 956-0108

FTP Software Inc. (Ethernet, token-ring)
2 High Street
North Andover, Mass. 01845

Hewlett-Packard Co. (Ethernet, token-ring)
8000 Foothills Blvd.
Roseville, Calif. 95747
(800) 533-1333
Fax (800) 333-1917

IBM DatagLANce Network Analyzer (Ethernet,
token-ring)
P.O. Box 12195, Department C09/8060
Research Triangle Park, N.C. 27709
(800) IBM-CALL
Fax (800 2-IBMFAX

Intel Corp. (Ethernet, token-ring)
5200 N.E. Elam Parkway
Hillsboro, Oreg. 97124
(800) 538-3373
Fax (800) 525-3019

LANQuest (Ethernet)
1225 Qume Drive
San Jose, Calif. 95131
(800) 487-7779
(408) 894-1000
Fax (408) 894-1001

Network General Corp. (Ethernet, token-ring)
4200 Bohann Street
Menlo Park, Calif. 94025
(415) 473-2000

The AG Group Inc. (Ethernet, LocalTalk, token-
ring)
2540 Camino Diablo
Suite 200
Walnut Creek, Calif. 94596
(800) 466-AGGP
(510) 937-7900
Fax (510) 937-7900

Triticom (ARCNET, Ethernet, tokenring)
Box 444180
Eden Prairie, Minn. 55344
(612) 937-0772
Fax (612) 937-1998

Wandel & Golterman Technologies Inc.
(Ethernet, token-ring, FDDI)
1030 Swabia Court
Reasearch Triangle Park, N.C. 27709
(800) 277-7404
Fax (919) 481-4372

NETWORK AND COMPUTER PUBLICATIONS

C

Byte Magazine
McGraw-Hill Inc.
Monthly
One Phoenix Mill Road
Peterborough, N.H. 03458
(603) 924-9281

Communications Week
CMP Publications Inc.
Weekly
600 Community Drive
Manhasset, N.Y. 11030
(516) 562-5530

ComputerWorld
CW Publishing Inc.
Weekly
375 Cochituate Road
Framingham, Mass. 01701-9171
(508) 879-0700

Data Communications
McGraw-Hill Inc.
Monthly
1221 Avenue of the Americas
New York, N.Y. 10020
(212) 512-2699

Datamation
Cahners/Reed Publishing Corp.
Biweekly
275 Washington Street
Newton, Mass. 02158-1630
(617) 964-3030

Information Week
CMP Publications Inc.
Weekly
600 Community Drive
Manhasset, N.Y. 11030
(516) 562-5898

InfoWorld
InfoWorld Publishing Inc.
Weekly
155 Bovet Road, Suite 800
San Mateo, Calif. 94402
(415) 572-7341

Internetwork
Cardinal Business Media Inc.
Monthly
101 Witmer Road
Horsham, Penn. 19044
(215) 957-1500

LAN Magazine
Miller Freeman Inc.
Monthly
600 Harrison Street
San Francisco, Calif. 94107
(415) 905-2200

LAN Times
McGraw-Hill
Biweekly
1900 O'Farrell Street
Suite 200
San Mateo, Calif. 94403
(415) 513-6800

NetWare Solutions
New Media Publications
Monthly
10711 Burnet Road, Ste. 305
Austin, Tex. 78758
(512) 794-8035

Network Computing
CMP Publications Inc.
Monthly
600 Community Drive
Manhasset, N.Y. 11030
(516) 562-5071

Network World
IDG Inc.
Weekly
161 Worcester Road
Framingham, Mass. 01701-9172
(508) 875-5400

PC Magazine
Ziff-Davis Publishing Company
Biweekly
One Park Avenue
New York, N.Y. 10016
(212) 503-5255

PC Week
Ziff-Davis Publishing Company
Weekly
10 Presidents Landing
Medford, Mass. 02155
(617) 393-3700

Stacks
Miller-Freeman Inc.
Monthly
411 Borel Avenue
San Mateo, Calif. 94402
(415) 358-9400

INDEX

F5NDES

NetWare SOLUTIONS
THE INDEPENDENT MAGAZINE FOR NOVELL SYSTEM MANAGERS

FREE SUBSCRIPTION APPLICATION

FREE subscription offer for buyers of *Networking the Desktop*

To apply, complete entire form, sign, date and mail to NetWare Solutions, 10711 Burnet Rd., Suite 305, Austin TX 78758-4459. Incomplete or unsigned forms will not be processed. International subscriptions are $50 for 12 issues. Please pay in U.S. dollars drawn from a U.S. bank.

☐ **YES** I want to receive *NetWare Solutions* free of charge.

☐ **NO**

Signature (required) _____ Date _____

Name _____ Title _____

Company _____ Phone _____

Address _____

City _____ State _____ Zip _____

1. Does your company provide a product or service to the LAN community?
☐ Yes   ☐ No

1A. Do you currently manage/supervise a NetWare LAN?
☐ Yes   ☐ No

1B. If yes, which product(s) do you use? (Circle all that apply)

A. NetWare v3.x	M. NetWare for SAA
C. NetWare v2.x	P. Novell DOS
G. NetWare for Macintosh	Q. NetWare Management Services
H. UnixWare	R. NetWare Connect
I. NetWare 4.x	S. NetWare Telephony Service
J. Personal NetWare	T. SFT III
K. NetWare NFS	Z. Other (please specify)
L. MHS NetWare or Global MHS	_____

2. How many users are on your LAN(s)? (Circle one only)
Users

A. Up to 10	E. 251-500
B. 11-25	F. 501-1,000
C. 26-100	G. 1,001-5,000
D. 101-250	H. More than 5,000

How many nodes are you responsible for? (Circle one only)
Connections

I. None	M. 126-200
J. 1-25	N. 201-325
K. 26-75	O. 326-450
L. 75-125	P. Over 450

3. What applications software is shared on your LAN(s)? (Circle all that apply)

A. Word processing	G. E-mail
B. Spreadsheet	H. Groupware
C. DBMS	I. Client-Server
D. Desktop publishing	J. Lotus Notes
E. CAD/CAM	Z. Other (please specify)_____
F. Accounting	X. None, not yet installed

4. Which best describes your job function? (Circle one only)
A. DP/MIS Management
B. Network/Communications Management
C. Systems Integration
D. Executive Management
E. Consulting
F. Marketing/Sales
G. Engineering/Technical Management
H. Research/Development
I. Education/Training
Z. Other (please specify)_____

5. Which best describes the nature of your business? (Circle one only)
A. Computer product manufacturing
B. Other manufacturing
C. Retail/Wholesale trade
D. Financial services/Insurance/Real estate
E. Medical services
F. Transportation/Utilities
G. Government
H. Education
I. Legal services
J. Computer retailer/Distributor
K. OEM/VAR/Software House
L. Media/Publishing/Information Services
M. Agriculture/Mining/Construction/Oil
N. Research and Development
O. Consulting
P. Engineering/Architecture
Z. Other (please specify)_____

6. How many employees at your company (all locations)? (Circle one only)

A. Up to 24	D. 500-999
B. 25-99	E. 1,000-10,000
C. 100-499	F. More than 10,000

7. Do you recommend, specify or purchase LAN-related products?
☐ Yes   ☐ No

8. At your location, are any of the following computer products used? (Circle all that apply)

I. Macintosh	Q. IBM System 36/38
J. IBM RS/6000	R. 386-based computers
K. Sun	S. 486-based computers
N. Other UNIX workstations	T. Pentium-based computers
O. IBM Mainframe	U. Power PC
P. IBM AS/400	

OSI Model	NetWare	TCP/IP	VINES
Application	• NLMs SAP • Shell Requester • File Systems Redirector • NCP	• File Systems • TELNET • SNMP	• File, Print, NetBIOS Emulation • VINES SMB • StreetTalk • Mail
Presentation	• NLMs • SAP • Redirector • Requester • Function Calls	• NCP	• SMTP • RPC
Session	• NCP		• Socket Interface • RPC
Transport	• SPX	• TCP	• VINES Internet Protocol

Windows NT	AppleTalk	LAN Server	Generic Characteristics
• File Systems • Named Pipes • Providers (NT) • Redirector	• AFP • AppleShare	• File Systems • Redirector	• Services • Directory and File • Interface to End-User
• RPC • SMB	• Redirector • Executive Services (NT) • Kernel Mode • Environment Subsystems	• AFP • AppleShare	• Conversion • Compression • Formatting • Encodes • Encrypts
• Redirector • NetBIOS • NetBEUI • I/O Manager • Transport Driver Interface	• ADSP • ASP • PAP • ZIP	• NetBEUI	• Synchronizing • Maintaining • Sequencing
• Transport Driver Interface	• RTMP		• Packet Delivery